The Organic Vegetable Grower

Phil Sumption

The Organic Vegetable Grower

THE CROWOOD PRESS

Contents

Firstly, thanks to Jason Horner for alerting me that *Organic Vegetable Production: A Complete Guide* had gone out of print. Secondly, thanks to Gareth Davies and Margi Lennartsson for giving the green light for me to write a completely new version of this old classic, and to Crowood for enabling it to happen.

The biggest thanks go to my partner, Isabeau Meyer-Graft, for help with proofreading, support and much more. Also, to Roger Hitchings, for many helpful comments and suggestions, and agreeing to write the Foreword. I am also grateful to Jim Aplin, Nathan Richards, Kate Collyns, Pete Richardson, Tony Little, Antonia Ineson, Kate McEvoy, Mark Measures, Pete Dollimore, Iain Tolhurst, Tamara Schiopu, Suzy Russell and Dom van Marsh for assistance with aspects of the text along the way.

Photographic Acknowledgements

Brian Adair: 103 (all)
Jayne Arnold: 86–87, 157 (bottom left and right)
Mandy Barber: 217 (both)
Adam Beer, Pitney Farm Market Garden: 15 (top right), 48 (left), 49 (bottom) right), 50 (top left), 50 (bottom) left), 90, 93 (all), 100 (right), 108 (left), 120 (top right and (bottom) left), 152, 206, 212, 222
Pam Bowers: 27 (bottom), 47 (bottom), 70, 115, 120 (top left), 162 (top left), 162 (top right), 162 (bottom) right), 163 (right), 173, 196, 13.32
CAWR: 116 (all)
Kate Collyns: 27 (inset), 72
Culinaris Saatgut: 215
Tim Dickens: 11 (right), 12 (right), 14 (top left), 15 (top left), 34 (left), 35, 153 (bottom) left), 162 (bottom) left), 178 (bottom), 179, 181
Pete Dollimore: 145, 150 (both), 157 (top right)
Ecological Land Cooperative: 39 (top)
FarmStart: 38
David Frost: 184
Groundswell: 16
Ed Hamer: 28
Chris Holton: 27 (top)
Jason Horner: 26, 121 (top)
Scott Hunter: 23

Antonia Ineson: 56 (left)
Paul Izod: 106
Debbie James: 110
Holly Jarvis: 39 (bottom)
Stephan Junge: 135 (both)
Landgilde and Wageningen University & Research: 41 (top)
Henryk Luka, 130
Marley of Bennison Farm: 40, 96, 132, 153 (bottom) right), 162 (middle left), 179 (both), 178 (top), 185, 211
Organic Research Centre: 13 (top left), 14 (top right), 17, 29 (left), 58 (right), 65 (both), 66, 75 (bottom), 76 (left), 82 (left)
Adam Payne: 41 (bottom), 46, 47 (top), 50 (middle left), 75 (top), 100 (left), 120 (top middle), 159, 161 (bottom) left), 186, 188, 190, 193, 195, 201
Morten Pederson: 14 (bottom) left), 24 (bottom)
Morten Pedersen/Trill Farm Garden: 94
permacultureprinciples.com: 20
Pitney Farm Market Garden: 21, 98, 153 (middle right), 165 (top right), 177
Ben Raskin: 109
Nathan Richards: 11 (left), 14 (bottom) right), 50 (top right), 71 (left), 105 (right), 1167 (top right), 170 (right), 202, 207
Pete Richardson: 37, 71 (right), 166 (top left)
Patricia Schwitter/FiBL: 155 (top)
David Shaw, Raindrops: 133 (bottom)
Jonathan Smith: 166 (bottom) left)
Claire Stapley: 32
Hans Steenbergen: 205
Emma Treanor, Sandy Lane Farm: 9, 25, 57, 133 (bottom) (potatoes), 161 (top left), 161 (bottom right), 162 (middle right) 170 (left), 182, 191, 203 (top), 214
Paul van Midden: 148, 1153 (top left)
Anja Vieweger/Organic Research Centre: 157 (top left)
Chloe Ward: 84
Ashley Wheeler: 24 (top), 34 (right), 73, 82 (right), 108 (right), 145, 146 (bottom), 153 (top right), 164, 165 (middle right and (bottom) right), 167 (bottom) right), 183, 1387, 189, 197, 199, 200, 203 (bottom), 210
Adam York: 48 (right), 124, 129 (right), 166 (top right), 220

Much has changed since the publication by Crowood of *Organic Vegetable Production: A Complete Guide* in 2005 and yet some things have stayed more or less the same. Notable changes include a greater focus on seed and food sovereignty, a much greater awareness of the realities of climate change, financial ups and downs and, more latterly, the COVID-19 pandemic and the war in Ukraine. All of these have affected organic food production and not always in a good way.

The amount of support for organic horticulture has increased. The Organic Growers Association was reborn as the Organic Growers Alliance (OGA) in 2007 and transitioned into a Community Interest Company (CIC) in 2019. It continues to provide support, representation and an increasing body of invaluable information for organic growers. Organisations such as the Soil Association and Garden Organic continue to provide valuable information and support, while the Landworkers' Alliance (LWA) campaigns to improve the livelihoods of all land-based workers, including growers.

The marketplace continues to be dominated by supermarket sales, but there is a much greater diversity of marketing initiatives at local and regional levels. Whichever part of the market you are supplying, or seeking to supply, there are challenges and these are increasing, not least because of the increasing variability and unpredictability of UK weather. Other factors to consider when working out marketing plans include addressing the increasing interest in veganism and tapping into interest in 'heritage' varieties and unusual vegetables.

A welcome, if belated, change is a significant increase in awareness of the importance of soil health and the fundamental importance of soils, both in terms of food production and as repositories of sequestrated carbon. Soil has always been at the heart of organic production, but there is now an increasing number of initiatives based on regenerative land management which seek to improve soil structure and health. There is no clear single definition of regenerative farming and many initiatives still rely on the use of herbicides and other inputs, but the change in emphasis is welcome.

This book not only builds on the very solid foundation of its predecessor, but also takes account of all the developments that have happened since. It is detailed and thorough and has drawn on the experiences and knowledge of a number of successful growers in different parts of the UK. It is also informed by research projects, many of which have been conducted in collaboration with growers. Another major source of information is the seriously impressive body of work contained in the 60-plus editions of *The Organic Grower*, all edited by the author.

This will probably be first and foremost a valuable reference book and should be essential reading for anyone starting out on the journey of commercial organic vegetable production on whatever scale. That said, there are also new things for old hands to learn, so the book should find its way on to a shelf in every packing shed and office in the country. It should not gather dust, but become well-thumbed as the seasons turn.

Roger Hitchings

Chapter One

Principles and Approaches

This is a book written for growers, or prospective growers, of organic vegetables for sale. The organic growing community is a 'broad church' and the 'organic' word can be off-putting for some. Many growers prefer to use other terms, such as agroecological, regenerative, biointensive and permaculture, to name but a few. There are zealots in every camp, but they have more in common than what separates them. It is essential to look at the principles rather than the jargon and for every grower, farmer or community to find the system that works best for them. It is the 'how' of applying those principles in practice that is important and examples of best practice will be given throughout this book.

Organic is not a trend or a fad, but a legally recognised system of food production. There are guidelines and regulations which may scare off those distrustful of authority, but they are there to protect the consumer and the grower from the fraudulent. It should also be noted that standards are a baseline and organic growers should – and mostly do – strive to improve their systems ecologically. Historically, growers played a huge role in the setting up of organic standards in the UK. Standards have evolved, but have always been a pragmatic representation of what was achievable on the ground. While some might argue that the standards have not evolved fast enough to eliminate or reduce contentious inputs, such as the use of peat, copper and plastics, or to include social and ethical dimensions, they are still useful as a starting point and as guidelines. However you choose to define yourself as a grower, please approach this book and your growing journey with an open mind and try to avoid dogma!

Embarking on a career as a grower can be a romantic notion. It can be, and might seem to others, a lifestyle choice. It is true that there are rewards to be gained from working in the fresh air, combining the joys of nature with the production of wholesome healthy food to be sold to a satisfied customer. But the sun doesn't always shine and growing is not without its stresses. Once in the hurly-burly of the season, it can seem relentless. Climate change is making the weather less predictable and the risks of losing crops to extreme weather events and/or pest and disease outbreaks are increasing.

There is also a huge amount of complexity involved with growing crops agroecologically. It is all about diversity – but that diversity demands an extensive knowledge of a large number of crops. Add in agroforestry, intercropping and perhaps livestock to the mix and the interactions between all those elements, and you have an organisational nightmare or a productive paradise, or maybe both! For that reason, this book focuses not only on the technical aspects of nurturing a healthy soil and bountiful crops, but also on the human side of vegetable production. The grower's health and that of their family and employees is as vital for sustainability as the health of the soil.

OPPOSITE: Harvesting carrots at Sandy Lane Farm, Oxfordshire. Precision sowing with an air seeder means that the carrots have the right space to grow for optimum size and yield, with no need for thinning.

The heart of the grower

The business of growing, as opposed to gardening or farming, is unique in terms of the relationship with the land and the direct contact with the soil and nature in addition to food production. Experienced grower Tim Deane expressed this eloquently in the first issue of *The Organic Grower* magazine in 2007:

Where is the grower in the scheme of things? Not a gardener, though we both grow plants, nor yet a farmer, though we both make our living from the ground.

Although in biodynamic practice and elsewhere commercial fruit and vegetable production may be characterised as 'gardening' and the term 'market gardener' is sometimes used, the divide between gardening and growing is simple and stark. One is a leisure activity, the other isn't. One is the pursuit of freedom, the other more a matter of survival. The impetus that leads to both activities may be the same, but the moment the notion of profit and loss appears the path forks, and the two ways soon lose each other.

Farmers and growers both make their living from the land. Alike we are caught up in the rhythms of the world, moving perforce to its humours and its seasons. We live on and with the land, while the rest of humanity seems merely to occupy it. We come to recognise its meaning and its mysteries even if we cannot pin them down, whereas the non-agriculturist sees only entertainment, decoration or a space to be passed over. In the face of this incomprehension, farmers and growers must surely stand in pretty much the same place.

And yet, and yet ... Of course, there are farmers who grow vegetables and growers who keep stock, but away from the edges, when you look at the two professions side by side and (as it were) en masse, there is a gulf between them. There may be some sympathy, but there is limited understanding. The differences all flow, I think, from the scale on which we work. A grower can make do with an acre or two (given enough plastic), whereas a farmer may just get by on a hundred acres and its subsidies, so long as his wife goes out to work. Scale implies status. It also has a huge effect on how we view the world.

Go to a farm sale and to a horticultural sale and you will see the difference right there – in the car park! In the one – Land Rovers, four-by-fours and macho pick-ups. In the other – battered vans. If you go further, you will see that the average weight at a farm sale is about two stone more than that at a grower sale. There will also be more beards at the latter, probably a lot more. And so on.

A grower might look on livestock as a literal waste of space; a livestock farmer tends to see vegetables, immobile in a field, as inanimate objects; the arable man's cereal crops are composed of plants beyond reckoning, each living and dying in perfect anonymity. The difference of scale runs all through this. Grass grows without much effort. It has to be managed, a matter of skill, but it doesn't have to be delved into. Just as well if several hundred acres are being farmed together. An arable field may only see a human presence for five or six days in the year. The value of what it produces may justify no more than that. If it wasn't for the need to relieve themselves, today's ploughmen could go from morning to night without their feet touching the ground.

The grower cannot live like that. The plants we grow may not move around, but the skill that brings them to life and husbands them through it is not different in essence to that entailed in stockmanship. Empathy, observation, attention to detail and not leaving things to chance – these are the same in both cases. Arable crops need space if anything is to be made of them. It's not just that there has to be a lot of them to add up to any value. The wind cannot weave its dance over a few square yards of barley. Even the swede is only really happy if it has enough of its kind around it to take up an acre or two. But horticultural crops are tame and with it tender. They demand attention and understanding. At least at stages in their life they are individual and distinct – as seed, transplant, harvested root, fruit and the rest of it. To make a place for them and to bring them to conclusion, the grower has to enter into the soil in which they root as well as to live the weather in which they grow.

While the farmer scans broad acres from his tractor seat, the grower is down on the ground and cannot live without the earth getting under his fingernails. I wouldn't say one is better or more valuable than the other. I do think though that, as farming is now, it is the grower who best preserves that vital link of mankind with the earth and its processes. The sun's energy, photosynthesis and the cycling of carbon – this is the basis of all life. In the growing of plants organically lies its truest human expression.

The sun doesn't always shine, especially in west Wales! Leek harvesting in the rain at Troed y Rhiw Farm, Llwyndafydd.

Growing has its fun moments, though.

Organic principles

Organic standards are guided by the principles and so should you be! Organic farming can often be defined or perceived by the negative – what you are not allowed to do, what is not permitted to be used and so on. I have heard growers say that they did not have a full grasp of what 'organic' was until they started down the road to certification and had to read the organic guidelines and standards. Understanding 'organic' is about recognising the wholeness and interconnectedness of the system.

After three years' work by a task force, IFOAM – Organics International came up with the following definition of organic agriculture:

Organic agriculture is a production system that sustains the health of soils, ecosystems, and people. It relies on ecological processes, biodiversity and cycles adapted to local conditions, rather than the use of inputs with adverse effects. Organic agriculture combines tradition, innovation, and science to benefit the shared environment and promote fair relationships and good quality of life for all involved. [IFOAM General Assembly, 2008]

IFOAM has also identified four principles of organic agriculture: The Principles of Health, Ecology, Fairness and Care. These are interconnected ethical principles composed to guide the global organic movement in policy positions, programmes and standards.

Organic growing is demonstrably so much more than the avoidance of artificial fertilisers and pesticides. By embracing the principles, organic growers can design systems from the ground up. If coming from a conventional growing or farming background, the biggest challenge can be converting what's between the ears. Rather than thinking; 'What product am I allowed to use to kill slugs instead of Product X?', the approach should be 'How can I redesign my system so that slugs are less of a problem?'

1. Principle of health

Organic agriculture should sustain and enhance the health of soil, plant, animal, human and planet as one and indivisible.

2. Principle of ecology

Organic agriculture should be based on living ecological systems and cycles, work with them, emulate them and help to sustain them.

3. Principle of fairness

Organic agriculture should build on relationships that ensure fairness with regard to the common environment and life opportunities.

4. Principle of care

Organic agriculture should be managed in a precautionary and responsible manner to protect the health and well-being of current and future generations and the environment.

Towards farmer principles of health

The farmers' principles of health as set out here are the results of the Health Networks project, conducted 2015–16. It was funded by the Ekhaga Foundation, Sweden, and led by the Organic Research Centre, UK; the Humboldt University Berlin, Germany; Leibniz Centre for Agricultural Landscape Research, Germany; and the University of Natural Resources and Life Sciences, Austria.

Over a period of two years, a group of sixteen farmers (including growers) from Germany, Austria and the UK identified their own principles of health in organic agricultural systems. The farmers have established personal philosophies and strategies of best practice that make them successful in running healthy farms and producing healthy food. In this context, 'farmers' and 'growers' are synonymous.

Statement 1 – Soil health

Farmers who aim to run healthy farming systems are aware that soil health is fundamental and the base for health in all other domains: plant, animal, human and ecosystem.

Statement 2 – Biodiversity

Farmers who aim to run healthy farming systems recognise and closely observe changes in biodiversity (particularly earthworms, farmland birds, bees and beneficial insects); and they aim for high and increasing biodiversity in their system, which contributes to the function of the agroecosystem.

Statement 3 – Systems thinking

Farmers who aim to run healthy farming systems are aware of working in and with nature's systems and feel that best health is achieved when all domains are included according to their being, as part of the agroecosystem: soil, plants, animals and humans.

Statement 4 – Observation skills

Farmers who aim to run healthy farming systems develop the ability to closely observe key health-related processes on their farm and react appropriately; they have a good overview of the system.

Statement 5 – Intuition and self-observation

Farmers who aim to run healthy farming systems develop the intuition and ability for self-observation (for example, daring to listen to an inner voice or gut feeling) as part of the observation process of the farm; and they are aware of their own strengths and weaknesses and know their own resources and those of the farm (for example, social network, basic trust).

Statement 7 – Long-term thinking and acting

Farmers who aim to run healthy farming systems improve health by planning in an increasingly broad and long-term perspective of the system. For example, through long rotations, perennials, habitats for wild animals, hedges or trees (generational structure and thinking).

Statement 6 – Overview

Farmers who aim to run healthy farming systems ensure the manageability and overview of land and processes (diversity, integrity and sustainability), their responsible organisation (design) and optimal organisation of capacities on the farm, so that the complexity and size of the farm does not negatively affect health (also social and societal health). Different scale farms require different processes and organisational structures to achieve health.

Statement 8 – Shifting goals

The main goals of farmers who aim to run healthy farming systems shift away from mass production towards quality production. In place of maximising productivity (for example with high performance breeds), optimal yields are aimed for. By selecting appropriate breeds and varieties suitable for the site and the farm, qualitative values and multiple outcomes can be achieved; such as quality, optimum yields, resilience, animal welfare, biodiversity, etc. Aiming for high productivity when it comes to achieving multiple outcomes.

Statement 9 – Impart health

Farmers who aim to run healthy farming systems are aware that they not only contribute to human health through their high-quality food products, but that they also deliver highly valuable outputs in other areas (for example, environment protection, public goods, cultural landscape, water quality and so on). They get across the story and value of the product and the farm through close communication with, and involvement of, customers, consumers, retailers, processors and so on.

Statement 10 – Indicators

The most apparent indicators of health on the farm are (in alphabetical order): biodiversity; economic sustainability (financial viability); external inputs; food quality; health of people on the farm; number of veterinarian visits and treatments; plant vitality; soil fertility; soil workability; weeds; pests and diseases; and yield.

Shades of green – approaches and philosophies

Regenerative agriculture

Regenerative agriculture is becoming a trend and there are many farmers or growers who prefer to call themselves regenerative rather than organic. The term has been around for a while, but has recently gained traction due to its emphasis on soil health. But what is regenerative agriculture?

According to the Regenerative Agriculture Initiative, California State University and The Carbon Underground: ' "Regenerative agriculture" describes farming and grazing practices that, among other benefits, reverse climate change by rebuilding soil organic matter and restoring degraded soil biodiversity – resulting in both carbon drawdown and improving the water cycle.'

The five principles of regenerative agriculture are summarised below, with my comments:

1. **Minimising soil disturbance.** The degree that this principle is adhered to can be a point of difference between some regenerative farmers who insist on no-till (and use of the herbicide glyphosate) and organic practitioners. There are, however, many successful examples of no-dig horticulture and systems that reduce tillage on a rotational basis.
2. **Keeping the soil covered.** Growing crops or stubbles will protect the soil from the impact of heavy rain, sun or frost.
3. **Keep living roots in the soil.** Living roots protect the soil from erosion – therefore cover crops are grown between cash crops, retaining nutrients and providing food for soil microorganisms.

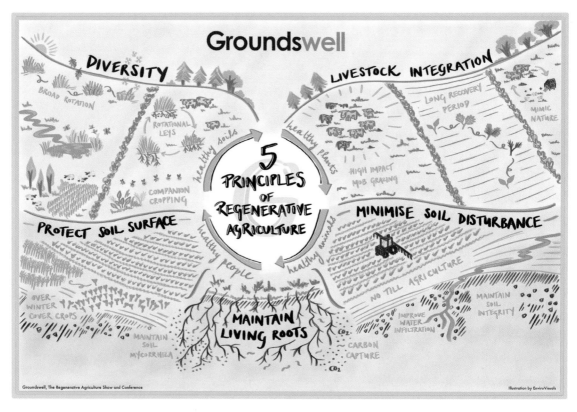

Groundswell's five principles of regenerative agriculture.

4. **Maximising plant or crop diversity.** The more diversity in the system, the more resilience to pests and diseases.

5. **Integration of livestock.** Livestock provide a source of organic matter, encourage new plant growth, create more carbon in the soil and drive nutrient recycling by feeding biology.

The term 'regenerative organic agriculture' was first coined by Robert Rodale (son of the founder of the Rodale Institute) in the US to recognise that farming should do more than just be sustainable. Some say that regenerative agriculture is 'beyond organic', but there is much of regenerative agriculture that is integral to organic farming in its truest expression. In the US, companies like McDonald's, Cargill and General Mills have jumped on the regenerative agriculture bandwagon. It makes good PR. Perhaps sensing this corporate encroachment, in 2018 the Rodale Institute went a step further and introduced Regenerative Organic Certified (ROC): 'a new, holistic, high-bar standard for agriculture certification' overseen by the NGO Regenerative Organic Alliance. The ROC takes the USDA Certified Organic standard as a baseline and adds: 'criteria and benchmarks that incorporate the three major pillars of regenerative organic agriculture (soil health, animal health and social wellness) into one certification'.

Stockfree organic

In contrast to regenerative agriculture, stockfree organic agriculture excludes animals or animal by-products from the farming system. It is partly a response to the difficulties in providing fertility through organic manures from within the farm, but it also coincides with the growing vegan movement and the demand that products vegans consume do not support livestock farming.

Iain Tolhurst of Tolhurst Organic, near Reading, has been a pioneer of vegan organic systems.

Stockfree organic systems aim to provide fertility through green manures and composts where livestock manures are not available; many stockfree organic farmers choose to farm without livestock for ethical reasons, as well. There are issues beyond the ethical concerns, with potential risks to human health from antibiotics and other drugs in manures – less an issue in organic farming – but the use of manure from non-organic (but not factory) farms is allowed in organic standards under certain conditions. Of course, animals can't ever be excluded completely from a system and stockfree organic growers could be considered farmers of earthworms and other below- and above-ground fauna.

The emphasis is on a systems-based approach. Stockfree organic standards have been developed and are currently certified by the Soil Association. There are currently two sets of standards: the Biocyclic Vegan Standard approved by IFOAM and supported by the International Biocyclic Vegan Network in Germany; and the stockfree organic standards held by the Vegan Organic Network (VON) in the UK. Both standards operate above and beyond the existing organic standards.

The first stockfree organic standards were developed by VON in the UK in 2007 and encourage practices promoting soil fertility and health through the use of plant-based inputs, such as compost and green manures, aligned with a well-designed rotation.

The Biocyclic Vegan Standard is based on the work of the German pioneer of organic farming, Adolf Hoops (1932–99). It takes a holistic approach, with an emphasis on using mature compost and humus, closing loops, working with nature and caring about the whole food chain.

Natural agriculture: Shumei and Korean style

The concept of Shumei Natural Agriculture was developed by the Japanese naturalist and philosopher Mokichi Okada in the 1930s in Japan. According to Okada, 'The principle of Natural Agriculture is an overriding respect and concern for nature.' Naturally, that precludes the use of fertilisers, but not just artificials – the belief is that any fertiliser inhibits the soil's natural ability to enrich itself. Soil is considered 'perfect', containing all that is needed for healthy plant growth. Health starts with healthy soils. The use of

Shumei Natural Agriculture at Yatesbury, Wiltshire, with brassicas continually grown in one place.

'natural compost' is permitted; it is not considered a fertility input, but is used for improving the soil temperature, keeping the soil 'temperate', and for 'softening the soil'. The principle of consciousness guides all life processes and extends to all that grows. Pests are not considered as such, with the principle of non-intervention extending to the prohibition of organic pesticides.

The most challenging aspect of Shumei Natural Agriculture is the absence of rotations. Continuous cropping allows crops to become accustomed to the soil they grow in and their wider environment, with plants building up resistance to pests and diseases. Seed-saving and adaptation is an important part of this. Science is starting to reveal how the seed biome adapts to its environment over time and we are learning more about mycorrhizal associations with crops, which can help to explain to an extent how these systems can work.

As with biodynamic farming, spirituality is integral to the philosophy, as is a pure mind, gratitude and humility. A caring attitude towards the soil and crops is key – water and soil respond to our hearts, according to Shumei Natural Agriculture precepts.

Korean Natural Farming (KNF) was developed in the 1960s by Dr Cho Han Kyu, who was influenced by the natural farming movements in Japan. The emphasis is on closed systems, limiting external inputs and recycling wastes on the farm. An important aspect is a focus on indigenous microorganisms (IMO), which are collected from woodland on site and nurtured with sugar and fermented plant juices as 'microbial seed for your land'. There are growers in the US and in the UK and Ireland who are adapting these methods, using local plants such as comfrey and nettle, fermented according to KNF guidelines.

Biodynamic agriculture

Biodynamics is claimed by the Biodynamic Agriculture Association to be the oldest defined system of organic growing. It has its roots in a series of lectures entitled 'Spiritual Foundations for the Renewal of Agriculture' given by Austrian philosopher Rudolf Steiner in 1924. According to Steiner, 'life forces' in the crops and animals also sustain the vitality of the person who eats the food. The use of chemical fertilisers reduces the vitality of the crops, he believed, so it is therefore important to increase soil life, with the use of composts and manures creating a biologically dynamic agriculture.

One of the best-known biodynamic preparations involves fermenting cow manure inside a cow horn that has been buried in the soil over winter.

Steiner introduced six herbal preparations for use on the compost heap and two additional preparations for spraying on the fields to increase vitality of the soil and crops. One of these is derived from manure buried in a cow horn during winter (500) and is designed to enhance the powers that come from the earth. The other (501) is made from a quartz crystal that is buried in the summer and said to be subject to the metabolic forces of soil life and the cosmos. A well-known aspect of biodynamics is its adherence to the rhythms of the sun and the moon – for example, planting by the moon.

Perhaps the most significant concept that Steiner introduced, and easier for the scientifically trained to grasp, is that of the 'farm organism'. Farms should be self-contained, mixed with livestock and with as far as possible closed nutrient and energy cycles. This can be problematic for horticultural units due to a higher land requirement unless part of a wider biodynamic farm.

Whatever you may feel about some of the more esoteric aspects of biodynamics, or misgivings you may have about some of Steiner's beliefs, farms practising their methods are often well run, with vibrant, healthy crops and animals. In the UK they come under the umbrella of organic certification, with additional requirements governed under Demeter certification.

Permaculture

Permaculture is a contraction of not only Permanent Agriculture but also Permanent Culture and was developed as a concept by the Australian Bill Mollison in the mid-1970s. He described it as a:

> design system for creating sustainable human environments. Permaculture is based on the observation of natural systems, the wisdom contained in traditional farming systems, and modern scientific and technological knowledge. Although based on good ecological models, permaculture creates a cultivated ecology, which is designed to produce more human and animal food than is generally found in nature.

The principles are sound: the use of polycultures (many species of plants and animals together); plant stacking (making use of different levels: trees, bushes, herbs); time stacking (starting one crop before another is finished); perennial vegetables (resilient and less soil disturbance); efficient energy planning; and energy cycling. It is the application of these principles to viable commercial production that can be challenging.

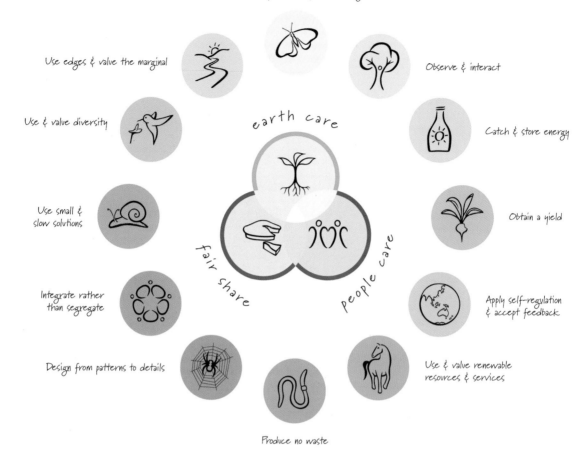

Creatively use & respond to change

Use edges & value the marginal

Observe & interact

Use & value diversity

earth care

Catch & store energy

Use small & slow solutions

Obtain a yield

fair share

people care

Integrate rather than segregate

Apply self-regulation & accept feedback

Design from patterns to details

Use & value renewable resources & services

Produce no waste

The foundations of permaculture are the ethics (centre) which guide the use of the twelve design principles, ensuring that they are used in appropriate ways. These principles are seen as universal, although the methods used to express them will vary greatly according to the place and situation.

Agroecology and Food Sovereignty

It has become common for growers who choose not to certify their holdings organically to describe themselves as agroecological growers. Agroecology has a comparatively wider meaning, but according to the UK Statutory conservation, countryside and environment agencies' Land Use Policy Group (LUPG) report, *The Role of Agroecology in Sustainable Intensification*: 'The term agroecology has been popularised more as an approach emphasising ecological principles and practices in the design and management of agroecosystems, one that integrates the long-term protection of natural resources as an element of food, fuel and fibre production.'

It was not until the early 1980s that agroecology became a discipline named by ecologists, agronomists and ethnobotanists. In essence, it encompasses all of the above approaches including organic farming, but more recently it has also been associated with more radical perspectives and linked to peasant agricultural movements such as *La Via Campesina* in South America.

Agroecology is based on applying ecological concepts and principles to optimise interactions among plants, animals, humans and the environment, while taking into consideration the social aspects that need to be addressed for a sustainable and fair food system (FAO).

There is a danger that the term could be hijacked by corporations as 'green wash', in the same way that some say the term 'sustainable agriculture' has been, and thus become meaningless. Indeed, in France the term 'agroecology' became a battleground in 2012 between the French Government's form of agroecology, which encompassed no-till methods with herbicides, and the version favoured by civil society organisations and small farmers, that is, a diversified organic agriculture on a human scale. Many argue that agroecology must go hand in hand with food sovereignty to enable transformation of the food system. *La Via Campesina* defines food sovereignty as:

> The right of peoples to healthy and culturally appropriate food produced through ecologically sustainable methods, and their right to define their own food and agriculture systems. Food sovereignty puts those who produce, distribute and consume food at the heart of food systems and policies rather than the demands of markets and corporations.

Chapter Two

It's All About the System

The system of production arises out of the principles outlined in the previous chapter, but it also relates to scale and to market. System design needs a degree of pragmatism and flexibility as ecological and commercial realities come into play, interacting with the individual circumstances of the particular holding. Certification, through adherence to standards, provides boundaries to the extent to which compromises can or should be made. The good grower will be continuously evaluating the functioning of their system and striving to improve it.

Sometimes more than one system can be employed on one farm. For example, a holding might have a bio-intensive no-dig system operating in polytunnels, an intensive market garden using a bed system and two-wheeled tractor, wheeled hoes and seed drills, plus field-scale vegetables with tractor-operated cultivations, planting, weed control and harvest. The intensity of the system and the degree of mechanisation is to an extent determined by the market and the value of the produce. If you are direct marketing and planning to grow all crops yourself, then you may need different systems – growing maincrop potatoes for hand harvesting on a no-dig system makes no commercial sense.

From market garden to field-scale production

Bio-intensive production

There is nothing much new under the sun and intensive bed systems are not new. Alan Chadwick in the 1960s in California and later John Jeavons in *How to Grow More Vegetables than You Ever Thought Possible on Less Land than You Can Imagine* advocated the biodynamic/French intensive method of horticulture. They drew inspiration from the French intensive techniques employed in the market gardens surrounding Paris in the nineteenth and early twentieth centuries. Crops were grown in 45cm of horse manure, which was readily available, and spaced closely together to exclude light and weed growth and to conserve moisture. Glass bell jars were used to provide individual cloches for winter and early crops. Using these techniques, up to nine crops per year could be grown.

Chadwick and Jeavons also drew on the biodynamic techniques of Rudolf Steiner, particularly the holistic growing environments of plants and their various companion relationships. Chadwick made a barren garden at the University of

OPPOSITE: Teign Greens, near Exeter, is an 80-member Biodynamic Community Supported Agriculture (CSA) veg-box scheme established in 2020, growing on roughly 1.5ha and using a mixture of methods from min-till with compact tractor to no-dig via a BCS walking tractor, As well as the CSA, they wholesale salad and greens to local pubs, retreat centres and so on, based on a larger 22ha mixed farm.

California – Santa Cruz fertile, using large quantities of compost. One technique he employed was to ensure that seedlings were always transplanted into progressively better soil, as well as sowing and planting by the phases of the moon. Yields were said to be four times higher than those produced by commercial growers. Jeavons describes biodynamic gardens using raised beds 90–180cm wide, themselves inspired by Ancient Greek observations of how plants thrived in landslides, with loose soil allowing air, warmth, nutrients and roots to penetrate the soil properly. Jeavons' system does involve double digging when setting up the beds, followed by the use of a U-bar – which has now come to be known as a 'broadfork'.

No-dig or minimum tillage

The model of growing food in undisturbed soil, thereby preserving soil structure and encouraging the absorbance of water and carbon while allowing soil health to flourish, is key to its appeal, coupled with the human scale of production and the possibilities of establishing a holding without huge investments in machinery. No-dig/no-till allows the soil biology to be more active and can help plant roots to find nutrients that are already in the soil. The mycelial network remains intact and serves as an extension to plant roots. Using compost on undisturbed soil is about feeding and encouraging the work of these valuable organisms.

Broadfork with intensive beds, mulched with compost at Trill Farm Garden in Devon.

Trill Farm Garden. Ashley Wheeler and Kate Norman have been running Trill Farm Garden since 2010. In 2022, they took on an additional hectare on top of the original 1ha market garden.

Charles Dowding has been a long-term practitioner of no-dig growing and his early systems involved initial cultivations with a rotavator, followed by bed-forming by hand using a spade. The system he has developed since 2000 at Lower Farm and now at Homeacres in Somerset involves laying cardboard on the ground (usually mown pasture), with 7–15cm of composted material on top. He is experimenting with different amounts and types of compost, including woodchip, and currently makes two-thirds of the compost he uses.

At Homeacres, the health of the crops, the lack of weeds and the reduction in hard physical labour are evident. The ongoing comparative trials (not replicated) between a dig and no-dig bed consistently show yield advantages for the no-dig system. It is, however, not a certified organic system and the use of cardboard plus the quantities of brought-in manures entails some challenges both for certification and for scaling-up to a commercial scale.

Inspired by Charles Dowding, many growers have adopted no-dig beds in protected cropping, or in intensive plots for high-value crops, such as salads.

More recently, growers have found inspiration in some of the (mainly) North American growers with intensive no-till market gardens. There are, though, a few notes of caution that should be raised. The North American models may not be replicable in UK conditions in terms of returns and profitability (for example, Curtis Stone's claim of being able to make $100K/year profit off his 0.1ha urban farm), as they are very reliant on a large urban market. Also, the systems depend on large inputs of manure or compost from off the farm, particularly when starting out. In the same way that the French bio-intensive growers of old relied on supplies of horse manure, the modern no-till grower may use green-waste compost from municipal composting, or manures from horse stables and livestock farming. This can be considered as 'closing the loop' by allowing the return to the land of nutrients that might otherwise go to waste. However, there is an ongoing debate about the addition of what some consider to be excessive amounts of

Setting up no-dig beds at Sandy Lane Farm.

Ghost acres

The term 'ghost acres' was coined in the 1960s by Georg Borgstrom in his book *The Hungry Planet* to refer to the area of land abroad that is used to grow feed for animals within a country. In horticultural terms, it relates to the land outside the holding that is producing the nutrients imported into the system. This can take many forms, not just the feed for animals on the holding, but also the manure, straw or mulches that are imported, which also need land to produce them.

organic matter and nutrients, and the problems this can cause (*see* Chapter 5).

Pedestrian rotavator/two-wheeled tractor

In the hinterland between the intensive no-dig market gardens and field-scale production lie intensive systems based on pedestrian rotavators, two-wheeled tractors or compact tractors. A little bit of mechanisation, though anathema to some, can enable a larger area to be managed by one person.

Two-wheeled tractors are mainly used for cultivations – preparing the ground for seedbeds and planting – but they can also be fitted with a range of implements for mowing, chipping and carting. A pedestrian rotavator or two-wheeled tractor can be used comfortably on cultivation areas up to 0.7ha, with much lower running and maintenance costs than a tractor and hence a lower carbon footprint. The easy creation of seedbeds enables seed drills to be used for precision sowing and row marking for efficient use of wheel hoes for weeding. Precision saves time when thinning crops, while optimum spacing maximises yields and quality, reducing wastage. The system lends itself to growing in plots rather than beds, though some systems have fixed paths, with the rotavator used to till narrow beds the width of the rotavator.

It is advisable to get the most powerful model you can afford. Avoid tillers and cultivators that are powered on the rotors, as they tend to bounce and can be difficult to control and need a lot more physical effort to use. That is not good when using anywhere near or inside a polytunnel!

Jason Horner of Leen Organics in County Clare, Ireland, using a two-wheeled tractor with ridging attachment in potatoes.

Compact tractor

A next step up is to the compact tractor. The advantages of small tractors are that, while good for seedbed preparation, you can expand the possibilities in terms of equipment like loaders for turning and moving manure and compost, fertilizer spreaders for lime, or broadcasting green manure and pallet forks for moving bulk bags around the holding. They are suitable for plot-scale growing, where a large field is subdivided into rotational plots.

Field-scale vegetable systems

Field-scale vegetable systems, where large plots or fields grow single crops, are normally associated with production for wholesale or packer (supermarket) sales. They are usually highly mechanised, with large capital inputs and economies of scale. There can be an assumption that these systems are not as agroecological as smaller intensive systems, but this is not necessarily the case. They can be every bit as focused on soil health and regenerative practices and are often very innovative in their approaches, for example the use of cover crops and integrated pest management.

A market grower may also have a few fields for growing the staples. It is still possible to source smaller field kit relatively cheaply and to grow staples profitably. There are indications that fewer new growers are coming into field production, plus there are fewer growers around with the necessary skills. Training and demystifying field-scale production is necessary, together with appropriate technology, if the gap between intensive market gardens and the supermarket growers, with increasing use of robotics and cutting-edge technology, is not to widen. There are opportunities, as well as a need for growers to work together through sharing machinery – for example through machinery rings – and planning field cropping strategically, something that UK growers have not always been good at doing.

Farmtrac FT25G HST electric tractor in demo at Grown Green in Wiltshire.

Kate Collyns (Grown Green) rents 1ha at Hartley Farm near Bath. Kate grows on a mini-field scale for local wholesale, to the farm shop and kitchen on site, as well as to nearby veg-box schemes, shops and restaurants. She uses a Kubota compact tractor with a 1.5m rotavator for the field and a BCS 740 two-wheeled tractor for cultivating polytunnels and smaller patches. Planting is done by hand, sowing with an Earthway drill, and weeding with a wheel hoe.

Field-scale vegetable production at Strawberry Fields in Lincolnshire.

Arable rotations with vegetables

While vegetables are normally grown on a vegetable holding with a permanent rotation, they can also be grown as part of a wider farming system, for example an arable farmer diversifying into vegetable production, or a grower entering into an agreement with an arable farmer to rotate vegetables around the farm. There are advantages for the grower, as the vegetables can be grown on ground that should be clean of pest and diseases.

It may be a few years before returning to the same field, which means that the usual need to balance crop families – there is often a need for more brassicas in the rotation than is healthy – don't apply. If it is a share-farming agreement, then primary cultivations and muck spreading could be done by the farmer, meaning fewer machinery requirements. On the other hand, arable farms are less likely to have irrigation and electric fencing may be required to keep rabbits, badgers and the like out of the crops.

Mixed farming systems with vegetables

A mixed farm that includes grazing land might also incorporate arable and vegetable crops into the rotation. In mild coastal locations like Cornwall, mixed farms would traditionally follow (at least) three years of grass/clover with early potatoes and winter cauliflowers and a summer reseeding of the grass leys. Animal manure from grazing animals, normally dairy or beef suckler herds, would provide fertility.

The Pioneer Homesteader in use at Chagford CSA in Devon.

Horse-powered vegetable growing

While for some the thought of powered machinery is scary, for others working with horses it is even more so! It may seem like a step backwards, but modern horse-powered vegetable farms combine new technologies with traditional ways. If you have an affinity with horses and the time and patience to learn the skills, it may be for you. A lot of the skills and knowledge about horse-powered systems come from the US, where there have been Amish communities keeping the skills alive.

In the UK, there are very few horse-drawn implements available and you may have to look to Continental Europe or North America for appropriate kit. There are toolbars, such as the French-made Kassine, which can be fitted with a range of different tools for weeding, tilling and ridging. It can be pulled by a range of draft animals, with either flexible traction, whereby the carrier is linked to the tool by ropes or chains, or rigid traction using a shaft or drawbar. Other tool carriers are available, such as the German–Swiss developed Univecus, which has a combined steering mechanism that is useful on sloping ground, and the US Pioneer Homesteader, which is good for heavier duty cultivations with two light or medium-sized horses.

The choice of horse is important – they need to be good natured and hardy, just like growers! Also of consideration is the care, housing and feeding that

is needed for working horses. A draft horse needs to consume about 2 per cent of its body weight in hay every day. The British Horse Society recommends a ratio of one horse per 0.4–0.6ha on permanent grazing.

Agroforestry

Agroforestry, put simply, is 'farming with trees'. More specifically, silvo-horticultural agroforestry is the practice of growing trees and vegetables or other horticultural crops as part of the same system. There can be many advantages of doing so. I planted rows of apple trees at Radford Mill Farm in the 1990s before I'd heard of the term agroforestry – it simply made sense to me. We needed more fruit for our markets and it was a good way to divide the rotational blocks in the field. It also made a difference to one's perception of the field, making it a less daunting, more human-scale space for those of us that worked there. In addition, the tussocky grass in-between the trees provided a beetle bank for pest control.

Many crops, such as beans, courgettes and squashes, can be vulnerable to wind and therefore benefit from the shelter. Trees can also protect vulnerable soils from wind erosion. Some trees, such as alders, are nitrogen-fixing, so they can benefit the crop rather than compete with it. However, agroforestry does though need careful planning in terms of

Vegetable agroforestry at Tolhurst Organic. Tree rows are spaced at 23m apart to fit the irrigation system and include apples on dwarf M26 rootstocks, oaks, hornbeam, birch, cherry, maple and alder.

Intercropping squash and sweetcorn at Cotesbach Gardens in Leicestershire. The two crops were then undersown with clover for a modern take on the 'three sisters'.

tree choice and planting design. Fortunately, there is a growing number of practitioners and guides on agroforestry out there to help.

Intercropping

Intercropping is the practice of growing two or more crops together, in the same space and at the same time. As with agroforestry, intercropping is a way of adding diversity into the system, using the benefits of shade from taller crops and making better use of light. Compatible plants – so called 'plant teams' – benefit each other rather than compete for resources and the combined yield is more than if the crops were grown on their own. Diversity almost always helps the biological functioning of the system, though it also adds complexity in management terms. As growers, especially on a small scale, we aim to make the best use of our main resources – land and light – by reducing the amount of bare ground. By intercropping faster growing crops with slower ones, we can get two or more crops from the same piece of land and adhere to the regenerative agricultural principle of the use of living roots.

Lettuces and radishes are good examples of fast-growing intercrops, that could be grown between taller-growing crops like tomatoes or kale. Agretti is a lesser known but increasingly popular vegetable that can also be suitable for intercropping under tall crops. Covering the ground with crops is a more agroecological approach than using plastic mulches for weed control in tall crops. There are well-known examples, such as the 'three sisters' which entails growing sweetcorn, climbing beans and pumpkins or squash together as a synergy of space and structure. Other forms of intercropping involve undersowing of taller crops with fertility-building crops to make better use of time and space.

Organic certification – do you need it?

When I started out as an organic grower, there was no legal definition of organic, so we could put a sign out for 'organic vegetables' and people had to take our word for it. There were organic standards – quite brief in those days (!) – and we followed them, but as we were not certified there was no mechanism to verify that we did so correctly.

In 1993, the EEC Council Regulation 2092/91 was adopted, which gave a legal basis for organic food production in the EU. This and subsequent regulations have set out the inputs and practices that can be used in organic farming and growing,

Is organic certification always appropriate for small-scale growers supplying local markets?

as well as the inspection system that must be put in place to ensure it. To call yourself organic, therefore, you need to be registered with an organic control body and be certified by them. This entails following organic standards that conform to the EU Organic Regulations. There is a conversion period, which is normally two years for annual crops and three years for perennial crops (Demeter, the biodynamic organic control body, requires a further year). The inspection process entails an annual visit by an inspector, which is a combination of a visual inspection and an audit of farm records (*see* Chapter 14).

While the days before an inspection can be preceded by long evenings, making sure that all paperwork is in order, as well as a certain amount of trepidation, it is a useful exercise to keep you on track and ensure you are heading in the right direction. As a grower, it should never be enough to aim for the baseline; good growers should always be looking at how they can improve their business and systems, both agroecologically and financially.

For many growers today, especially small-scale or part-time growers, the cost of certification can seem a big barrier. If you can sell directly to the consumer

Checklist for conversion

1. Do you or any staff have experience of vegetable growing or organic systems? Are they on board/motivated for change?
2. Is the business in good heart economically?
3. Do you have a market?
4. What changes need to be made and how much will they cost?
5. What are the boundaries of the farm? Buffer zones may be needed to prevent spray drift.
6. Is the land in good heart? Are there any legacy issues, for example high populations of perennial weeds and/or soil-borne diseases?
7. Is the farm infrastructure suitable? Irrigation, manure handling, appropriate farm buildings for packing/storage. Fencing for livestock.

None of these may be barriers to conversion, but it is important to be well aware of the challenges ahead!
Adapted from Davies, G. and Lennartsson, M. (eds) *Organic Vegetable Production: A Complete Guide* (Crowood, 2005).

and are transparent about your methods, do you need it? If you can call your produce 'agroecological' or 'regenerative', maybe you don't need the 'O-word' at all? There may also be an anarchic streak in a lot of growers that shuns away from bureaucracy and regulation.

There are concerns, however, that unverified organic claims, such as 'grown according to organic principles' or even 'better than organic', could damage the reputation of certified organic as 'food you can trust'. There is a strong case that paying for certification helps to support the long-term sustainability of the organic market and the promotion of organic values and products by the control bodies – or, in the case of the Soil Association, its associated charitable arm.

Participatory guarantee schemes

Lawrence Woodward, who founded the Organic Research Centre (as Elm Farm Research Centre) and played a part in the development of organic standards in the UK, believes that the answer lies in developing a participatory guarantee scheme to cover those growers that: a) follow organic standards but are not certified; b) aspire to follow organic principles/practice and wish to indicate they are under the 'organic umbrella'; and c) those using organic techniques, but identify as 'agroecological' or 'regenerative'. According to Woodward, 'The scheme would be built on the published organic principles and standards but adapted to grower conditions and concerns. At its core would be the active engagement of regionally based peer group growers in partnership with their consumer/citizen community.' Participatory certification falls outside of the scope of European Organic Regulations, though it has a history in a number of countries. There would be legal issues to resolve, but Woodward thinks it could be done.

In the past, there have been some group certification schemes aimed at reducing costs for small growers, for example by the Soil Association, but these have not been continued.

Chapter Three

Getting on the Land

In 2020, the Landworkers' Alliance conducted a survey of 156 new entrants to farming in the UK, 76 per cent of whom included vegetable production. The survey showed a surprising diversity: 54 per cent of new entrants were female and 9 per cent identified as BBIPOC (Black, Brown, Indigenous and People of Colour). The average age of new entrants was 37.

However, it is not easy to get on to the land and become a grower, especially if you are not in the fortunate position to inherit land or the family farming business. When asked about barriers to setting up or expanding production, 61 per cent cited 'access to land' as a limiting factor. Other barriers mentioned were: 'training or experience' (54 per cent); 'access to finance' (46 per cent); and 'accommodation and planning permission' (35 per cent).

Getting the skills

Of the new entrants questioned in the 2020 survey, 77 per cent were educated to degree level or above, but only 21 per cent had agricultural qualifications at Level 2 or higher, which suggests a lack of appropriate training available to new entrants. Those who have developed an interest in growing as a progression from gardening need to be aware that a whole new set of skills is required, as well as a change of mindset. Malcolm Gladwell in *Outliers:*

The Story of Success states that to become masterful at any task requires 10,000 hours of practice, or about ten years of dedication to your field – literally for growers.

When I started my organic growing journey there was not much training available and commercial horticulture courses gave little time or credibility to organic alternatives. After graduating with an environmental degree and volunteering on an organic farm and market garden in east Devon, I was inspired by a ten-week part-time organic gardening course. Following that, it was all about learning on the job and attending as many farm walks and conferences as I could. I devoured all the books and publications that were out there, learning and adapting knowledge from the conventional sector, as well as organic. There is no substitute for practical on-farm experience, so the best learning pathways will probably combine the practical with online methods, networking, mentoring and more. In the words of Ric Bowers, an organic grower since 1975 and now an international consultant in fresh produce and processing:

> Learn by observation, trial and error – the latter is a wonderful leveller. Don't have a closed mind that restricts self-growth and understanding. Don't take advice as sacrosanct, go and challenge and draw your own conclusions as we did, and still do.

OPPOSITE: The Apricot Centre runs the 13ha Huxhams Cross Farm in Devon, which was acquired by the Biodynamic Land Trust in 2015. This farm has been developed with a 15-year renewable tenancy, designed using permaculture and biodynamic principles. The Centre employs eight people on the land and provides training for farmers and growers.

WWOOFing/volunteering

Originally 'Working Weekends on Organic Farms', then 'Willing Workers on Organic Farms' or 'World Wide Opportunities on Organic Farms' (WWOOF) and now known just by its initials, WWOOF is a worldwide movement, linking visitors with organic farmers, aiming to promote a cultural and educational exchange and to build a global community conscious of ecological farming and sustainability practices. Many of the holdings that participate are smallholdings, or on the semi-commercial end of the scale. Many growers would agree that 'WWOOFing' is a good way to start and a good way to visit and learn from a large range of different farms, though it can be a world away from the sharp end of commercial production.

There may also be local Community Supported Agriculture (CSA) schemes that take volunteers, often on specific days of the week.

Traineeships

Where traineeships exist, they can be a great way to learn, especially when they span over one or two seasons and when the trainee works alongside the grower. It is important that there is clarity of what is expected on both sides. The Biodynamic Agricultural College offers work-based full-time certified two-year training across the UK – the trainee joins a biodynamic farm, working and learning alongside an experienced practitioner and in parallel attends residential study seminars.

At the time of writing, the Kindling Trust is running a FarmStart programme in Manchester, which is a year-long training programme. Trainees work at the Trust's 0.6ha organic market garden two days a week, learning how to become a commercial organic grower. Combining classroom and practical training, trainees gain knowledge on everything from soil nutrition, managing pests and disease, to crop planning for a commercial operation. The Kindling Trust's FarmStart also runs short courses for commercial growers, as do Trill Farm Garden, ChagFood, Cae Tan CSA (Grow Your Own CSA) and the CSA Network UK.

In Wales, the LWA has been working with Lantra to pilot a network for Welsh horticultural trainees – the Resilient Green Spaces Wales Future Farmers Network, funded by the Welsh Government. The aim is to teach key skills and connect trainees to the wider network of organic growers in Wales.

Tuesday is volunteer day at Teign Greens CSA. Here the Tuesday team shows off the first pick of broad beans of the season.

Trill Farm Garden runs a range of courses aimed at new entrant growers, or those who are looking either to add or develop their skill set.

A trainee at Teign Greens CSA learning how to operate a two-wheeled tractor.

There has been an emphasis on developing practical and management/business skills, but there are also less tangible benefits, such as exposure to different business models and approaches, as well as mutual support amongst the trainees.

The Apricot Centre CIC in Devon offers an accredited one-year Level 3 course in Regenerative Agriculture and Land Based Systems, which combines three days per week on a placement farm with two days per week training.

In addition, many farms are running their own informal apprenticeship schemes, based on the model of the now sadly defunct Future Growers programme, trail-blazed by the Soil Association. There are some attempts to support and coordinate these disparate on-farm training schemes through the OGA, the LWA and others. At present, they are not regulated, so potential trainees need to assess if what is offered is really training or a synonym for cheap labour.

Online learning

In recent years, there have been a number of online courses aimed at new growers, mostly emanating from North America. They often combine video with webinars and Q&A sessions and discussion groups, so can be quite accessible (though sometimes the time differences mean that they can be scheduled for the middle of the night, UK-time) and offer a huge amount of content. They can also involve a not inconsiderable expense, which needs to be paid up front or in regular instalments. Examples, at the time of writing, are: the JM Fortier Masterclass; the Neversink Online Market Farming Course; Elaine Ingham's Soil Food Web Foundation Courses; Michael Kilpatrick's Small Farm University; Ben Hartman's Lean Market Growing Masterclass; and, from Sweden, Richard Perkins' Making Small Farms Work and Permaculture Design Course.

There is also a huge volume of free farming videos on YouTube and some useful podcasts available. One 'benefit' of the Covid-19 pandemic has been a growing library of recorded webinars and conference sessions on various topics available online.

Academic learning

The grower is a 'Jack of all trades', but a Master's degree can be good for some. An understanding of biological principles is important, as can be marketing and communications. Agricultural and horticultural degrees or Master's qualifications can give a good grounding in the science; the lecturers might be more amenable to organic and agroecological approaches than they were in my day! Either way, an open mind to learning and a quest for knowledge are vital.

At the time of writing, Writtle College offers undergraduate courses in Horticulture, as do Greenwich University (Hadlow College) and Nottingham Trent University. Bridgend College offers a Higher National Diploma in Horticulture, which includes an organic module, and Chichester College offers a Higher National Certificate in Horticulture. The University of the Highlands and Islands, University Centre Myerscough and Cornwall College also have undergraduate horticulture courses. Schumacher College runs a Regenerative Food and Farming BSc.

Scotland's Rural University College's long-running part-time distance learning Organic Farming MSc can be compatible with part-time or even (at a push) full-time growing. Harper Adams' Masters in Agroecology also has part-time as well as full-time options.

Advice and mentoring

It is important to take every opportunity to get good advice. A professional adviser has a weight of experience and knowledge to draw upon. It goes without saying that the adviser should have organic experience, though there may be specific fields where it is less relevant (for example. irrigation, business advice and so on). A fresh pair of eyes can see things that you may not and potentially save lots of wasted time and money. According to Jim Aplin of Hotchpotch Organics:

> We were lucky enough to catch the days of free OCIS [Organic Conversion Information Service] advice and get a visit, tailored advice and a written report from [experienced horticultural adviser] Roger Hitchings. This was worth its weight in gold – an expert eye looking in can help you to focus on key issues fundamental to your enterprise, and not be over-distracted by secondary matters. It's a good investment.

With an ageing population of growers, there is a recognised need for mentoring schemes so that new growers can learn from the experienced and in some cases pioneer growers. There have been formal mentoring programmes pairing up new entrants in their first five years of business with experienced farmers, such as through Nourish Scotland and the CSA Network UK.

Working as a grower

There can be many job opportunities for growers and assistant growers (sometimes seasonal posts), once a certain amount of experience has been gained, and

this can be a good stepping stone towards growing in your own right. You have the security of a regular income and can continue to learn and put your ideas into practice and make mistakes at others' expense – though don't say that at the interview! Opportunities come up for growers with CSA schemes, established box schemes, community projects, farms and estates that have farm shops and cafés or restaurants.

In recent times, some of those vacancies requiring field-scale or tractor-driving experience have been more difficult to fill. Organisations that provide care farming and therapeutic horticulture or training may also employ growers. These jobs are advertised on: the OGA forum; e-news and social media; the Soil Association Marketplace; WWOOF; UK Organic Market Gardeners Facebook page; Organic Farmers & Growers (OF&G) newsletters; and through the LWA and CSA Network UK.

Access to land

Unless you are lucky enough to inherit land or be part of a farming family, access to land can be the biggest obstacle to setting up on your own as a market gardener. You may aspire to be growing on your own land, providing security and the ability to plan long term. However, the reality of high house prices, and particularly houses with land, can make that a pipe dream. In many places, the demand for pony paddocks, with or without a house, can price you out of the market. Land prices continue to rise, despite, or maybe because of, global uncertainty.

The Knight Frank Farmland Index cited an average value of bare farmland in England and Wales as £20,509/ha in Autumn 2022. The unit price of small parcels of land will be considerably higher. Many of the organic pioneers chose to seek land and accommodation in cheaper areas, such as Devon, Cornwall and West Wales. This is still where most organic growers are concentrated, with few in the traditional horticultural heartlands of Lincolnshire, Bedfordshire, West Sussex and Kent, where better or more suitable land is located. Just owning any piece of land is not enough, however; ideally, you need good-grade agricultural land with easily workable soils on level ground, or with good aspect.

Renting land

There can be many more opportunities to rent than to buy land, even though you may have to be proactive to make them happen. Large landowners like the National Trust and private country estates may have walled gardens or small farms for rent. If an estate is diversifying, its owners may be keen to rent out land that can grow produce to supply a farm shop, café or restaurant. There are organic and/or regenerative farmers that are keen to add enterprises to their farms or estates, but don't have the skills themselves. For them, a tenancy agreement or share farming might be appropriate.

Tenancy agreements

Every agricultural tenancy agreement is unique. It is recommended to seek independent expert advice before entering into a new tenancy agreement or arrangement, or when changing an existing one. The regular form for a horticultural business is a fixed-term

Walled gardens provide great micro-climates for market gardens and are sometimes available to rent. This one is rented by Coleshill Organic from the National Trust.

farm business tenancy. There is no minimum tenancy period, but where the agreed term is two years or longer, a year's notice must be given on either side.

At the end of the fixed period, if no notice is given, it becomes a periodic tenancy under the same terms. Rent reviews can take place at no less than three-year intervals. At the end of the agreement, compensation can be made to the tenant for any physical improvements, provided that the landlord has given prior consent. This can be particularly important for tree planting, rabbit fencing and so on.

Share-farm agreements

With share farming, two parties come together in a mutually beneficial agreement to farm an area of land, while remaining as two separate businesses. Often, one of the parties will own the land, while the other is given the opportunity to grow on it. For organic or regenerative farms that are looking to embed more diversity into their systems, it can work well.

The basis of shared-farming agreements is a ratio, which sets out how much each party is responsible for putting in and is entitled to take out; this is established by assessing the annual value of the assets and expertise that each person brings to the table. The landowner might contribute the land, farm buildings and fixed equipment, with the grower contributing field kit and labour. Cost of inputs might be shared or separated. The owner does not receive rent for the land and the grower is not paid for their time. Both parties submit separate VAT returns. For the grower, less upfront capital is needed compared to taking on a tenancy or an own holding. The share in the business can be built up by reinvesting profits.

The new entrant can learn from the farmer's experience, while for the farmer it can be a way of ensuring that the land is worked without relinquishing possession, for example for a phased retirement or succession. It is important to nail down a written agreement at the start, with no grey areas, and to make sure that the aims and objectives of both parties are aligned.

Starter farms

In the UK, 'county farms', or 'council farms', were set up at the end of the nineteenth century to provide a way into farming. Some of these still exist, though more than half have been sold off in England since the 1970s. There are also council smallholdings – for example, the City of Bristol possesses around 263ha of smallholdings and agricultural land. In addition to the council land, there are also large public land-owners in the city such as the University of Bristol, the University of the West of England and the NHS. Through the Fringe Farming Project, the LWA, together with SUSTAIN and Shared Assets, have presented key asks to Bristol City Council, including providing resources to manage the smallholdings once more and recognising the important role they could perform in feeding the city.

In North America, FarmStarts, or incubator farms, have a long history of enabling access to land, mentoring and training new entrants. In France, RENETA is the National Network of Farm incubators and has around 58 incubator farms, aiming to enable prospective new farmers to experiment, innovate and determine if farming is for them. In England, Farm-Start in Manchester has modified its approach. It started off with two sites divided up into quarter-acre plots where people could run their own businesses. Following feedback, it decided to simplify operations, with trainees now growing alongside a coordinator at the central site and as part of a team, rather than on their own. FarmStart, together with OrganicLea from London and Tamar Grow Local from Devon, have been learning lessons from RENETA to support and develop the growth of FarmStart projects in the UK. The LWA has developed a guide for establishing and running FarmStarts.

The Ecological Land Cooperative supports new entrants into ecological farming through a model it has designed for creating affordable ecological smallholdings. The model involves the creation of small clusters of three or more residential smallholdings with permission to build a sustainable home, and

A couple of FarmStarters at Woodbank in Stockport with kale for sale to an ethical partner, such as Veg Box People, who deliver fresh, organic veg across Greater Manchester, or Unicorn Grocery based in Chorlton.

with off-grid utilities and road access. By purchasing larger sites at a lower price per hectare, shared infrastructure and planning expenses, the costs are kept down. Each new smallholding cluster is established with a binding ecological management plan drawn up by an expert group. The smallholders can work together and support each other, while the cooperative retains the freehold on the land. At each site, each smallholder receives, in addition to a land unit of between 1.2 and 3.6 hectares:

- permission to build a low-impact dwelling
- a shared timber-frame barn
- road access and an internal stone track
- on-site renewable electricity generation
- water via rainwater harvesting and borehole
- one year's business mentoring from a sector expert.

The cooperative now has six sites in East Sussex, Glamorgan, Carmarthenshire, South Somerset, Devon and Cornwall in various stages of development, some with full planning permission, others with temporary planning, and some still going through the planning process where applicable. Each site is, or will become, home to three sets of agroecological smallholdings.

Cae Tan CSA growing crops on the Ecological Land Cooperative's Furzehill site on the Gower, South Wales.

Land trusts

The Soil Association Land Trust safeguards legacies of productive land, providing a safe haven and preventing land being lost from farming and growing. Land is donated by retiring farmers and landowners, often those with no dependants, who wish to see their life's work continue into the future.

The Biodynamic Land Trust is a charitable community benefit society working with communities to secure UK land in trust, protect and develop biodynamic, organic, community-connected farms and provide further opportunities for sustainable agriculture and entrant farmers/growers. The Trust encourages entrant farmers or growers with viable farm business plans who are looking for help finding land to get in touch with them.

Living on your land

Living away from your holding comes with a number of difficulties: tools and equipment need to be stored securely, while in some areas vandalism may be an issue. Unsocial hours, watering and the need to open and shut tunnels morning and evening, as well as early morning harvesting, can make for further problems if you are living off site.

Many growers start by buying land, then apply for temporary planning permission for a mobile home, later applying for full planning permission for a permanent dwelling. The regulations vary between devolved Nation, County and National Park authorities. Usually, as a prerequisite for granting planning permission for building a house on your land, you have to be able to demonstrate viability and the essential need to live on site. Chapter 7 (the planning office of The Land Is Ours), the Landworkers' Alliance and others have worked hard to support growers' applications and to raise

The first step towards 'living the dream' is often to live on site in a caravan or mobile home.

awareness amongst planners and Government of the viability and productivity of small-scale horticulture. It can be a long process; with in some cases repeated appeals and applications, plus consultants' fees running into thousands of pounds. Detailed preparation and research are vital and can make the difference, though success is not guaranteed.

Community Supported Agriculture

Community Supported Agriculture (CSA) is defined by the CSA Network UK as a partnership between farmers and consumers in which the responsibilities, risks and rewards of farming are shared. CSA schemes not only benefit the land, soil and planet, but also bring clear benefits to the grower(s) through solid finances and a mutually supportive relationship with customers, or members as they are more commonly known. Growing can be an isolated profession and CSA means not only a more stable and secure income, but also (some or all of) sharing the costs of production, shared ownership or investment in the business or land, volunteer labour and emotional support.

CSA is not for every grower – if you enjoy working on your own and find larger groups hard work, then it is probably not for you. However, for those who enjoy interacting with others, and are happy to delegate and share decision-making, it can offer a much more supported role, where much of the stress of managing is done by others. Most CSAs allow a high degree of autonomy on day to day decisions by the grower, while well-managed volunteers can be a real benefit to the enterprise. Some of the key factors of success identified in the CSA Network UK's starter guide include:

- a clear vision for the CSA
- a clear structure (legal and actual)
- security of land tenure
- a suitable site for growing
- access to an appropriately large population
- good communications; understanding the motivation of members and keeping them involved
- provision of a range of social engagement opportunities and events
- realistic pricing and pragmatic forecasting
- an able and competent workforce
- an understanding and control of growing costs and a focus on production of quality produce
- an understanding of finances – don't be too reliant on grants, use them for start-up or capital investment.

Bennison Farm CSA is a 3.5ha organic market garden in north Essex. The CSA was started by Danny Steele (left) and Meg Brooks-Steele in 2013.

Farm succession

Farm succession is not just about inheriting or taking on a farming business within a family; it can also involve transferring businesses outside of a family. Many organic farmers or growers, having built up a business, find themselves at retirement age, wanting to retire but also wishing for the farm to continue to be managed organically. While this transition might happen within the family, the business could also be passed to an intern or an employee. This is not an easy process, however, especially as farming involves a lot of emotional investment in the land and letting go can be difficult.

There can be benefits from bringing in an independent adviser or facilitator to help the process. Good communication between all parties – especially with family members that are not directly involved – is key. There may be differences in expectations and the question of accommodation: Who lives where? Establishing how the farm assets are owned, as well as the present and future roles and needs of each party, are all important. Tax issues, particularly Inheritance Tax and Capital Gains Tax (in the UK), need serious consideration, as do pensions and investments. It may be possible for the younger generation to use their pension funds to buy land and/or property from the older generation through a Self-Invested Personal Pension Fund.

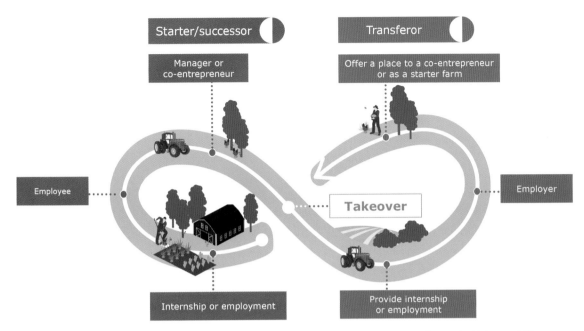

Landgilde and Wageningen University & Research in the Netherlands have developed a 'Roadmap to Succession'. It is a model for new entrants to gain experience and learn how to run a business and decide if they wish to take over a farm. The established farm takes on an intern and increasingly shares responsibilities with the intern, who progresses to an employee and then manager, or co-entrepreneur. Finally, if all goes smoothly, a transfer of the business can take place. Graphic: Landgilde and Wageningen University & Research

Finance

Having a good business plan is crucial to success and it may be worthwhile gaining advice or training on this before getting going. See the LWA's (2022) *Business Planning Guide* for the ecological farm and forestry businesses. Also see the Organic Research Centre's *Organic Farm Management Handbook*.

The LWA report, *Supporting the Next Generation of Farmers*, outlined the economic, social and environmental cases for supporting agroecological farming. The report stated that the costs of starting up agricultural businesses are significantly higher than for start-ups in other sectors. Estimates for required initial investments for agroecological start-ups range from £25,000 to well over £500,000, with lower profit margins than for most businesses, whilst annual risk is higher. The low and unpredictable returns of farming make borrowing money an unrealistic option for many new entrants. The report recommends the Government to provide start-up grants and loans for new entrants.

Meanwhile, some not-for-profit organisations are taking up the slack. The Dean Organic Fund, administered by the Organic Research Centre,

Southern Roots Organics in Pembrokeshire received a Dean Organic Fund loan to go towards building essential infrastructure, such as a packing shed, processing barn, machinery store and access road.

has been providing interest-free loans of between £5,000 and £25,000, repayable in instalments over up to five years. The Fund is able to lend to companies, sole traders, community/social enterprises or charity-owned businesses, including ones that are not certified organic but are closely aligned with organic principles. The windows for funding are variable, but are announced in the organic farming media.

The Real Farming Trust also runs the 'Loans for Enlightened Agriculture Programme' (LEAP), which offers a mix of low-interest loans between £20,000 and £100,000 and grants, with mentoring and business advice included. It is aimed at community food businesses – Community Interest Companies (CICs), Community Benefit Societies (CBS), cooperatives or Companies Limited by Guarantee (CLGs) – but not sole traders, partnerships or Companies Limited by Shares (CLS). LEAP will, however, provide support for those who wish to change their governance models.

Ethical banks, such as Triodos, may be worth approaching, as they finance many organic farming projects. Private funders, which can include friends, family, benefactors and entrepreneurs, might be able to offer grants or loans – however, be clear as to contracts and understandings, motivations and expectations.

The Community Supported Agriculture model is worth looking at. As well as shared costs of production, many CSAs incorporate elements of shared ownership or community investment in the business or land. It can be easier to attract funding as a CSA, and the experience and contacts of Board members can be tapped into to help fund-raising.

Crowd-funding options are also possible, using internet-based platforms such as Kickstarter and Crowdfunder. They need good planning to make them work and an estimated three-month lead-in time. The rewards – the offer – need to be carefully thought about and you must make your project stand out from the rest. Having good social media networks, built up over time, is also an advantage.

Organic conversion

Control bodies

Once the decision has been made to become organic, the first step is to decide which organic control body to register with. The approved control bodies in the UK are at present:

- Organic Farmers and Growers CIC (GB-ORG-02)
- Organic Food Federation (GB-ORG-04)
- Soil Association Certification Ltd (GB-ORG-05, GB-BIO-142)
- Biodynamic Association Certification (GB-ORG-06)
- Quality Welsh Food Certification Ltd (GB-ORG-13)
- OF&G (Scotland) Ltd (GB-ORG-17).

These control bodies are regulated by UKAS – the UK Accreditation Service – to comply with UK and EU law. Post-Brexit, the UK incorporated the EU legislation on organic farming into UK law and is expected to continue to align closely with the EU Organic Regulations. It is advisable to research the different control bodies and make an informed decision based on what fits best with you. In terms of horticultural standards, there is not much difference among the various bodies, so your decision may be based on what your customers need or recognise. If your system includes livestock, the standards may differ in terms of stocking rates and housing.

Initial inspection

The next step is to arrange an initial organic certification inspection. Ahead of the visit, if you have not previously done so, you should familiarise yourself with the organic standards and think about how you would establish an organic system, or the adjustments you would need to make to become organic. At inspection, the Inspector will carry out an audit of your farm to see how compliant it is with organic standards and what changes you may need to make to ensure full compliance. When that is achieved, you can enter the conversion period, which is normally two years for annual crops and three years for perennial crops. The Biodynamic Association also certifies to biodynamic standards, which entails an additional year's conversion period before you can use the Demeter trademark.

The conversion period

The purpose of the conversion period is to allow time to establish organic management practices, build soil fertility and create a functioning agroecosystem. For those already following agroecological approaches, the need for a conversion period can seem less clear and a little burdensome. Before the days of the Organic Regulations, it was possible to sign an affidavit to confirm that no prohibited inputs had been applied in the previous two years, then go straight into organic production, but that is no

Conversion normally starts with a grass/clover ley to build fertility and kick-start biological processes.

longer permitted and the conversion period must be a monitored one. There are, however, good reasons for giving the land a rest and it also allows the grower time to gather information, learn new skills and put in the infrastructure that is needed (*see* Chapter 4). For many, particularly those converting from arable, it should be a time to kick-start the biological systems, through fertility building with green manures and grass leys.

During the conversion period, the land must be managed according to organic standards, which have to be documented through record-keeping. It may be frustrating that you can't get on and grow and sell organic vegetables right away. There is no market for in-conversion organic produce, though if you are selling directly to the public, you can communicate this to your customers.

Chapter Four

Setting Up

Whether you are starting from scratch or taking over an existing operation, there will be lots to do and it can be quite daunting. It is worth taking time to plan and set up properly, rather than rush in and make mistakes that may be difficult to rectify later. Not everything needs to be done at once and you may need time to get to know your site. Start small and build up slowly, get things right and do things better, rather than doing more. Take care to ensure that you build in the aesthetic and give the place a human scale. Use permaculture principles for design – or common sense, as some might say. Think towards the future and allow for expansion, if needed. Imagine what the holding could look like five or ten years down the line.

Market research

Everyone agrees on the importance of market research and your business plan will depend on it. Indeed, finding a market and your niche in it can be far more of a challenge than the growing bit. We outline the different options for routes to market in Chapter 11. A passion for growing vegetables should be a given, but some growers are reluctant marketeers, while others are natural at selling and love the customer interface. You need to find a balance – either within yourself, or with others, as both sets of skills are important.

The market you choose will dictate what crops you grow, and to an extent the complexity of your business. What is clear, though, is that you need to understand the organic market and the organic consumer, together with the local landscape of growers, shops and markets. Geen and Firth state that market research is a process that:

- identifies opportunities and customers
- develops products that satisfy opportunities and customers at a suitable price
- presents and promotes the product to appeal to customers.

In the context of the organic vegetable market, that might entail mapping existing producers and their markets/delivery areas, organic shops, farm shops and supermarkets selling organic produce. It is a good idea to get to know other growers in the area; although they could be seen as competition, there may be opportunities to work together. What farmers' markets exist locally and do they have an organic produce stall? What is the demographic and profile of your local population? Statistics from the Soil Association's annual *Organic Market Report* will give a 'direction of travel' that might be useful for a business plan, but meeting and talking to people is the best way to gauge interest locally. In the words of Reuben Chesters, founder of Locavore, speaking at the Oxford Real Farming Conference in 2022: 'All the best market research in the world doesn't compare to just giving it a go.'

OPPOSITE: Planting hedges and establishing agroforestry early on can have ecological benefits later.

To find out more about your potential customers, a simple questionnaire or online survey, distributed via local shops, surgeries, pubs and the like may help. Alternatively, you can conduct an online survey using Google forms or similar and connect with local groups via social media. Be wary of leading questions, however, as people may just say what they think you want to hear! A questionnaire can help to define your target consumers. Who are they? What is their profile? What do they want? What are their motivations and needs? How do they want what they want? What are their buying habits?

Another way of engaging with your potential local customers, particularly if you are going down the CSA or box-scheme route, is to organise a meeting and invite green groups and others to attend.

Infrastructure

Buildings

It is useful if you have a range of farm buildings that can be adapted for your purposes. There may be buildings that are not suitable for large-scale industrial farming, but you may be able to use for workshops, machinery and equipment storage, potting and packing. There may also be a need for communal space for meetings or staff breaks. It makes sense logistically to combine as much as you can, except for machinery storage, under one roof and to enable multiple uses of given spaces. You need to check with your local planning authority on what is allowed. There can be permitted rights for development on agricultural holdings over 5ha, with reduced rights for smaller holdings.

Workshop

Having a good workshop can save money in the long term. It is worth spending time in the winter, servicing and maintaining equipment, in order to save wasted time when stretched and stressed in the busy summer

months. Those with the skills and an innovative bent can also adapt and create machinery and tools that fit their systems. FarmHack has some inspiring examples, as does the French collective *L'Atelier Paysan*, with a number of open-source designs for appropriate technology for growers available in English on its website.

Greenhouses and polytunnels

We will cover protected cropping in Chapter 10. Greenhouses and polytunnels can be crucial for extending the season and maximising income, when growing on a small area. They provide an escape from the rain when field work is impossible and are also useful for plant-raising, chitting potatoes, drying crops and machinery storage, as well as lambing and raising poultry.

Washing, packing and storing

A central accessible area for processing and packing vegetables is essential – especially for direct sales and vegetable boxes. Build in a silt trap, so that you can reclaim any soil washed from your vegetables. If planning from scratch, ensure that you have enough space to allow for expansion. Cool areas for vegetable

Multi-span polytunnel construction at Southern Roots Organics.

storage are important, for example for root crops. You may also need a refrigerated cold store for longer-term storage and for taking field heat out of harvested produce. This could be built into an existing building, or alternatively you can buy a used refrigerated lorry body (*see* Chapter 11).

Staff room/meeting rooms

It may be that you live on site and are happy for staff to join you for breaks and lunchtimes, but you may also want to separate work from home life. In any case, the importance of a shared brew should not be underestimated! Temporary structures, such as yurts, can serve as comfortable spaces for team gatherings, while straw-bale roundhouses or other lower impact ecological buildings could be considered. Green construction can be a good communal activity for CSAs.

Irrigation

In an increasingly unpredictable climate, access to irrigation is essential for vegetable production. In dry periods, it can mean the difference between a crop and no crop; it also gives the grower an element of control. For many vegetables, irrigation is essential for establishment, while for others it can make a difference to quality and yield. If you have sufficient water pressure from the mains supply, you could run a sprinkler line, usually having a diameter spread of around 14m, with sprinklers spaced 6m apart. Drip lines work with lower pressure and are more suitable for perennials, or in protected cropping.

Watering off mains can be expensive, so consider collecting as much water as you can off buildings and think about sinking a borehole (consent may be needed), or creating a pond for irrigation. Solar pumps can be used to pump water to a header tank to provide pressure for irrigation. Reel systems consist of a big coil of polyethylene pipe with a large sprinkler (cannon) mounted on a trolley, which is pulled in slowly while the water is cannoned over a wide area. They are popular in field-scale production as they are a lot less work and can irrigate large areas in a short period of time. If you plan to abstract more than 20cu m (20,000ltr) a day from a river, stream, canal or borehole, you are likely to need an abstraction licence from the Environment Agency.

Borehole being dug at Southern Roots Organics. The borehole provides the farm with water security to back up rainwater harvesting in a changing climate.

Irrigation of field vegetables at Strawberry Fields, Lincolnshire.

Weeds, wireworm and 'wabbits'

It is a common scenario for a new grower to take on a pasture field for vegetable production. You should plan to deal with what Iain Tolhurst calls 'the three w's' – weeds, wireworm and w(r)abbits ...

While there can be a rush of fertility due to the incorporation of decayed organic matter, there may also be problems with weeds and almost inevitably wireworm. If the field has been grazed by horses, or otherwise abandoned, there are likely to be an abundance of docks, thistle and couch, as roots and as seeds in the weed seed bank.

Wireworm can be a devastating pest and needs to be taken seriously, especially in the first three years after breaking a pasture. Almost all horticultural crops are susceptible, with some destroyed at seedling stage, while potatoes, alliums and root crops can be made unmarketable due to tunnelling. The primary options for tackling wireworm are through cultivations and growing mustard – biofumigation (*see* Chapter 9). Trap-cropping and the use of a naturally occurring insect pathogenic fungus (*Metarhizium brunneum*) are also being researched.

Tim Deane has developed a sequence of cultivations that should also give good weed control. Starting as soon as dry enough to cultivate in the spring:

1. Shallow rotavate with fast rotor speed to cut turf away from the roots.
2. Repeat across direction of travel, slightly deeper than the first pass.
3. Use harrows, with spring tines, to stir the broken turf around, so that it dries out and dies off. This may take a couple of months.
4. Sow mustard in mid-June and again in August, followed by overwintered rye in the autumn. If an early seedbed is needed in the following spring, delay the second sowing of mustard until September and leave for the winter.

'Wabbits' are not so easily dealt with by cultivations. But they will surely find your new lush vegetable plantings sooner, rather than later. If you can, rabbit-fence your whole area, or consider protecting plots with electric rabbit netting.

Mowing of mustard at Pitney Farm Market Garden, south Somerset, prior to incorporation.

Rabbit fencing at Glebelands Market Garden, near Cardigan. Although the rabbits disappeared, the fences provide wind protection for intensive salad beds.

Tools and accessories, tractors and implements

The tools and equipment you require relate to the type of system you have decided on (*see* Chapter 2). Careful decisions need to be made, as tools can be expensive and something that works on one farm, may not work on another. Gaining practical experience of tractors and tools on other farms before committing to purchases, as outlined in the previous chapter, cannot be overemphasised.

By starting small and expanding slowly, you can work out what equipment you really need. You can start market gardening with almost no capital investment using basic gardening tools and a wheelbarrow. You can share equipment with other growers, though if this is done informally make sure the share is fair and that you return equipment clean, promptly and in one piece!

Equipment does not have to be new. Sign up to some agricultural auction sites, as you may be able to bid online, set up alerts on eBay for things you need, and keep an eye on the OGA forum and the UK Organic Market Gardeners Facebook group.

Hand tools/small-scale

Drill-powered electric tilther.

Broadfork.

Two-wheeled tractor with trailer at Pitney Farm Market Garden.

Manually pulled Treffler harrow for greenhouses and market gardens.

Roller in action at Pitney Farm Market Garden.

Webb seed drill units sowing into ridges at Troed y Rhiw farm.

Transplanter at Southern Roots Organics.

Spring tine cultivator at Troed y Rhiw.

Tractor and front-loader with harrows.

Table 1: Tools for the organic vegetable grower

Tool	Description	Suitable for:				Cost Range (guidance only)	Notes
		Protected crops	Intensive no-dig	Intensive Market garden	Field-scale		
Stirrup/ oscillating hoe	Has a U-shaped blade that oscillates as you push and pull, working in both directions.	✓	✓	✓		£33–42	Units available for interchangeable use, e.g. Wolf tool.
Colinear hoe	Light and precise tool designed by Eliot Coleman.	✓	✓	✓		£41	Allows a comfortable upright position for hoeing small weeds.
Wire hoe	Fine tool for hoeing in confined spaces.	✓	✓			£31	Can be very effective; easy to use if there's a good fine tilth around plants. Good for no-dig tunnels and first strike on carrots. Easy to make.
Draw hoe	Chopping action for bigger weeds, paths and ridging up potatoes, etc. by hand.	✓	✓	✓		£15–20	
Flame weeder	Thermal weed burners using LPG/propane gas for killing small annual weeds in false or stale seedbeds.	✓		✓	✓	Hand-held: from £70 Carts: £1,000 Tractor-mounted: £3,000+	Can be available at any scale from hand-held, trolley-mounted to tractor-mounted. Less suitable for grass, weeds and perennials.
Broadfork	Two-handled fork, nor-mally 60cm wide with five 30cm long tines, used for aerating the soil without damaging the soil structure.	✓	✓			£180	Bespoke versions can be created for different bed widths. Could it damage mycelial networks?
Paperpot transplanter	Japanese-developed system for manual transplanting; hand-pulled.			✓		£2,000+	Single- or double-row versions available. Need to buy complete kit with trays and paper. Issues with glues and ingredients of the paper chain at time of writing – need to check with organic control body before use. Very expensive if crops are not closely spaced in the row, but very quick way to plant by hand.

(continued)

Tool	Description	Protected crops	Intensive no-dig	Intensive Market garden	Field-scale	Cost Range (guidance only)	Notes
		Suitable for:				**Cost Range (guidance only)**	**Notes**
Leaf harvester (drill-powered)	Cuts leaves into a bag at consistent height.	✓	✓	✓		£650	Quick harvesting of young, closely planted leaf crops. Requires clean and weed-free crop to be effective.
Tilther	Works top layer of soil into a fine tilth.	✓	✓			£650	Drill-powered. Most suited for no-dig beds in tunnels.
Seed fiddle/ spreader	Broadcasts seed.			✓	✓	£70	Suitable for broadcasting green manures.
Strimmer/ Brushcutter	Petrol-powered hand tool for grass and small bushy growth.	✓	✓	✓		£75–£200	Useful for field and hedge margins and beetle banks, also between and around polytunnels (with care!) and sheds. Consider scythes and jungle knives as alternatives.
Wheel hoe	The wheel hoe is simply a wheel (or sometimes two or four) with handles so that it can be pushed and has a toolbar for attaching hoes, discs or ridgers.	✓		✓	✓ (in small areas)	£50–£400 Also easy to make your own.	Versatile tool for inter-row weed control, ridging, etc. for scales up to 2ha. When weeds are small can be operated at fast walking pace. About ten times faster than a hand hoe. Keeps you fit!
Rotavator/ two-wheeled tractor	Power unit with a range of attachments for use around the holding.	✓		✓		£1,500 (second-hand) Power unit £2,500–£3,000 Implements: rotavator £650–£1,500 power harrow £2,000 flail mower £1,800	Suitable for cultivation in smaller areas, although can damage soil structure in the wrong conditions. Can struggle in heavy soils and can be demanding work, especially when turning, or working for extended period.
Sprayer	Knapsack or tractor-mounted versions available at different scales.	✓	✓	✓	✓	Knapsack sprayer £30–£150 Tractor-mounted £500–£3,000	For application of bio-pesticides, biodynamic preparations, biostimulants, etc.

(continued)

Tool	Description	Suitable for: Protected crops	Intensive no-dig	Intensive Market garden	Field-scale	Cost Range (guidance only)	Notes
Seed drill	Precision-seeding saves time and improves quality of crops through correct spacing.	✓		✓	✓	hand drills £150–£600 Stanhay precision drill £2,000–£3,000+ Set of discs £100	Range from simple Earthway seeder with interchangeable plastic plates for different crops to more sophisticated and precise models (e.g. Terradonis or Stanhay). Can also be tractor-toolbar-mounted.
Tractor	15–35hp tractor	✓		✓		£2,500+	Suitable for cultivations in smaller areas and protected cropping; also for reducing soil compaction when harvesting in wet conditions. Very useful on smaller holdings, but can struggle with powerful equipment and heavy soils.
Tractor	35–40hp tractor	✓		✓	✓	£5,000–£10,000	Creeper gearbox needed for planting, etc.
Tractor	40–60hp tractor					£10,000+	
Tractor	80–90hp+				✓	£20,000+ (80–90hp) prices rising and holding value	
Frontloader	Bucket, or pallet forks mounted on front of tractor	✓	✓	✓	✓	£500–£1,000	Very useful equipment for handling and moving heavy items, turning and handling compost, FYM, etc.
Linkbox	Heavy duty transport box for front or rear linkage of tractor	✓	✓	✓	✓	£150	Saves a lot of time and work.
Trailer	For harvesting crops and transport around the farm and beyond.			✓	✓	£900	Tipping trailer useful for compost.
Plough	Traditional tillage tool – inverts the soil.				✓	three-furrow plough £450+	There may be a place for shallow ploughing. Most contractors' ploughs are too big for shallow ploughing; try other organic farmers in your area.

(continued)

Tool	Description	Suitable for:				Cost Range (guidance only)	Notes
		Protected crops	Intensive no-dig	Intensive Market garden	Field-scale		
Spring tines	Frame-mounted steel tines under tension for secondary cultivations.				✓	£100–£300	Traditional 'go-to' equipment for weeding and light cultivation. Simple and easy to repair. Cheap and cheerful!
Tractor-mounted rotavator	Power-driven rotating blades mix the soil and residues to a fine tilth suitable for sowing.				✓	£500–£800	Excessive use and use in wet conditions can damage soil structure and leave a pan.
Disc harrow	Rotating gangs of discs on a frame driven by ground speed to chop and incorporate residues and break up the soil. Suitable for larger areas.				✓	£500–£800	Useful tool as it doesn't get clogged by grass. Fast and less damaging than a rotavator.
Power harrow	PTO-driven machine with vertical blades that stir the soil to break it up rather than mixing it, preserving soil structure more than a rotavator.	✓ (small models)		✓ (small models)	✓	From £800 (small/rare) – £8,000	Prepares ground for planting following primary cultivation. Can be used to break out green manures and incorporate crop residues before planting without other cultivation in the right conditions.
Subsoiler	Tractor-mounted deep tillage tool for breaking up soils at depth.			✓	✓	£500–£2,000	Useful in conjunction with a plough and a rotavator to remove compaction and pans. Widely available – could use contractor or borrow from a neighbour.
Roller	Useful for breaking clods or creating good contact for seedbeds, particularly for small seeds such as clovers.				✓	Field roller £800–£1,000	Hand-rollers filled with water can be useful/ appropriate on a small scale. Flat roll plus markers good for drilling. Cambridge Roller very good for green manure establishment and for preparing beds for mechanical planting.
Transplanting machine	Pulled behind a tractor while workers on the back drop transplants down a chute.			✓	✓	£1,000–£4,000	Best suited to fine soils and flat ground.

(continued)

Tool	Description	Suitable for:				Cost Range (guidance only)	Notes
		Protected crops	Intensive no-dig	Intensive Market garden	Field-scale		
Potato planter	Rear-mounted, ridges and plants seed potatoes and other tubers.			✓	✓	£700	Basic models are manual with 2 seats and a bell so tuber is dropped at right distance. Automatic models also available.
Bed lifter	Undercutter for harvesting roots and leeks.			✓	✓	£450	
Mulch-layer	Manual or tractor-drawn. Lays and secures plastic or biodegradable mulches on beds.			✓	✓	£800	Some mulch layers can also bed-form and lay drip-tape in one pass.
Flail mower	Tractor-mounted heavy-duty mower.		✓	✓	✓	£1,500	Useful for cutting green manures prior to incorporation.
Manure spreader	PTO-driven trailer for efficient spreading of manure or compost. Loaded with tractor/frontloader.			✓	✓	5t rear discharge PTO £1,500–£3,000	Rear discharge models are most appropriate for vegetable systems.
Finger weeder	Toolbar-mounted. Rubber disc 'fingers' rotate and weed intra-row.					Set of finger weeders £2,200	Works best on loose soils. Crop needs to be well-established to avoid up-rooting.
Brush weeder	PTO-operated inter-row steerage weeder with rotating nylon brushes. Crop protected by tunnel covers.				✓	£2,000–£5,000	Not a pleasant job in dusty conditions!
Toolbar weeder	Tractor-mounted bar which various implements can be added.			✓	✓	£500–£1,000	Interchangeable hoe attachments.
Harrow comb weeder	Flexible-tined weeders under tension mounted on a frame. Dragged through crop to a depth of 1–3cm.	✓		✓	✓	£800	Suitable for small weeds. Don't look back! Treffler also produces a 'tiny' harrow series for pedestrian use in greenhouses and intensive production.
Tool carriers with vision guided hoes	Precision weeding tractor-mounted hoeing systems to 10–15mm accuracy.				✓	£30,000+	Suitable for serious field production.

What is appropriate technology for organic or agroecological horticulture? With widespread problems around sourcing labour in horticulture, there is push for innovation focusing on robotic solutions. These technologies have the potential to be lighter on the land and replace some of the drearier elements of the job – such as weeding. They may be too expensive, or too large scale, for small growers. GPS-guided systems and electric vehicles that can carry people for weeding or harvesting, as well as pulling implements, are becoming increasingly available. According to Eliot Coleman, pioneer American organic grower:

> The reason I invent better tools and systems is because I'm congenitally lazy and I'm out working, doing some job harvesting or cultivating, and the whole time I'm doing it, I'm thinking, gee, there could be an easier way to do this. What if we tweaked that or made a new such and such here? I think that's what all growers should be doing. They should be not satisfied with what's available and saying, okay, we could do better than that.

Ecological infrastructure

This may sound like a jargon phrase, but providing homes and habitats for birds, pollinators and other wildlife is not just a 'nice to have', but is vital for a fully functioning agroecosystem. As necessary as the buildings, roadways, tunnels and plant-raising facilities are, it is also important to design your holding to include features for the predators and wildlife that will make your system work agroecologically. Your holding may already have biodiverse hedgerows and ponds and species-rich grass margins, but, if not, you will have to think about creating them. The more diversity of habitat you have, the better. You should also try to curb the 'tidiness' impulse; not mowing grass as often will encourage insect life.

Hedges and shelterbelts

Hedges not only support birds, mammals and other wildlife, but also smaller creatures, including predatory insects such as ground beetles and earwigs. Of course, pests like carrot fly may overwinter in

The French GPS-guided Toutilo electric vehicle for planting, weeding, harvesting and transporting viewed at the Tech & Bio show in France. At a price of around €25,000 in 2019, it was said to be viable on farms of 2ha and above.

Ecological infrastructure at Radford Mill Farm in Somerset. Hedges provide lots of food and habitat for birds and predators, beetle banks under agroforestry strips act as plot dividers, and cornflowers within the brassicas provide a multifunctional landscape.

hedgerows too, but promoting diversity is key. Hedges provide protection from wind and salt blast in coastal areas; such shelter can help the growth of sensitive crops like runner beans, French beans and squashes. Research shows that pollination by insects of flowering crops is superior in sheltered fields. Lighter sandy and peaty soils, particularly in East Anglia, the Vale of York and the East Midlands, can be vulnerable to wind erosion.

Although cultural practices and building up organic matter can help to reduce the risk, vegetable fields can be susceptible to wind erosion when fine seedbeds are prepared for drilling crops. Therefore, re-establishing hedges or planting shelter belts can protect your soils. Trees and shrubs can also trap water, soil and sediment washing off fields during increasingly frequent extreme weather events. Hedges and shelterbelts can also be useful in providing physical boundaries to neighbouring farms, particularly where bordering with conventional arable fields may create the potential for spray drift.

The area protected by a shelterbelt is proportional to its height and therefore the shelterbelt should be as tall as possible. The most effective shelterbelts allow approximately 40 per cent of the wind to penetrate and flow through, with the remainder deflected over the top of the trees. The shelterbelts are best planted at right angles to the direction of the prevailing wind. The length of the belt should ideally be around ten to twelve times the projected height and gaps (for example, gateways) should be avoided or planned carefully to avoid tunnelling effects. Irregular canopies are better at breaking up and reducing wind eddies, which is best achieved by planting a mix of species.

Deciduous trees are preferable, as they are more permeable. Native species generally support more wildlife, while locally sourced planting material is best in terms of adaptation and avoiding disease risks from imported material. Faster growing trees

Harvesting hazel for bean poles at Sandy Lane farm, a more sustainable alternative to imported Chinese bamboo.

like poplars, willows, alders (great for wet sites and nitrogen-fixing), the much-maligned sycamore and birch can establish quickly, though will have a relatively short lifespan. It may be best to avoid ash due to ash-dieback disease, unless resistant stock can be sourced. It is also important to include an understorey of shrubby trees such as hawthorn, if intending the belt to grow tall, otherwise the wind will come through at the base. Alternatively, coppicing of hazel, chestnut, ash, oak, sycamore, alder, hornbeam, lime, birch or willow can provide thickness at the base.

One of the additional advantages that hedges and shelterbelts provide is from the tussocky grasses and mixed habitat of the hedge margin, which acts as a resource and refuge for many beneficial insects, birds and wildlife. They can act in the same way as beetle banks (below).

Planting the agroforestry system at Eastbrook Farm, Wiltshire,

Beetle bank at Tolhurst Organic in full flower with lots of umbellifers, chicory and tall grasses providing nectar for beneficial insects. Iain Tolhurst considers the ploughing method to be too disruptive for small fields and establishes his beetle banks on the flat, either by natural regeneration, or by sowing wildflower mixes. He avoids sowing grasses, as he has a wide range of suitable species within the seed bank that colonise the strip naturally.

Beetle banks

Beetle banks are mid-field refuges, like hedge banks but without the woody and shrubby element, where predators can overwinter and spread out to crops in the spring. Developed as a tool for arable farmers, the Game & Wildlife Conservation Trust (GWCT) recommends an earth bank 40cm high and 2m wide. It is normally created by careful two-directional ploughing and sown with a mixture of tussocky and mat-forming grasses such as cock's-foot, timothy and red fescue. Beetle banks can encourage winter insect densities of more than 1,000 individuals per square metre.

Tall-growing wild flowers such as umbellifers can be added to encourage hoverflies and predatory wasps.

The need for beetle banks will depend on the size of your fields and quality of existing boundaries. The GWCT says that, as a rough guide, a square 16ha field would not need a beetle bank, as insects will be able to cross the whole field in reasonable numbers, while in a 20ha field one beetle bank in the centre is needed to achieve uniform cover of insects in the spring. The GWCT estimates that it takes two to three years to develop good habitats for beetles and spiders to overwinter and to see benefits in the crops by reduction of pests.

Flower strips

Another option is to grow strips of herbaceous perennials as magnets for beneficial insects. Some species could also be cut as flowers. Examples include bergamot (*Monarda* spp.), echinacea (*Echinacae pupurea*), rudbeckia (*Rudbeckia* spp.), goldenrod (*Solidago* spp.) and aster (*Symphyotrichum* spp). Plants with night-scented flowers, such as honeysuckle (*Lonicera periclymenum*) or evening primrose (*Oenothera biennis*), are particularly good for bats.

Ponds

Water is obviously important for organic vegetable growing, but you should also consider water in your landscape for wildlife and beneficials. Even a small pond in a polytunnel or glasshouse can help by attracting frogs and toads. Ideally, a farm reservoir that provides for all your irrigation needs can also provide good wildlife habitat and leisure opportunities. A clay-lined reservoir can incorporate shallow muddy margins for plants and wildlife, as well as deeper areas for fish. Synthetic-lined reservoirs offer fewer opportunities to create natural water habitats, but they can still have some ecological value. Healthy ponds can be really good for birds, bats, pollinators and moths, in addition to supplying water for mammals in dry summers.

Other actions

Birds, while primarily encouraged by habitat provision, can also be helped by providing nest boxes, perches and winter-feeding stations. Barn owls will feed on voles (which make up 45 per cent of an average British barn owl's diet – a pair and offspring will consume 4,000 prey items per year). Nesting boxes for a range of birds and winter-feeding stations can also encourage a variety of birds.

Bat boxes can be put up to provide roosting opportunities for bats, whose populations have been negatively affected by tree loss and barn conversions. A single bat can consume 3,000 gnats, mosquitos and other insects in one night. Bats feed on a number of insect pests such as cutworm (nocturnal moths), chafer, wireworm (click beetles), weevils and leatherjackets (crane flies). Bat boxes can be built from scratch, or are available to buy. They can be fixed to buildings (avoiding lit areas), or trees at a height of 2–7m above ground.

The late Lin Tolhurst picking flowers at Tolhurst Organic. Flowers provide a potential crop, as well as a biodiversity gain.

Ideally, farm ponds should be multifunctional. This pond at the Seed Co-operative at Gosberton Bank Nursery in Lincolnshire collects water from the greenhouse roofs for use for irrigation.

Chapter Five

Soil Health

Until relatively recently, the concept of soil fertility was foremost, with a fertile soil defined as one that simply supplies sufficient nutrients to the crop to allow maximum growth and yield. However, the definition of soil fertility needs to encompass all soil functions, including biological activity and physical condition, as well as the ability to provide nutrients to the crop. This interpretation is associated with the idea of soil health (Lennartsson and Davies, 2005).

Soil health is a fashionable topic – that has to be a good thing. We have come a long way from the stuffy lectures on soil science that I sat through at college. Concepts of soil health have been popularised by the likes of Dr Elaine Ingham in the US, but they are not new and lie at the beating heart of the organic movement. The principle, attributed to Lady Eve Balfour, that 'the health of soil, plant, animal and human are one and indivisible' is fundamental to organic farming. It is enshrined in the IFOAM Principles of Health (see Chapter 1), which points out that the health of individuals and communities cannot be separated from the health of ecosystems – healthy soils produce healthy crops that foster the health of animals and people. As touched on in Chapter 1, it can seem that the proponents of regenerative agriculture and agroecology are all battling for the moral high ground on soil health, but what does it actually mean?

Soil health has been defined by the UN Food and Agriculture Organization's (FAO) Intergovernmental Technical Panel on Soils (ITPS) as 'the ability to sustain productivity, diversity and environmental services of terrestrial ecosystems'. Soil health is a dynamic concept, applicable to both managed and unmanaged soils. In managed systems, the ITPS goes on to say that 'soil health can be maintained, promoted or recovered through the implementation of sustainable soil management practices'. An earlier definition of soil health, also from the FAO, may be more useful:

> Soil health is the capacity of soil to function as a living system. Healthy soils maintain a diverse community of soil organisms that help to control plant disease, insect and weed pests, form beneficial symbiotic associations with plant roots, recycle essential plant nutrients, improve soil structure with positive repercussions for soil water and nutrient holding capacity, and ultimately improve crop production.

The nature of soil

Soil parent material

Soils form as a result of the weathering of parent materials (rock) through physical and chemical alteration and biological activity. Soil profiles

OPPOSITE: Hungarian grazing rye, just emerging in the autumn, is a nitrogen lifter and will hold on to nitrogen, preventing it leaching in the winter. It is the latest green manure that can be sown, well into October.

are the result of a series of complex interactions between climate, geology, topography and biological activity. Where these factors are stable over time, distinct layers or horizons can form. The parent material determines the soil texture, with the relative proportions of sand, silt and clay contributing to the degree of ease of cultivation and management.

Soil structure

Soil structure has been defined (Arriaga *et al.*) as the combination and arrangement of primary (individual) soil particles into secondary structural units that form aggregates. This arrangement of solids and air spaces is determined to an extent by the soil texture. Aggregates are formed by the colloidal humus, the finest fraction of soil organic matter (SOM), which acts as a binding agent with soil particles to form large clusters. These combine further to form crumbs or clods in the soil, with their size and form determining the soil structure. The structure is important for root growth and the movement of air and water, which has effects on nutrient availability, 'workability' and on pest and disease severity. Issues of structural damage can be more serious in organic farming, as there is no quick fix of 'chucking on a bit of artificial' fertilizer.

A biologically active soil is more predisposed to better aggregate stability and the addition of SOM generally promotes that (*see* SOM below). Compaction, caused by traffic and cultivations, especially when the soil is too wet, or too dry, can cause serious damage to the soil structure, which is often difficult to rectify. So, any inclination to force the soil into a seedbed through additional passes with powered machinery should be avoided, as should driving on the land in wet conditions. Restricting where you drive, for example by using a bed system with wheelings, can help. This can be assisted using the Global Positioning System (GPS) and is known as Controlled Traffic Farming.

Plant nutrients

There are sixteen elements necessary for plant growth. Carbon, hydrogen and oxygen, which make up 95 per cent of plant biomass, are supplied by carbon dioxide and water. The other 5 per cent consists of nutrients derived from the soil. The macronutrients, needed in highest concentrations, are primarily nitrogen (N), phosphorus (P) and potassium (K), but also Calcium (Ca), Magnesium (Mg) and Sulphur (S). Micronutrients are also necessary for plant growth, but in smaller quantities. They include iron (Fe), zinc (Zn), manganese (Mn), copper (Cu), boron (B), chlorine (Cl) and molybdenum (Mo). They are not normally limiting to growth, apart from on nutrient-poor sandy soils.

Nutrients are present in the soil in the form of primary minerals originating from the bedrock, secondary minerals formed by chemical weathering, in organic matter, in living soil organisms, as ions in soil water, or attached to organic matter by electrostatic attraction. However, the presence of nutrients in soil does not tell the whole story, as they may be strongly bound to soil components such as soil minerals and some humus, and thus effectively unavailable to plants. Nutrients held on the surface of clay minerals and organic matter are released more easily; those present in soil microorganisms are some of the most available to plants, as their populations turn over rapidly and are released into the soil water. To make things more complicated, high levels of some elements (for example, molybdenum) can cause lock-up of others – in this case copper. Soil pH can also influence nutrient availability. For example, high pH increases the release of cations, but reduces the solubility of salts such as carbonates and phosphate.

Whereas a conventional grower will have access to fertilizer recommendations based on the nutritional requirements of the plants, the organic grower needs to take a more holistic approach. It is important, however, to understand the individual needs of the crops grown and to maintain necessary nutrients levels, without accumulating excesses that could cause pollution.

Soil organic matter

Soil organic matter is any material produced originally by living organisms (plant or animal) that is returned to the soil and goes through the decomposition process. It can be in various stages of decay – the stable fraction is known as humus. The important functions of SOM are:

- SOM acts as a store of plant nutrients, with humus holding nutrients in plant-available form. In order to maintain levels of SOM, the rate of organic matter addition from plant residues, cover crops, manures and other amendments must equal the rate of decomposition.
- SOM improves soil structure, maintains tilth and minimises soil erosion, through aggregation – binding soil aggregates together. However, it is only part of the total SOM – generally younger SOM with a larger content of polysaccharides, roots and fungal hyphae – that stabilises aggregates. Therefore, optimal aggregate stability requires frequent turnover of organic matter residues.
- SOM also feeds soil organisms – there is a strong correlation between SOM and the number of soil organisms.

Therefore, regular additions of SOM are usually recommended and claims are often made about increases of carbon contents in soil through raising SOM levels. Clay soils will tend to have higher SOM levels than sandy soils. But very high additions of SOM can mean a build-up to levels where there are significantly more nutrients available in the soil than plants can use. If this happens, nutrients can leak and cause pollution problems.

A handful of decaying organic matter from cut and mulch green manure at Tolhurst Organic.

Biological fertility

Soil life is incredibly important, yet relatively little is known about the complex ecosystems beneath our feet. However, the study of the soil biome is developing. The Plant Soil Microbial Community Consortium (PSMCC) states:

> The plant soil microbiome is the dynamic community of microorganisms associated with plants and soil. This community includes bacteria, archaea, and fungi and has the potential for both beneficial and harmful effects on plant growth and crop yield. The composition of any particular microbiome is influenced by many factors, including environmental, soil physical properties, nutrient availability, and plant species.

As with above-ground ecosystems, the principle of enabling as much diversity as possible holds.

Bacteria and archaea

Bacteria are the largest microbial group found in agricultural soils, both in terms of population and biomass. They are responsible for the breakdown of organic matter and releasing nutrients for crop use. They also produce gums that stick soil particles together, important for soil structure.

Archaea are single-celled organisms widely found in soils and may comprise up to 10 per cent of microbial cells in temperate soils. The difference between archaea and bacteria lies mainly in their genetic make-up.

Fungi

Fungi are the second largest microbial group present in soils and are a vital part of many processes, including the breakdown of organic matter and the release of nutrients. Arbuscular mycorrhizal fungi form symbiotic relationships with most crops – exceptions being brassicas and chenopods. They can increase the uptake of nutrients and help to protect plants against pathogens. Care should be taken, as mycorrhizal populations can be suppressed by intensive cultivation and high nutrient levels, especially phosphorus. Fungi can participate in nitrogen fixation, hormone production, biological control against pathogens, protecting against drought and stabilising SOM. Not all fungi are good, though, and soils can host pathogenic fungi such as *Fusarium* and *Verticillium*.

Soil micro- and mesofauna

Microfauna is less than 0.1mm in size and includes protozoa and nematodes. Protozoa are unicellular organisms, which mainly predate on microbial populations. Nematodes are microscopic roundworms that occur widely, particularly in sandy soils. They divide into three functional groups:

- plant-feeding herbivores – primary consumers; these can be crop pests and can also transmit viruses to plants
- bacterial and fungi-feeding nematodes – secondary consumers
- predatory and omnivorous nematodes.

Soil mesofauna is between 0.1–2mm in size and includes arthropods, such as mites, collembola and enchytraeids. They feed on a range of living and decaying plant material and release nutrients.

Soil macrofauna

Soil macrofauna is any soil fauna larger than 2mm. This includes pests such as wireworms and leatherjackets. The most important are earthworms, which break down organic matter, incorporate surface material into the soil profile and improve soil structure and drainage through creating deep channels. There are a number of different species of earthworm, each with their different niches. As well as their abundance and biomass, the diversity and structure of earthworm communities is indicative of soil health. Earthworm numbers are adversely affected by tillage, as most people are aware, but some studies have shown that the use of organic manures, composts and green manures can offset these effects and have a greater positive impact on earthworms than any other soil-management practices. Earthworm numbers can recover quickly after ploughing, especially when organic matter is incorporated. Soil compaction can also negatively impact earthworm populations.

Getting to know your soil

Whether you are assessing a field with a view to establishing a market garden, or simply familiarising yourself with your plot, getting to know your soil is vital. A healthy soil should smell like the forest floor – wholesome and 'earthy', indicating a well-aerated and biologically active soil. A rank, marshy smell suggests poor aeration and a low level of biological activity. Touch and feel are important, not just by hand, but how the soil feels under the feet – a springy softness being optimal. Observe not only the soil itself, but the appearance of the crops (vigour and variations in colour) and the weeds (species and condition), which can give indications of soil health and any deficiencies. Chickweed and fat hen, for example, imply good friability and nitrogen content, whereas sorrel points towards acidity and horsetail is linked with poor subsoil drainage.

The spade-diagnosis method

Taking a sample

The samples taken should be representative of the field. You might need to do several tests if the field is very variable, especially if you know that it contains more than one soil type. In all cases, soil should be examined that is representative of the field.

To use the spade-diagnosis method, at least one – and preferably two – spades are required. One spade will be used to lift out the soil sample. Insert it into the ground vertically using side to side movements, rather than backwards and forwards, so as to avoid compressing the sample. Use the other spade to dig a trench in front of the sample. The result should be a block of soil about 30 × 20 ×10cm, which can be moved without undue disturbance or compaction.

Remove the block of soil, using the spade with a block of wood or your hands at the front to hold it together. With a simple claw, the various parts of the soil can be separated without damaging the structure of the block.

Time of sampling

It is really important to carry out the sampling when the soil is moist, usually in the autumn or spring, so that compaction problems are obvious.

Examining the sample

Observations should be noted immediately in the field and photos taken for future reference.

Within the layer of coarse material identify:

- soil type; sand, loam and clay
- stone content
- soil layers, depth and colour of topsoil, subsoil, compaction layers
- size of clumps when the block is thrown on to the ground, for example on to a polythene sheet.

Within the layer of fine material (tilth) assess:

- number of earthworm burrows
- extent of visible soil-life activity.

Spade analysis is a useful, practical way of assessing the structure and health of soil, visually and by touch and smell.

Earthworm tunnels are a clear indicator of worm activity.

(*continued*)

These observations should be used to guide subsequent choices for cultivation and fertilisation. If there are dead layers or compacted horizons in the soil, they should be loosened at the earliest dry weather opportunity, using a chisel plough, deep tines or a subsoiler. It is possible to gain a lot of information from this, but the focus is an assessment of the structure of the soil in the profile.

A range of actions can be taken to address identified problems, but it should be remembered that there is generally no immediate success with the various measures that can be taken – it can take several years before improvements can be seen. It is, however, well worth the effort, as soil structure and soil condition are fundamental to the productivity of the soil.

Source: Roger Hitchings, 2007.

Earthworm counts

Earthworms are widely accepted as an indicator of soil fertility, soil health and organic matter. Earthworm counts can be useful, but need to be done in the spring and/or autumn when worms are most active and repeated regularly for long-term monitoring. The Open Air Laboratories (OPAL) *Soil and Earthworm Survey* and *Earthworm Identification Guide* (OPAL, 2015a and b) include a key for identifying the twelve most common species of British earthworms. Worm counts help to get a feel for the 'normal' numbers and natural fluctuation of populations in your fields.

Scanning a soil sample for earthworms as part of trials in the GREATsoils project.

Assessing soil compaction

Assessing infiltration rates can be useful for determining soil structure and compaction and is easy to carry out. All that is needed is a 20cm length of 10cm diameter drainpipe, which you hammer halfway into the ground, then pour in water to a depth of 10cm and measure the time taken for it to drain away. This can be repeated at different locations. If the soil is in good health, water should drain away in two to five minutes for light or medium soils, whereas a heavy clay soil could take twenty minutes or longer.

A quick and easy way of locating areas of compaction in a field is to press a blunt knife, soil probe or corer into the soil to get an impression of the pressure needed to reach a certain depth.

Laboratory soil analysis

Laboratory soil analysis can be useful to monitor pH, organic matter and available nutrients over time. Results can help to keep an eye on long-term trends and to assess if the system is functioning properly. It is recommended to do soil analysis at least once in every rotation, prior to cropping.

Soil pH will determine nutrient availability and whether adjustments are needed through liming. It is important to ascertain if any plant nutrients are lacking, not only for optimum crop health, but also for soil organisms. For example, boron is needed by nitrogen-fixing rhizobia, which are crucial for the functioning of organic systems. It is equally vital to avoid excess levels of nutrients, such as phosphate, which can be a pollution risk. Organic control bodies require evidence of analysis before allowing the use of external mineral inputs. There is an increasing range of soil analysis services available, but which to go for?

Soil samples should be taken systematically. Follow the guidance from testing services, as it may vary. One way is to walk a 'W' through the field or plot, taking samples with a soil auger to 15cm (four on each arm of the 'W') and mixing them to form a sample. Avoid gateways and compacted area such as headlands.

Standard soil analysis

Standard soil analysis is the cheapest option available. It provides an estimate of crop-available phosphorus (P), potassium (K) and magnesium (Mg), as well as soil pH. Having been developed for conventional farming, there are some limitations. There are no assessments of organic matter (sometimes available as an optional extra), soil biology and nutrient reserves stored in humus and soil organisms.

Interpretation of the analysis generally includes recommendations of fertilizer and organic amendments necessary to raise P and K to appropriate levels for the rotation (target indices). Organic soil specialists have proposed that these indices should be lower for organic farming in order to reflect higher levels of biological activity and lower yields.

NRM Laboratories offer a more comprehensive analysis, which is recommended for new fields/farms. This includes sulphur (S), organic matter and trace elements. However, according to Mark Measures, organic adviser and former head of the Institute of Organic Training and Advice (IOTA):

> Analysis is only an aid to good organic soil nutrient management; the absolute priorities are to ensure good soil structure and drainage, develop a diverse rotation with sufficient legumes, avoid excessive tillage and support a thriving biological activity by feeding

Table 1: Conventional Target Soil Index for K (AHDB, 2021) with proposed revision for organic (Measures, 2020)

Conventional	Organic	
Grassland	2–	1
Arable crops	2–	1
Vegetable crops	2+	1+/2– Crop-yield dependent

the soil organisms with large quantities of organic matter from fertility building leys, green manures and compost. In short, a systems-based approach to soil management. Dig, walk, look, smell and grow!

Soil health analysis

Soil health analysis services are now available. They provide a spot check on the overall health of the soil. Usually these are relatively crude and based on an assessment of soil biological activity (respiration). Some laboratories offer analysis of mycorrhizal populations, which can be a good indicator of soil biology and with frequent analysis over time can help to build up knowledge of the farm's mycorrhizal populations and practices to improve them.

Some soil labs can provide more information on soil microbial life, including numbers of bacteria, actinobacteria, fungal pathogens, ratio between fungi and bacteria, protozoa and nematode numbers and types. However, they require proper interpretation and we need a reference library of values to gain deeper understanding. Recommendations can often be very general, such as 'add more organic material, 'plough only when necessary' and 'grow deep-rooted plants like lucerne'.

Albrecht analysis

The Base Cation Saturation Ratio (BCSR), or Albrecht analysis, was developed in the US in the 1930s. It puts emphasis on the development of soil biological activity and on achieving the correct balance of nutrients for plant health. Organic adviser Mark Measures (2020), in his review of soil analysis options, says that it can be useful for growers of high-value crops, but points out that most recommendations following BCSR analysis advise regular use of humates, mined carboniferous material and other fertilizers to stimulate biological activity and to balance the cation ratios. 'Is this really organic farming?', he questions.

Plant-tissue analysis

Plant-tissue analysis can be a useful diagnostic tool in helping to understand why plants are not performing well (sometimes despite good soil analysis results), as it shows what has been taken up by the plant (and thus is truly available).

Feeding the soil

Organic growing is all about feeding the soil, rather than the plant. For that reason, we talk about 'heavy feeders', rather than the specific nutrients needed to grow a crop. The source of the food is also important and growers should try to be as self-sufficient in nutrients as possible. For the intensive market grower on a small patch of land, this will be more of a challenge. It is not always easy to incorporate livestock into horticultural holdings, though a laying-hens enterprise can often be a good fit. Green manures and leys are valuable tools for the grower, using legumes to fix nitrogen from the air and sunlight to produce green material for incorporation.

When planning nutrient input, it needs to be considered that, through harvesting crops, nutrients are removed from the system and these must be replaced in order to keep the system in balance. In principle, it makes sense to source materials as locally as possible so as to keep transport and environmental costs down. There are some caveats, however, as not all organic inputs are acceptable in an organic system, due to ethical considerations of the systems of production and there may be risks of contamination. In the following section, I will outline some pros and cons of various materials that may be available.

Farmyard manure

Animal farmyard manures (FYM) enable the recycling of nitrogen, phosphorus, potassium and other nutrients on organic farms, as well as supplying

Table 2: Typical total nutrient content of manures and composts (fresh-weight basis)

Figures from the table in the AHDB *Nutrient Management Guide (RB 209)* (AHDB, 2021)

	Nitrogen		Phosphate			Potash			Sulphur	Magnesium
	Dry matter %	Total nitrogen (kg N/t)[a]	Total phosphate (kg P$_2$O$_5$/t)	Availability (%)	Available phosphate (kg P$_2$O$_5$/t)	Total potash (kg K$_2$O/t)	Availability (%)	Available potash (kg K$_2$O/t)	Total sulphur (kg SO$_3$/t)	Total magnesium (kg MgO/t)
Manures										
Cattle	25	6.0	3.2	60	1.9	9.4	90	8.5	2.4	1.8
Pig	25	7.0	6.0	60	3.6	8.0	90	7.2	3.4	1.8
Sheep	25	7.0	3.2	60	1.9	8.0	90	7.2	4.0	2.8
Duck	25	6.5	5.5	60	3.3	7.5	90	6.8	2.6	2.4
Horse	25	5.0	5.0	60	3.0	6.0	90	6.4	1.6	1.5
Goat	40	9.5	4.5	60	2.7	12.0	90	10.8	2.8	1.9
Poultry	20	9.4	8.0	60	4.8	8.5	90	7.7	3.0	2.7
	40	19.0	12	60	7.2	15	90	14	5.6	4.3
	60	28.0	17	60	10.2	21	90	19	8.2	5.9
	80	37.0	21	60	12.6	27	90	24	11	7.5
Compost										
Green waste	60	7.5	3.0	50b	1.5	6.8	80b	5.4	3.4	3.4
Green/ food	60	11	4.9	50b	2.4	8.0	80b	6.4	5.1	3.4
Ramial chipped wood		4.6–11.5	1.4–5.3			3–13			–	0.26–1.1
Digestate										
Food-based -whole	4.1	4.8	1.1	60c		2.4	90c		0.7	0.2
Farm-sourced whole	5.5	3.6	1.7	60c		4.4	90c		0.8	0.6

Notes:

[a] The crop-available nitrogen supply will depend on the application timing and the delay between application and incorporation.

[b] Estimated value from *RB209*, extrapolated from livestock manures.

[c] Estimated value from *RB209*, extrapolated from slurries.

[d] Source: Westaway (2020) *Ramial Woodchip in agricultural production. WOOFS Technical Guide 2.* Organic Research Centre.

significant amounts of organic matter that stimulate the biological activity of the soil and improve soil structure. If the FYM is from your own farm you can control the feed and bedding material that is used.

Increasing the amount of straw used in bedding will not only improve the welfare of the animals, but also increase the carbon content of the manure and make it go further. Arrangements can be made with organic poultry producers, who are obligated to spread their manure on organic land.

Non-organic manures are allowed to be used in organic systems, but must not be derived from 'factory farming origin', nor from livestock raised with GM feed. Manures should have been stacked for at least six months, or composted for at least three months, prior to use. Non-organic manure, particularly of the 'help yourself to the pile in the corner' kind, can contain weed seeds and roots, as well as microplastics (silage wrapping and baler twine). There can also be risks of herbicide contamination from aminopyralid or clopyralid, in particular.

Nutrient contents of manures will vary according to the animals' diet, bedding and storage. Not all nutrients are readily available to the crop, with composted manures also being more stable (no pun intended), in that nutrients are released more slowly over time. The well-managed composting of manures – regular turning with a front-end loader or purpose-built compost turner – can also be effective at controlling microbial pathogens and killing weed seeds and roots.

FYM is best applied at, or before, times of maximum crop growth, that is, from late winter to early summer. It should be incorporated as soon as possible after spreading to avoid gaseous losses of nitrogen. For vegetable crops, in particular salads, the Food Standards Agency (FSA) guidance is that mature or composted manure can be applied any time before drilling/planting, but fresh manure should not be spread within twelve months of harvest and at least six months before drilling/planting. Where livestock grazing is part of the farming system, as it often is in organic systems, the FSA recommends a minimum six-month gap between livestock grazing and harvest.

The total amount of manure that you can apply to organic land, according to the EU Organic Regulation, must not add more than 170kg of nitrogen per hectare per year, averaged over the whole farmed area. If you are in a nitrogen-vulnerable zone, the field limit is 250kg of nitrogen per hectare per year.

Spreading manure on overwintered rye and vetch in March at Strawberry Fields, Lincolnshire.

Home-made compost

Composting is always a good thing – right? Well, it may not always be so clear-cut. Some, like Edward Faulkner, author of *Plowman's Folly*, believe that the soil benefits much more if organic matter decomposes within the soil: 'There can be no advantage in composting over surface incorporation of the equivalent organic matter … losses of carbon dioxide are at a minimum within the soil, thus assuring a maximum of carbonic acid for releasing minerals from the mineral portion of the soil.' More than half of carbon and nitrogen can be lost to the atmosphere during composting, while significant potassium (more than half) and some nitrogen and phosphorus can be lost to leaching. The nitrogen is also stabilised and not so readily available to the crop. Charles Merfield, Head of the Future Farming Centre in New Zealand, maintains that undecomposed crop residues on the soil surface are far better (than compost) for soil health, breaking down quickly and providing a good food source for soil microbes.

Composting takes fuel and energy to turn the heaps, and when moving the finished compost back to the plots. Before barrowing materials across your site to the compost heap, ask yourself if they can be left *in situ*. Woody brassica stalks can be cut at ground level, reducing the weight of material carted

Troed y Rhiw Farm collects seaweed from the local cove after storm events and it is mostly used as an additive to compost. It is gathered by hand into crates and then lugged into a tipping trailer or rear-discharge muck spreader parked just above the beach. After late storms, it has also been used as a mulch on potatoes, spreading directly on to the ridges. It quickly dries and is incorporated with the power ridger.

Table 3: Typical C:N ratio and moisture content of common compost ingredients

Material	C:N ratio	Moisture (%)
Vegetable crop residues	13:1–30:1	75
Cattle FYM	10:1–30:1	65–90
Poultry manure	3:1–10:1	60–75
Grass clippings	17:1	82
Straw	50:1–150:1	5–25
Sawdust	200:1–750:1	20–25

Source: Davies *et al.* (2005).

and avoiding removing soil that will cool down the heap.

Where leaving plant residues on the surface or incorporation is not practical – for example, when large amounts of material are produced in a polytunnel – or not desirable due to containing weed seeds or perennial weed roots, then composting can be useful. 'Waste' material (weeds, straw, crop residues, manures, woody material, pack-house waste, food waste) is converted into a homogeneous product that feeds the soil. If done well, it can also control pathogens and kill weed seeds and perennial roots. To achieve this, the mix should have the right balance of carbon to nitrogen (20:1–40:1), moisture content (50–65%), particle size (1–1.15cm) and pH (6.0–9.0).

Composting works better on a large scale and is best when done in batches at a time when sufficient material has accumulated to make a heap. Turning it several times will maintain aerobic conditions and

speed up the process. Temperature probes can be used to indicate when a heap has cooled down and needs to be turned – wireless probes can relay the data direct to your phone!

On a small scale, turning can be done by hand with a fork; at larger scales, a tractor and front-end loader, or tractor-mounted windrow turners can be used. Making your own compost on site means that you can control what goes into it. If you have access to lots of food waste, for example from a pack-house or greengrocery waste, you may want to consider in-vessel composting to reduce odours and risk of rat problems.

Compost bays can be created using pallets; at least three bays are needed to allow turning and different

Composting in action. Turning compost with a frontloader at Coleshill Organic. This provides compost that is used as mulch in the no-dig polytunnels.

stages of decomposition. Metal grids used for reinforcing concrete floors can also be bent into a circle for hot composting; these are easy to move around, allowing aeration and so on. For ease of turning with machinery, heaps can be created directly on the soil (or on a concrete base). The heaps can be covered, once cooled down, between turnings. They may need to be watered during dry periods. Composting operations should be sited carefully, so that they are not near watercourses. Larger operations may need approval by the Environment Agency.

The Johnson-Su Composting System, developed in the US, is gaining popularity. A 'bioreactor' is used to create a fungal-rich compost, for use in compost teas and to increase overall soil health and function.

Green-waste compost

Green-waste compost is produced on a large scale by, or on behalf of, local authorities to recycle garden and landscaping green waste, in order to reduce landfill. Green waste needs to be PAS100 certified to be used on organic farms, which should ensure (in theory) that it has been properly processed and separated from non-biological waste. It can be a cheap and readily available source of nutrients when locally available, especially if you can pick it up in

Every compost heap needs a 'Sid'. Grown Green's compost monitor.

bulk. The biggest associated cost is transport. If you have a reliable source of green-waste compost and an analysis to show that it is not contaminated with heavy metals, it would seem to be a perfect fit for horticultural systems.

There is, however, very little crop-available nitrogen in green-waste compost; in fact, for practical purposes the AHDB *RB 209* (2021) guide considers it to be zero. The nitrogen will become available in subsequent years with regular applications. It can be a useful source of phosphorus and potassium, in conjunction with growing leguminous cover crops that supply the bulk of the nitrogen in the rotation. If rates of application are calculated in order to provide N, then it is likely that excess P and K will be applied. Because it is normally clean of weed seeds compared to FYM, it can be tempting to use it as a mulch. However, for regular use this is likely to be too much P and K and may lead to pollution.

One problem with green-waste composts that people are becoming increasingly aware of is plastic contamination. Often it is visible, but, even if not, there may be high levels of microplastics, which can pose problems for soil life. Another issue in recent years has been the use of feedstocks in the compost that are contaminated by aminopyralid and/or clopyralid weedkillers, which can even survive robust composting processes and can pose a real risk of damage to many vegetable crops. Testing compost samples by sowing runner or French beans can determine if there is a problem before using with sensitive crops.

Woodchip compost

Woodchip is fashionable, but for a good reason, as it is great for building the biological and particularly the fungal activity of soils. For a long time, growers have been shy of using woodchip through fear of nitrogen robbery (that is, the lock-up of nitrogen, which is needed to break down the carbon and thus becomes unavailable to crops). However,

Green-waste compost at Trill Farm Garden.

Soil obesity

Many no-dig market gardens are using high quantities of compost as mulch. Is this sustainable? Could it be causing problems? The term 'soil obesity' has been coined by renowned grower Iain Tolhurst, who says:

> Soil obesity is used to refer to soils that have been excessively overfed with large amounts of organic matter, usually over fairly extended periods of time. The most obvious result of soil obesity is very high N, P and K (in some cases P indices of 8–9) with usually a very high SOM content of over 10 per cent. The effects of soil obesity are usually seen as trace element deficiencies in crops due to lock-up in soil. This condition has been seen in tunnel and glasshouse crops where there has been a long-term no-dig and heavy annual surface mulching, and sometimes on some soil types in outdoor cropping where the organic material inputs have been high over long periods of time.

More research is needed, but anecdotal evidence shows that, where soil drainage is poor, particularly on heavy soils, excessive additions of compost can lead to soils becoming 'porridgey' and growing moss and algae.

Iain Tolhurst has been composting woodchips for many years with great success. He has a good relationship with a local tree surgeon, who regularly delivers 2cu m loads of woodchip (mostly coniferous). The material heats up quickly, especially when it contains any green material, and he consolidates it into windrows (3m wide × 2m high) and turns it after six to eight weeks with a small digger. Thereafter, he turns it three or four times a year to produce a well broken down and friable material. He spreads it at 50m³/ha on to green-manure crops during the growing season, allowing for further breakdown and incorporation by worms. An increased rate of 200m³/ha is applied in the polytunnels.

Ramial woodchip

Ramial Chipped Wood (RCW) is fresh, uncomposted woodchip made from small (less than 7cm) diameter tree branches. Nutritionally these are the richest parts of trees, with young tree branches containing as much as 75 per cent of the minerals, amino acids, proteins, phytohormones and enzymes found in the

Woodchip compost at Tolhurst Organic.

Woodchip composting at Tolhurst Organic. Material is windrowed and turned with a mini-digger.

entire tree. The advantage of RCW over composting is that you can chip and spread immediately without the time, costs and space needed for composting. Spreading should take place soon after chipping in the autumn/winter to provide optimum conditions for decomposition. Ideally, RCW should be applied

to a fertility-building ley, to reduce the risk of nitrogen lock-up.

Studies have shown increased soil biological activity – in particular fungi but also bacteria – and SOM when RCW is applied to farmland. Trials as part of the WOOFS project (Woodchip for Fertile Soils) showed that phosphorus levels in the soil increased with RCW applications. The trials also showed that RCW may reduce slug damage to crops. Trials in Canada suggest that RCW can increase saprophytes, which can reduce pathogen incidence such as scab on potatoes.

The WOOFS project concluded that compost and RCW act in slightly different ways when applied to soil and could be used in a complementary way; either by mixing RCW into compost, or by alternating applications according to availability to get the best out of both.

Fertility-building leys

Legumes are the basis of most organic farming systems and organic standards require that rotations include a legume to provide nitrogen for subsequent crops. Usually this takes the form of a long-term fertility-building ley, such as red or white clover and grass. The advantages of a long-term grass/clover ley are:

- For converting farmers, it can help to kick-start soil fertility and provide time needed for building infrastructure, markets and knowledge.
- It is a break in the rotation, allowing soils to recover after intensive cropping and reducing risks of pests and diseases in the rotation.
- It is an opportunity to reduce weed burdens through suppression/competition and to control perennial weeds through cultivations.
- It provides grazing opportunities for livestock.
- It provides food for pollinators.

However, for intensive stockless horticultural systems it is a period of the rotation that does not directly bring in money through cash cropping, so

Mowing grass/clover ley at Southern Roots Organic.

the temptation can be to keep the period as short as possible. One option is to use it as an undersow, so that it is ready to grow when the crop is removed. Another option is to use shorter bursts of green-manure crops such as vetches, which can be grown over winter and produce high biomass in the spring.

The grass component is usually perennial ryegrass, due to its ease of establishment, yield, persistence and quality (grazing) in the maritime climates of western Britain. However, on dry sandy soils cock's-foot is a better choice, while timothy is particularly suitable for cutting regimes. Grass is an important component of leys, as it takes up the nitrogen fixed by the legumes, reducing the risk of leaching and stimulating the legume rhizobia to fix more nitrogen. The grass also raises the C:N ratio, prolonging the release of N to following crops. The inclusion of grasses can build leatherjacket and wireworm populations, however. Also, it is more difficult to get rid of in no-till situations and may

Spreading Ramial Chipped Wood at Tolhurst Organic.

require multiple cultivations for incorporation to prevent regrowth.

The clover component is usually red clover, due to its productivity, but it can be susceptible to pathogens and parasites, such as stem eelworm (*Ditylenchus dipsaci*) and sclerotinia. 'Double cut' varieties are needed for quick regrowth after cutting. Large-leaved white clovers are better suited to cutting than smaller-leaved varieties. White clovers can also get white clover fatigue, associated with clover cyst nematode, so it may be sensible to alternate the clovers in mixes, use lucerne (alfalfa), or go with more diverse mixes including bird's-foot trefoil, lucerne, yellow trefoil, sainfoin and crimson clover. More complex mixtures can provide greater resilience to extreme weather events, better suppress weeds and extend forage availability for pollinators. They also decompose more slowly, with better utilisation of N by subsequent crops.

Management is key, as the fertility-building ley can be considered the most important 'crop' in the rotation. That entails providing a good, firm seedbed for establishment, with irrigation if necessary. On fertile soils, leys may need to be mown every two to three weeks – the normal advice is to mow when the height of the ley reaches knee height, cutting to ankle height above the ground – but of course your knees and ankle will be different to mine! Regular cutting will keep the ley productive and the weeds under control. If the ley is allowed to grow too high, there can be an excess of material which mulches out regrowth. Cutting and removing (for example as silage, or as transfer mulch) will increase nitrogen fixation. Undersowing tall crops such as beans, sweetcorn and brassicas can be a good way to save time and get the ley established. Otherwise, early autumn sowing will avoid peak weed flushes.

The length of time the ley is in the ground will depend on the intensity of the farm system and whether the ley has another purpose, for example grazing. In any case, the annual accumulation of nitrogen in the ley will decrease after two years.

'All species mixture' at Wimpole Hall Farm, in Cambridgeshire, as part of the LegLINK project led by the Organic Research Centre. The mixture contained red, white, crimson and alsike clover, black medic, sainfoin, meadow pea, lucerne, large bird's-foot and bird's-foot trefoil, timothy, meadow fescue and Italian and perennial ryegrass. It was found to be more productive than the standard, simpler mixes.

When cutting leys that are in flower it is good practice, as here at Tolhurst Organic, to leave strips that are uncut (to be cut later), in order to maintain food supply for pollinators and beneficials.

Table 4: Green manures, cover crops and fertility-building crops compared

Name	N-fix (kg/ha)	Biomass	Sowing time	Frost-hardy	Period	Persistence	Topping?	Weed suppression	Gap between crops in rotation	Notes
Alsike clover (*Trifolium hybridum*)	150	Medium	Spring or early autumn	Yes	Medium-term	2–3 years	Yes	Medium	4 years	Low-growing – suitable for undersowing. Good on acid and heavy soils.
Berseem/ Egyptian clover (*Trifolium alexandrinum*)	125–200		Late Mar– Early Sep	No	Summer	2–8 months	Early	Good		Killed by frost, useful for no-dig.
Bird's-foot trefoil (*Lotus corniculatus*)	150 (1st year)	Medium. High root biomass	Spring or autumn	Yes	Medium-term	2–4 years	Yes, but avoid severe defoliation	Slow to establish		Performs better at higher pH. Usually grown as part of a mixture.
Crimson clover *Trifolium incarnatum*	100–150	High	Mar-May/ late Aug/ early Sep	Some (to −5°C)	Summer+	Annual, dies after flowering	No	Good, once established	None	Spectacular. Good early nectar source for bees. Low lignin content. Shade intolerant.
Fenugreek (*Triginella foenum-graecum*)	Not known	Medium	Mar–Aug		Summer	6–8 weeks	Early	Good	None	Useful for polytunnels, can also be sold as a herb 'Methi'. Needs inoculation.
French serradella (*Ornithopus sativus*)	Not known	Medium	Spring	No	Summer	Annual	Yes	Poor		Grows well on acid sandy soils. Adapted to summer drought. Suitable for undersowing.

(continued)

Name	N-fix (kg/ha)	Biomass	Sowing time	Frost-hardy	Period	Persistence	Topping?	Weed suppression	Gap between crops in rotation	Notes
Lucerne/alfalfa (*Medicago sativa*)	150	Slow in 1st year, high after	Mar–May/ Aug	Yes, dies down over winter	Long-term	2–3 years	2–3 times / year	Slow to establish	4 years	Prefers alkaline soils, drought tolerant. Best as pure stand. Does not tolerate grazing. Needs inoculant.
Persian clover (*Trifolium resupinatum*)	100	High	Mar–late Aug	No	Summer	5–12 months	Early	Good	None	Will need irrigation to germinate if sown in summer.
Red clover (*Trifolium pratense*)	150	High, especially when sown with grass	Mar–May/ late Aug	Yes	Medium-term	Up to 3 years	Regularly (knee height to ankle level)	Good	4 years	Beware of clover sickness. Can be alternated with white clover.
Sainfoin (*Onobrychis viciifolia*)	100	High	Apr–May	Yes	Medium-term	3–4 years	2–3 times / year	Slow to establish	None	Thrives on alkaline soils. High lignin so breaks down slower than some.
Sweet clover (*Melilotus officianalis*)	150	Very high	Mar–May/ Aug	Yes	Short- to medium-term	Biennial, dies after flowering	No	Poor at start	None	Needs inoculation

Name	N-fix (kg/ha)	Biomass	Sowing time	Frost-hardy	Period	Persistence	Topping?	Weed suppression	Gap between crops in rotation	Notes
Subterranean clover (*Trifolium subterraneum*)			Spring or early autumn	Yes		Annual but can persist due to self-seeding (underground) if autumn sown	Yes	Good		Drought-resistant alternative to white clover. May be suitable for tunnels. Good living mulch.
Vetch (*Vicia sativa*)	150	High	Mar–May/Sep	Yes	Over winter	6–8 months	No	Excellent		Very competitive against weeds. Allelopathic.
White clover (*Trifolium repens*)	150	Medium	Mar to Aug	Yes	Long-term	7–8 years	Regularly (30cm)	Slow to establish	None	Can be undersown but may need irrigation.
White sweet clover (*Melilotus albus*)	80–180	High	Spring to autumn	Yes	Short- to medium-term	Biennial. Dies after flowering	No	Poor to moderate until canopy cover		Strong taproot – good drought resistance. Low tolerance of flooding. High lignin content.
Yellow trefoil/Black medick (*Medicago lupulina*)	150	Medium	Mar/May–Sep	Yes	Short- to medium-term	Annual	Regularly (20cm)	Good		Low-growing – good for undersowing. Good for alkaline soils. High lignin content

(continued)

Name	N-fix (kg/ha)	Biomass	Sowing time	Frost-hardy	Period	Persistence	Topping?	Weed suppression	Gap between crops in rotation	Notes
Buckwheat (*Fagopyrum esculentum*)		High	Apr/May–Aug	No	Summer	Annual.	No	Good		Prevents leaching, makes P available, suppresses weeds including couch.
Chicory (*Cichorium intybus*)		Medium	Mar–May/Aug–Sep	Yes	Medium to long-term	3–4 years	Regularly (around 3 weeks in summer) or grazed	Good, once established	None	Deep-rooting, pan-buster
Cock's-foot (*Dactylis glomerata*)		Medium	Mar–May/Aug–Sep	Yes	Medium to long-term	2–10 years	Regularly or grazing	Good		Usually sown with red clover. Good storer of N, excellent root structure for improving soil. Drought-tolerant.
Fodder radish (*Raphanus sativus*)		High	Mar–May/Aug–Sep	Some	Summer	Annual	No	Good	3 years	Brassica, so be careful in rotation.
Grazing rye (*Secale cereale*)		High	Sep–Oct	Yes	Over winter	6 months	No	Excellent		N scavenger, prevents leaching. Allelopathic effect when incorporated.
Italian ryegrass (*Lolium multiflorum*)		High	Mar–Apr/Aug - Sep	Yes	Medium-term	1–2 years	Regularly/grazed	Excellent		Grown in mixes with red clover or vetch.

Name	N-fix (kg/ha)	Biomass	Sowing time	Frost-hardy	Period	Persistence	Topping?	Weed suppression	Gap between crops in rotation	Notes
Mustard *(Sinapsis alba)*		High	Mar – Autumn	Little	Summer/ autumn	4–6 weeks	No	Excellent	3 years	Nitrogen lifter. Brassica, so be careful in rotation. Can reduce soil-borne pests and diseases (especially *Caliente* types).
Perennial ryegrass *(Lolium perenne)*			Apr or Sep	Yes	Long-term	Up to 6 years	Regularly/ grazed	Slow during establish-ment		Grown as mixture with clovers for long-term grass/clover leys.
Phacelia *(Phacelia tanacetifolia)*		High	Mar– Autumn	Hardy from autumn sowing	Summer/ over winter	Short-term	No	Excellent		N-holder: Good at attracting bees.
Tillage radish *(Raphanus sativus)*		High	Apr–Aug	Some	Summer	6–8 weeks	No	Good	3 years	Deep-rooted annual for improving sol structure. Brassica, so be careful in rotation.
Westerwolds ryegrass *(Lolium westerwoldicum)*		High	Autumn	Yes	Over winter	Annual	Regular, or grazing	Excellent		N-holder reduces leaching over winter.

Source: Information adapted from *Sort out your soil* (Rosenfeld and Rayns, 2010) and *AgroDiversity Toolbox* (Kassel University).

Cover crops and green manures

The terms 'cover crops' and 'green manures' tend to be used interchangeably, as crops grown for the benefit of the soil. Their aim is to retain nutrients (reduce leaching), boost nitrogen through fixation and feed the soil by adding organic matter. They tend to be short-term in use, filling gaps in rotations, whereas fertility-building leys are in for longer periods. While it is easy to focus on leguminous green manures such as vetches, clovers and trefoils, they will not fix much nitrogen over the winter period, making the timing of incorporation crucial, as an extra few weeks in the spring can make a big difference to the amount of nitrogen fixed. Therefore, it is crucial to plan them in properly to rotations to make the best use of them.

Also, there are many non-leguminous green manures that have useful functions. Cereal or 'grazing' rye (*Secale cereale*), with its large fibrous root system, is extremely effective at retaining nitrogen and can be sown as late as mid-October in some areas. Buckwheat can be an effective tool against couch grass and is also a P lifter, making phosphorus available to subsequent crops. Phacelia is another quick-growing summer green manure that is also an excellent nectar provider for bees and other beneficials. *See* the Table, 'Green manures, cover crops and fertility-building crops compared' for the characteristics of different options.

There can be many advantages to growing single-species green manures – simplicity of sowing, establishment and management. It is worth getting to know what species work well on your land. However,

Buckwheat at Purton House Farm. Grower Ed Sweetman took part in the Innovative Farmers trial, testing to see how effective buckwheat is at controlling couch grass. He found it 'a joy to grow' and effective at controlling couch – the critical factor being to follow it with a winter cover crop that will out-compete couch in the spring.

Cover crop mix of phacelia, crimson clover, Persian clover, black oats, millet, sunflower and buckwheat at Trill Farm Garden, five weeks after sowing. This will be flailed after flowering and covered with black plastic ready to plant straight into.

Crimson clover and phacelia in full flower at Tolhurst Organic.

we can also extend the principle of diversity to green manures. There is increasing interest in green-manure mixtures, backed up by growing evidence that diversity above the ground is linked to diversity below ground.

Australian soils ecologist Dr Christine Jones emphasises the importance of fungi in transporting carbon compounds around the soil and supplying energy to the bacterial community. Diversity of plants is needed, as a variety of different leaf structures can intercept more light, increasing photosynthesis and the rate at which root exudates draw down carbon through the fungal pathway. Below ground, plants from different groups cooperate with each other, sharing microbes from each other's microbiome. Dr Jones's message is to prioritise diversity and she recommends including at least one mycorrhizal plant in a cover-crop mix.

There are some simple established mixes that work well, such as vetch and rye for over winter, but it is worth experimenting with different species that grow well in your sowing or cropping window. Many growers also throw out of date vegetable seeds into the mix for added variety!

Mobile green manures, or transfer mulch

One approach is to harvest a green-manure crop in one place and use it as a mulch in another – this is known as transfer mulch. This can be useful when material is required as a mulch and not enough material can be produced *in situ*, or for protected cropping, where cropping space is at a premium (*see* Chapter 10).

Comfrey has been a favourite of organic gardeners since being championed by Lawrence Hills in the 1950s. It is a perennial crop, with nitrogen and phosphorus in comparable concentrations to, and potassium levels much higher than, farmyard manure. It has often been used as a mulch for fruiting crops such as tomatoes, as well as a liquid feed.

Danish researchers have trialled a range of plant species to deliver high concentrations of specific nutrients to particular crops. Their results showed that, for example, Dyer's woad, salad burnet and stinging nettle showed high boron, whereas dandelion, chicory and garden sorrel showed high potassium levels. The researchers concluded that it is possible to produce green manures with high concentrations of S, P, K and B, with low C:N ratios, and that these properties have a great impact on the value of the green manure for vegetable production.

Work by Chloe Ward on perennial mobile green manures at Bangor University focused on three nitrogen-fixing perennials, alder, gunnera and gorse. She argued that growing these crops on marginal land and applying to the soil to meet crop demand could

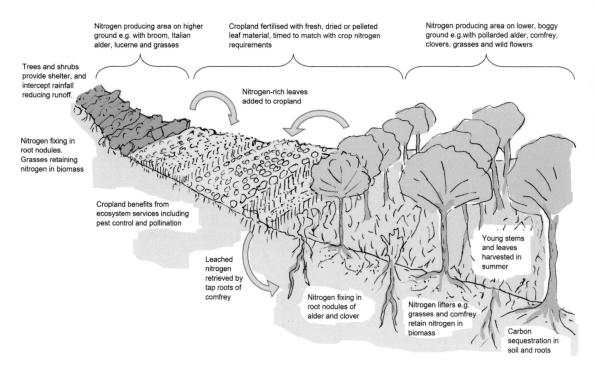

Nitrogen producing area on higher ground e.g. with broom, Italian alder, lucerne and grasses

Cropland fertilised with fresh, dried or pelleted leaf material, timed to match with crop nitrogen requirements

Nitrogen producing area on lower, boggy ground e.g.with pollarded alder, comfrey, clovers, grasses and wild flowers

Trees and shrubs provide shelter, and intercept rainfall reducing runoff.

Nitrogen-rich leaves added to cropland

Nitrogen fixing in root nodules. Grasses retaining nitrogen in biomass

Cropland benefits from ecosystem services including pest control and pollination

Young stems and leaves harvested in summer

Leached nitrogen retrieved by tap roots of comfrey

Nitrogen fixing in root nodules of alder and clover

Nitrogen lifters e.g. grasses and comfrey retain nitrogen in biomass

Carbon sequestration in soil and roots

Fertilising crops using perennial mobile green manures. Diagram produced as part of the research at Bangor University.

be more efficient than incorporation of clover and could reduce leaching and gaseous emissions.

Green manures for no-till market gardening

Green manures (aka cover crops) can be incorporated into no-till systems, with care and an understanding of how best to kill, or 'terminate', the crop. Buckwheat is a great summer cover crop for no-till systems, as it easy to kill by mowing, or by frost. Annuals like mustard, field peas, Persian clover, berseem (Egyptian clover) are also useful, especially when an early planting is needed in the spring. The trash on the surface can be raked off, or planted through.

For overwintering green manures where the emphasis is on ensuring that there are living roots and to avoid nitrogen leaching, rye and vetch are good for sowing as late as mid-October/early November,

depending on where you are in the country. Phacelia can also overwinter as a young plant if sown late, while oats, winter wheat and crimson clover are other options. In some situations, broadcasting seed, especially with diverse mixes, is convenient, but it is always important to get good contact of the soil with the seed, otherwise there will be germination losses. For that reason, drilling can be a more successful way to establish cover crops in no-till.

Termination of winter green manures is not easy. For rye and other grains, it is best done at the 'milk stage', which is when the grain is just starting to form and expresses a milky liquid when squeezed. This gives a two-week window for terminating it by crimping, that is, squeezing the vascular system of the stems to prevent water and sugars flowing from shoots to roots. Similarly, other non-grain green manures can be killed by crimping when they are starting to flower. On a tractor scale roller-crimpers are used, which

Persian clover at Cotesbach Gardens in September and the following March.

consist of a roller that flattens the crop and blades that crimp the stem.

Jesse Frost of Rough Draft Farmstead, Kentucky in the US, has tried different techniques of terminating rye cover crops on his no-till holding and found the best way is to run over the top of the rye with a two-wheeled tractor and power-harrow, but not breaking the ground. This clobbers the rye, pinches the stems and spreads it on the ground. Tarps can also be used in conjunction with this technique, especially when terminating the cover crop early, when it can have a tendency to regrow.

Organic fertilizers

You should plan your production system to mini-mise the need for brought-in nutrients. There are, however, a number of fertilizers permitted for use in organic farming. Some of these are mineral-based but naturally occurring, such as rock phosphate, mag-nesium carbonate and calcium carbonate, which can be used where deficiencies have been identified. You may need evidence of need to justify the use of sup-plementary nutrients.

Bagged and pelleted fertilizers are labelled in the same way as conventional ones, with nitrogen, phosphorus and potassium content percentages in order, for example 4.5(N):3.2(P):3.1(K) for a pelleted poultry manure.

Animal-based fertilizers are a contentious input. While there are many products available, such as hoof meal, horn meal, fish meal and blood meal, their use is under review by the Soil Association, to ensure that they do not contain products from intensive facto-ry-farmed systems. The nitrogen in these products is often highly available and poses risks of pollution if not handled carefully.

Diversity with a smile

Jayne Arnold of Oxton Organics in the Vale of Evesham has been an organic grower since the 1980s, but has only recently transitioned to no-till. Over the last couple of years, she has introduced green manures due to quality problems with the green-waste compost that she had been using. Her approach is to broadcast green manures wherever she can into summer crops as well as winter crops. She doesn't use too many legumes, as she thinks too much nitrogen can bring problems. She loves flowers and while the fields have a joyful eclectic appearance, a lot of thought has gone into the plants included in the mixes. Jayne stresses that the mixes are work in progress and that she changes them as the soil changes, and as she observes and learns more.

- **Cover crops for sowing under tall crops in the field:** oats, corncockle, millet, phacelia, linseed, buckwheat, nigella, sheep's parsley, sweet william, cornflower, calendula, trefoil and crimson clover.
- **Cover crops for shorter outdoor crops:** trefoil, flax, home-saved mix (tagetes, nigella, alyssum, dwarf Californian poppy, linaria)
- **Winter green-manure mix for bare plots or undersowing at end of August:** vetch, flax, buckwheat, oats, sunflower seed, daikon radish, fodder kale, crimson clover, calendula, cornflower annuals (any other hardy annual seed), sheep's parsley, phacelia, old vegetable seed.
- **Later plots, winter mix for September to November sowing:** rye, vetch, phacelia

'Tall mix' sown under kale.

Winter green-manure mix, left to flower until June, when mown off.

'Short mix' under leeks, grow slowly through the winter and left to grow after the leeks are harvested.

Jayne has seen a noticeable improvement in her soils since using the cover crops. In addition:

> The wildlife absolutely love it and we've got a lot more insects and birds, so the diversity below ground and above ground is really beneficial. There have been fewer issues with pests and diseases, plus other benefits such as no splitting in the tomatoes even when the irrigation had been left on over-night! It makes me very happy; it's not all about the money.

Chapter Six

Rotations and Crop Planning

Rotations entail keeping closely related crops together and growing them sequentially on one plot of land over different years. Rotations have been around as long as agriculture itself. In terms of history, they have only briefly gone out of fashion with the 'green revolution' and monocropping made possible by high levels of external inputs. Rotations are traditionally very important to organic farming systems and are fundamental to ensuring that diversity is designed into the farming system in time and space. Despite 'natural farming' systems challenging the paradigm (*see* Chapter 1), rotations remain the principal tool in the organic grower's box for managing soil fertility, weeds, pests and diseases.

Fundamentals of rotation design

Inclusion of legumes

The use of legumes that can fix nitrogen biologically is a crucial element of rotations, in order to replace nitrogen extracted from the soil by crops (*see* Chapter 5).

Balancing fertility-building and exploitative cropping

The fertility-building period is crucial to the whole rotation and grass/clover leys and cover crops should be considered as important crops and managed accordingly (*see* Chapter 5). It is also a good time to apply phosphorus and potassium through manures and composts, and, when needed, lime.

On a small scale, it can be tempting to focus on cash crops and provide nitrogen primarily through imported manures or composts. This is, however, contrary to the organic farming principle of self-reliance. There are opportunities to fit short-term fertility-building crops, including quick-growing legumes, into the rotation as alternatives to the traditional two-year grass/clover ley. It is a misconception to consider cropping legumes, such as broad beans, runner beans and peas, as fertility-building crops, as any nitrogen that they fix is removed in cropping. In nitrogen terms, they should be considered as 'neutral' crops.

Separating plants according to family or needs

Crops within the same family groups are subject to the same pests and diseases. Allowing time to pass before similar crops return to the same piece of land breaks the reproductive cycle of pests and soil-borne diseases. For alliums, brassicas and potatoes, a minimum three-year gap is recommended (up until 2019 it was mandatory in the Soil Association organic standards), but where possible it should be longer, especially when there are known problems. In intensive market gardens there is often

OPPOSITE: Squash undersown with red clover at Tolhurst Organic. Iain Tolhurst has perfected what he calls 'relay green manures'; setting off the green manures during the productive cycle of cropping, so that once the crop has died back or been removed, the green manure can race on, keeping the ground covered over winter and being better placed to fix nitrogen in the spring. A couple of weedings are necessary prior to sowing the clover – ideally just as the plants are starting to throw out lateral shoots.

a demand to fit more brassica cropping into the rotation, as these are popular crops. As a result, we are seeing many new growers getting club root problems, which may be due to too many brassicas in their rotation with insufficient time periods between them.

Heavy feeding crops, such as brassicas and potatoes, should usually be placed at the start of the rotation after the fertility-building period. Rotations should alternate, or balance, deep-rooting crops with shallow-rooting ones in order to improve soil structure and allow access to nutrients from different parts of the soil profile.

Biodynamic growers also classify their crops into leaf, root, flower and fruit groups. The principle is that though crops such as spinach, lettuce and cabbage are from different families, they share similar needs, so the grower can concentrate on practices that are focused on those needs, such as nitrogen supply for leaf development. For root crops, nitrogen should be restricted and supply of potassium is more important. The groupings are used to plan work, based on the biodynamic sowing and planting calendars.

Weed competition

Some crops are more competitive against weeds than others, so it is good practice to include in the rotation some 'cleaning crops', such as potatoes, which will be easy to manage and will suppress weeds. Fertility-building leys and green manures/cover crops also give a break from the cycle of annual weeds, during which weeds are controlled by mowing and/or suppressed by competition. Most weeds have peak times of year for germination, so by growing a range of crops with different sowing or planting times should help to avoid particular weeds proliferating.

Keeping the soil covered

Good planning of the rotation is needed to maximise cropping and avoid bare ground and potential nutrient losses due to leaching.

Other factors

There can be other good reasons for particular sequences of crops in rotations. One example is to crop alliums after brassicas, as when brassicas are incorporated into the soil this can have a suppressing effect on allium white rot. In Continental Europe, many organic growers avoid growing potatoes or roots directly after a fertility-building ley due to the risk of wireworm damage.

Harvesting times also influence the order of crops in a rotation: for example, leeks planted in midsummer are best to follow an early harvested crop, for example early potatoes or spring cabbage, or a green manure. For the no-till grower, the sequence of cropping needs to consider the bed preparation requirements of following crops. Following a cover crop that is not killed in the winter with a drilled crop such as carrots is not recommended.

Some cover crops can have an allelopathic effect (releasing biochemicals that inhibit the germination and growth of other crops). This can inhibit crop germination in the following two to three weeks, but does not affect transplanted crops.

Kale undersown with clovers at Pitney Farm Market Garden.

Table 1: Plant families (field veg) and their rotational characteristics

Crop	Feeding requirement	Root depth	Weed competition	Biodynamic grouping	Years between crops
Alliums					
Onions	Low	Shallow	Weak	Roots	At least three, preferably longer.
Leeks	Medium	Shallow	Weak	Stem	
Garlic	Low	Shallow	Weak	Roots	
Chenopods (Beets)					
Beetroot	Medium	Medium	Medium	Roots	
Leaf beet/chard	Medium	Medium	Medium to strong	Leaf	
Spinach	Medium	Shallow	medium	Leaf	
Compositae					
Chicory	Low	Deep	Medium	Leaf/root	
Lettuce	Medium	Shallow	Medium	Leaf	
Endive	Low	Shallow	Medium	Leaf	
Brassicas					
Brussels sprouts	High	Shallow	Strong	Leaf	
Cabbage	High	Shallow	Strong	Leaf	
Calabrese	High	Shallow	Strong	Leaf	
Cauliflower	High	Shallow	Strong	Leaf	At least three, preferably longer.
Kale	High	Shallow	Strong	Leaf	
Kohlrabi	Medium	Shallow	Medium	Stem	
Swedes	Medium	Medium	Medium	Root	
Oriental brassica salads	Medium	Shallow	Medium	Leaf	
Radish	Medium	Shallow	Medium	Stem	
Cucurbits					
Courgettes	Medium	Deep	Strong	Fruit	
Squashes/pumpkins	Medium	Deep	Strong	Fruit	
Legumes					
Peas	Low	Medium	Weak	Fruit	
Broad beans	Low	Medium	Medium	Fruit	
Runner beans	Medium	Medium	Strong	Fruit	
French beans	Medium	Medium	Strong	Fruit	
Solanaceae					At least three, preferably longer.
Potatoes	High	Shallow	Strong	Roots	
Umbellifers					
Carrots	Low	Medium	Weak	Roots	
Celery	High	Shallow	Strong	Stem	
Celeriac	Medium	Shallow	Medium	Roots	
Fennel	Medium	Shallow	Medium	Stem	
Parsnips	Low	Deep	Weak	Roots	
Miscellaneous					
Sweetcorn	Medium	Shallow	Strong	Fruit	

Practical considerations

The market will determine what crops you grow, but the rotation will set the limits. The quantities of each crop grown may be tweaked according to demand or performance on your site. If you are farming on a specific piece of land, the amount of one crop, or crop family, you can grow will be limited by the size of your rotational blocks. Therefore, the longer the rotation (number of years), the less of each group you will be able to grow in one year. For crops that have no restrictions in the standards as to length of time between crops you can be a bit more flexible, especially with quick-growing crops like lettuce, which can be fitted in wherever.

There may be other occasions when flexibility is needed. Mechanical harvesting may cause soil damage, which needs to be addressed through use of deep-rooted cover crops, such as lucerne. Time out of the rotation may be required to deal with an infestation of perennial weeds through cultivations and/or the use of cover crops (see Chapter 8).

The more intensive the market garden, the more complicated the rotational planning will be. It can be sensible to have a separate rotation for the more labour-intensive crops, alongside a rotation for field crops. Fields are rarely equally sized or uniformly shaped, so you may need to be creative when setting up your plots. If rotational blocks are not equally sized, there will be years when there is too much of one crop group and not enough of another. Field corners or odd shapes that don't fit easily into a plot plan can be planted with perennial vegetables, fruit or energy crops, or used for nature conservation. Rotational plots can be marked out clearly with beetle banks, agroforestry strips or paths. It is important to allow enough space for vehicular access, irrigation considerations and to avoid shade from trees or buildings. Nature may not like straight lines, but evenly sized rectangular blocks do make the grower's life a lot easier! Daniel Mays, author of *The No-till Organic Vegetable Farm*, recommends beds of thirty metres length, with plots containing ten beds for ease of calculation.

Nutrient budgeting

Nutrient budgets are useful tools to help farmers and growers make the right nutrient management decisions. They can help to evaluate the viability (in nutrient terms) and sustainability of rotations, to make optimum use of available nutrients and to indicate surpluses of nitrogen that could leach

Table 2: Nutrient offtake for vegetable crops

Crop	Approximate yield (t/ha)	N		P		K	
		Approximate offtake					
		Kg/t	Kg/ha	Kg/t	Kg/ha	Kg/t	Kg/ha
Potatoes	36	2.7	97.2	0.6	58.32	4.9	285.8
Cabbage	30	3.4	102	0.4	40.8	10	408.0
Calabrese	7	2.3	16.1	0.3	4.83	22.2	107.2
Lettuce	20	1.4	28	0.2	5.6	25	140.0
Leek	12	2.8	33.6	0.4	13.44	8.2	110.2
Onion	20	1.4	28	0.3	8.4	9.6	80.6
Carrot	36	1.2	43.2	0.3	12.96	8.3	107.6
Swede	30	1.1	33	0.4	13.2	9.1	120.1

Source: Adapted from Watson *et al.* (IOTA, 2010).

All grown at Pitney Farm Market Garden.

Alliums: garlic.

Brassicas: Red Russian kale.

Chenopods (beets): beetroot.

Cucurbits: squashes.

Solanaceae: potatoes.

Compositae: lettuce.

Legumes: peas.

Umbellifers: carrots.

and pollute ground and surface water. As part of the budget, the quantity and nutrient content of all inputs (seeds, manures, mulches, animal food) is calculated, including nitrogen fixation, together with outputs as crops, meat and livestock. Losses due to leaching are also included.

Example rotations

A typical rotation will be at least five years in length and should start with a two-year fertility-building period, normally consisting of a grass/clover ley. The cash cropping phase of the rotation will normally

Rotation on the ground at Trill Farm Garden.

Crop planning

Crop planning is a good job for the winter months. The more direct your marketing is, the more complicated the process will be. The table developed by Roger Hitchings is a good place to start to help work out the areas of crops you will need to grow. You may decide not to grow all of these crops yourself, or your land may not be suitable for all.

Spreadsheets, phone/tablet applications and software can assist with planning. Alternatively, you can do it the old way on large sheets of paper. Having the full cycle of the rotation marked out and divided into months will help visualise where the gaps are – which will be bare soil – and where the opportunities are for short-term cash crops or green manures to be squeezed in. The sheet can be filled in with more detail, such as varieties, numbers of plants needed and seed required, as well as timings for successional sowings and plantings. It is important to allow 'wriggle room' for crop failures and it is always worth having spares.

Once you have a plan, it should be printed out and put somewhere prominent, so that it is visible to all involved with the business.

commence with a high nutrient-demanding crop, such as brassicas or potatoes. The second crop, for example alliums, should be able to use residual fertility and can benefit from the weed competitiveness of the first cash crop. In the final place would be the least nutrient-demanding vegetables, such as the root crops, before returning to fertility-building. Short bursts of six to twelve months of green manures can also be strategically placed in the rotation.

Table 3: Example vegetable field rotation

Year	Crop	Notes
1	Grass/clover fertility-building	Add compost/manure.
2	Potatoes	Hungry crop – weed competitive.
3	Grazing rye/vetch overwinter green manure	Dependent on harvesting potatoes by mid-October. Add lime at this point if needed – will benefit brassicas.
4	Brassicas. Undersown with overwinter green manure	Another hungry crop, needs to feature early in rotation.
5	Alliums. Undersown with overwinter green manure	Less hungry and less competitive.
6	Carrots/parsnips	Least demanding nutrient wise, less competitive.
7	Squash – undersown with fertility-building ley for years 1 and 2	

Source: Table adapted from *Organic Vegetable Production: A Complete Guide,* Table 7.1 (Davies and Lennartsson, 2005), incorporating elements of Tolhurst Organic field rotation.

Table 4: Weekly produce requirements for 50 customers (could be for box scheme or market stall)

Crop	Unit size	Quantity for 50 customers	Frequency	Sales period	Average weekly requirement	No. of weeks	Total requirement	Total area in ha	Areas allowing for field factors	Rotation blocks	Area of rotation block
Potatoes	1.5kg	75kg	Weekly	Jul–Mar	75kg	40	3t	0.1	0.15	Potatoes	0.15
Calabrese	400g	20kg	Fortnight	Jul–Oct	10kg	9	180 kg	0.036	0.054	Brassicas	0.162
Cabbage	1 head	50 heads	Weekly	Sep–Mar	50 heads	32	1,600	0.06	0.09		
PSB	300g	15kg	Fortnight	Feb–Mar	7.5kg	4	60kg	0.012	0.018		
Onions	500g	25kg	Weekly	Sep–Mar	25kg	32	800kg	0.04	0.06	Alliums/ cucurbits	0.176
Squash	1 no.	50 no.	Monthly	Aug–Dec	12 no.	11	550	0.01	0.015		
Leeks	600g	30kg	Fortnight	Sep–Mar	15kg	16	480kg	0.04	0.06		
Courgettes	500g	25kg	Fortnight	Jul–Oct	12.5kg	8	200kg	0.027	0.041		
Carrots	450g	22.5kg	Weekly	Jul–Mar	22.5kg	40	900kg	0.025	0.038	Roots/ legumes/ salads	0.157
Lettuce (gem)	twin pack	100 heads	Weekly	Jul–Oct	100 heads	17	1,700	0.022	0.033		
Beans (various)	500g	25kg	Weekly	Jul–Oct	25kg	16	200kg	0.01	0.015		
Spinach	450g	22.5kg	Fortnight	Jul–Oct	11.25kg	8	180kg	0.02	0.03		
Beetroot	bunch	22.5kg	Fortnight	Jul–Oct	5.5kg	8	180kg	0.009	0.014		
Parsnip	450g	22.5kg	Fortnight	Oct–Mar	11.25kg	14	315kg	0.018	0.027		
Grass/clover										Grass/clover	0.34
TOTALS								0.429	0.645		0.985

Crop: A typical range of crops though this can vary according to the market.

Unit size: These are fairly typical but could vary.

Quantity for 50 customers: Simple unit size × 50.

Frequency: Another factor that will vary according to demand.

Sales period: This will depend on variety choice, storage, etc.

Average weekly requirement: Customer quantity × frequency as a fraction.

No. of weeks: Weeks in the supply period.

Total requirement: This assumes harvest success.

Total area in ha: Area needed in ideal terms (OFMH data).

Areas allowing for field factors: Realistic increase (×1.5) to account for problems.

Rotation blocks: Potatoes and brassicas clearly need own blocks.

Area of rotation block: Rounding block sizes to 0.17ha to even it out = 1ha.

Source: Hitchings, R. (2009).

Chapter Seven

Seeds and Plant-Raising

Giving your plants a good start will go a long way to ensuring the success of your crops in terms of yield and quality. This begins with the choice of variety and the quality of the seed. Then you need to provide the optimum conditions for germination and enough moisture, but not too much, plus warmth to get them going.

It starts with the seed

Organic versus non-organic

The use of organic seed is, when available, obligatory in organic farming, but growers can apply for derogations from their control bodies on the grounds of availability, and sometimes quality, to use non-organic seeds. Organic seed may not always be available in the varieties you want, particularly for speciality crops, such as salads, or in the quantities you may need. Supply problems have been exacerbated by Brexit, as a lot of organic seed was imported from the EU. Under the Organic Regulation EC 848/2018, it has been set out that these derogations will be phased out by the end of 2035; whether the UK will still be working to the EU Organic Regulation at that stage remains to be seen.

Seeds are a very small input into the system and organic seed can often be more expensive. There are, however, many good reasons for buying organic seed whenever possible. Firstly, you are minimising the 'upstream pollution' created by growing seeds conventionally. Secondly, you are supporting the organic grower who is growing the seed, as well as the relatively small independent organic seed and plant breeding sector. For me, it feels right to use organic seeds and science is starting to back up that gut feeling. Work as part of the European Horizon 2020-funded LIVESEED project stated:

> Use of seeds produced under organic conditions can also have benefits, as organic soils may have a richer and more diverse microbiome and part of this microbiome enters the seed during development. Although much more research is needed, there are indications that certain microorganisms in this seed microbiome play a role in tolerance of the emerging seedling toward biotic and abiotic stress in the field. Beneficial microorganisms isolated from the seed microbiome can be applied in seed coating as biocontrol agents.

Research from LIVESEED shows that plant breeding can directly and indirectly shape and select the seed microbiome. If organic breeding is conducted under stressful conditions (for the plant), it can result in a shift to a more beneficial microbiome.

Hybrid or open pollinated seeds

There can be a lot of politics and emotive language around seeds. Let's start with some definitions.

OPPOSITE: Propagation at Bennisons Farm CSA.

Seed-sowing time at Pitney Farm Market Garden.

F1 hybrid varieties

F1 hybrids (filial 1 hybrid) are the first filial generation of distinctly different parental types. They are produced by crossing two stable seed lines (called inbred lines) and give rise to especially uniform progeny and 'hybrid vigour'. However, any seed produced by F1 plants will not come true to type and will be unstable and considerably less vigorous. Plant breeders have applied the theories developed by Gregor Mendel in the nineteenth century and by the 1930s the first hybrid sweetcorn varieties were available in the US. Now, hybrid crops dominate commercial production in many crop species. The benefits of hybrids are:

- **Uniformity:** It is this characteristic that makes hybrids so important for commercial producers. Consistency of size and timings of maturity enable efficiency of harvesting and more predictability and reliability for marketing.
- **Yield and vigour:** Not all crops demonstrate hybrid vigour, but those that do, may emerge more vigorously, mature earlier and perform better in adverse climatic conditions, and produce higher yields.
- **Disease resistance:** It can be easier to breed disease resistance into hybrids than open-pollinated varieties.

Open-pollinated varieties

Open-pollinated varieties are those which, if properly isolated from other varieties in the same species, will produce seed that is genetically 'true to type'. Open-pollinated varieties carry a wide genetic diversity and contribute to the biodiversity of food crops. The advantages are:

- **You can save your own seed:** Seed-saving means that you can adapt and select to produce a strain that is adapted to your region, climate and even farm. You will need to pay attention to separation distances to allow proper isolation for some species.
- **Cost:** Because they are less complicated to produce than hybrids, they tend to be cheaper. This can be particularly important when sowing directly in the field, especially if not using precision drills.
- **Flavour:** It is often stated or assumed that open-pollinated varieties have better flavour than hybrids, and this can be the case. However, many modern hybrid breeding programmes are now putting more emphasis on taste than they have in the past.

Heritage or heirloom varieties

Heirloom or heritage varieties are also open-pollinated. The terms can be used synonymously and embrace landrace varieties that have become adapted to specific growing conditions (for example, Shetland cabbage), heirloom varieties that have been passed down over many generations and varieties that have been dropped from seed catalogues and the UK National List of registered varieties over many years. The term 'heritage' can be mis-used, as it is often applied to any vegetable that looks a bit different – for example, the purple carrots on the supermarket shelf may be a product of modern breeding!

The stunning, crimson-flowered broad bean – a heritage variety.

Not many growers would be without F1 hybrid Crown Prince, which is the most reliable squash in terms of yield, together with being the best tasting for roasting and also storing well.

Mixing and matching

Most growers will produce both hybrids and open-pollinated varieties. For some crops, the quality of open-pollinated varieties does not compare favourably with the hybrids. Many winter brassicas, such as cabbages, cauliflowers and Brussels sprouts, are much more consistent, predictable and better quality than the open-pollinated ones. In some ways, it is no surprise – the breeding of open-pollinated varieties has been neglected for years and the maintenance of many has also been poor, with growers reporting declines in quality of certain varieties. However, there is a resurgence of open-pollinated varieties among many breeders, particularly in Europe with work on programmes to dehybridise crops. Sativa in Switzerland has been working on sweetcorn with some impressive results.

Seed-saving

For many growers, life can be complicated enough without saving seeds, but there are good reasons to do so. Vigour of the seed will usually be better than that of bought in; you can also adapt and select what performs best on your site. There may also be varieties not easily available as organic seed that you can produce yourself. Organic or biodynamic seed production can also be a business opportunity, growing for specialised small-scale seed companies, like Real Seeds, Vital Seeds and the Seed Co-operative. Flowering plants are also great for biodiversity around the holding.

Plant-raising

Direct sowing versus transplanting crops

There are some crops, such as carrots, parsnips and radishes, which are always direct-sown. There are other crops that are almost always grown as transplants, such as winter brassicas and celeriac. However, a lot of crops can be either direct-sown, or raised as transplants. Raising plants under protected conditions for planting out later can help to extend the season and save space.

For intensive systems, where a quick turnaround between crops is needed, a few weeks can be saved by using transplants that are grown in advance. In no-dig systems it is not always easy to achieve a fine seedbed for drilling, so transplanting is often preferred.

Although there can be risks in exposing the germination and emergence processes to the elements and pests, when conditions are favourable, direct-sown crops can be more robust than when transplanted. They can quickly catch up with transplanted crops in the warmth of summer. With precision drilling, for which graded seed works best, target populations for optimum spacing and quality can be achieved, so that thinning of crops is not needed.

Plant-raising or buying in plants?

Raising your own plants is a real skill, or even an art, which may become an all-consuming passion. I always enjoyed plant-raising and would never have countenanced contracting it out to someone else. However, there are very professional plant nurseries out there and it can sometimes be a good decision, especially when starting out, to buy in plants; it frees up time and allows you to concentrate on the growing crops. Doing your own plant-raising gives you control of the process, but also all of the risks. If mistakes are made, it can mean the loss of a crop for a year, or at least a gap in the cropping plan. Plant-raising also needs specialist equipment and facilities, such as a greenhouse and germination boxes. Nevertheless, with a minimum of kit, plants can be raised reasonably cost-effectively. There can be a middle way – perhaps buying in plants that need heat (and sometimes light) to start them off, such as peppers and aubergines. If you are part of a network of growers, one member might take on the role of plant raiser for the group.

The potting shed is a vital part of the plant-raising process. It needs to be tidy, clean, spacious, warm and light. Warmth is necessary for the comfort of those carrying out the tasks – cold fingers make mistakes. Good direct lighting is needed for seed-sowing. Growing media should not be cold, so bring in a few bags to warm up, in advance of sowing. Water should be easily available for wetting growing media and should also not be too cold.

It can be tempting to take benches outside if the sun is shining, but beware – a gust of wind can blow your expensive hybrid seeds into the nearest hedge!

Transplanting in progress at Southern Roots Organics. On a larger-scale, tractor-mounted planting machines can significantly reduce labour costs.

Plant-raising at Pitney Farm Market Garden.

Modules

Plastic-moulded modular trays have been the mainstay of horticultural transplant production since the 1980s. Trays consist of a number of individual cells that are filled with a growing medium for growing individual or groups of plants. Good-quality rigid plastic trays can last 20 to 30 seasons, so it is best not to economise on quality. The more rigid the tray, the more easily the module will pull from the tray, thereby speeding up the transplanting process. The standard tray size is 400 × 600mm, with the number of cells per tray varying according to the crop. Because in organic systems the intention is to provide all, or most, of the nutrition needed by the transplant through the growing medium, cell sizes need to be bigger than for conventionally grown transplants. Trays can be filled by hand, or on larger holdings by proprietary filling lines.

Blocks

Blocks are compressed square blocks of substrate for sowing into. The system is particularly suited to growing media containing high levels of dark (humified) peat. Large celery and salad growers use blocks that are mechanically planted on a large scale. At present, there is no reliable peat-free growing media that works well enough for commercial production, so blocks are best avoided.

Winstrip® trays

This is an American product made of rigid plastic that is said to make blocks obsolete: 'providing all the benefits of blocks without any of the downsides'. Unlike other module trays they are designed to provide airflow above and below the plants, for air pruning of roots and good robust plants. They are sold through Neversink Farm and are available through Reagtools in the UK. Downsides may be the cost, plus a larger area needed compared to stand-alone blocks.

Pots

For many higher-value plants, such as the summer Solanaceae (tomatoes, peppers, aubergines), cucumbers and the like, it is usual to prick out into pots, or transplant from modules into 7 or 8cm pots. Square pots make better use of space than round ones and are less wasteful of water.

Rootrainers

Rootrainers are like deep module trays, consisting of segments known as 'books', which open up for easy extraction of plants. They use a lot of growing medium, so are best for high-value crops that need the space for roots to develop, or require a bit longer to grow before planting out. They can be suitable for

Table 1: Types of module tray and their suitability for different crops

Cell number	Volume (ml)	Cells per m²	Crop
126	55	525	Beans, courgettes, squash, asparagus, tomatoes.
216	30	900	Brassicas, celeriac, sweetcorn, Beetroot, swedes and turnips, leaf beet, herbs.
345	15	1,439	Leeks and onions.

Sources: Vaughan, 2008; Teagasc, 2020.

early plantings of runner or French beans, whose growth could be checked when grown in smaller modules or blocks, but would take up too much space in pots.

Paperpot system

The paperpot transplanting system has become very popular, spreading from Japan thanks to some beguiling YouTube videos that went viral. The system consists of a manual transplanter that you pull along a ridge and it unfurls a row of linked paper pots at the perfect spacing. Designed for a variety of crops, such as onions, beet, spinach, lettuce, broccoli, cabbages, beans, sweetcorn and so on, it is great for small farms or solo operations. It does entail buying into the whole system of trays and supplies of pots.

The first few growers to adopt the system in the UK fell foul of the organic standards when it was shown that the pots contained plastic microfibres and there may also have been issues around the glues used. Chain pots are now being produced from hemp, but at time of writing had not yet been approved for organic use. They do need a well-prepared seedbed with no clods, stones or plant debris. The system is less suited to no-till situations, though if the surface is prepared with an electric tilther it could work.

Bare-root transplants

A lot of vegetable transplants were produced as bare-root transplants, or 'peg plants', prior to the uptake of peat blocks and modules. Bare-root transplants are most suited to brassicas and leeks, but onions,

Bare-root brassica transplants at Growing with Nature, in Lancashire.

Soil-assisted modules

This is a hybrid system developed by Brian Adair on Jersey. Recognising the problem of leeks running out of nutrition when grown in modules, but not wanting the hassle of weeding seedbeds, Brian sows leeks in module trays with heat in February in a greenhouse. Once the roots start poking out from the bottom of the cells, he transfers the trays to a polytunnel and nestles them on the surface of a well-prepared seedbed, watering them in to make the connection between the module content and the soil. The leeks draw their nutrition from the soil, so no feeding is necessary. This technique produces transplants four weeks earlier than when raised on benches and no weeding is needed! The trays are undercut with a spade, excess soil sliced off and the plants graded and bunched for planting.

Module trays sown and placed on well-prepared soil.

Roots grow through into the soil, accessing nutrients.

When ready to plant, trays are undercut with a spade.

Modules are pulled from the trays as normal.

Excess soil and roots can be sliced away with a knife.

Modules are ready to plant out in the field.

celery and celeriac are also possible. They allow more flexibility for the grower, as they can hold longer in the soil, simply growing bigger, without getting too stressed or needing additional feeding. This can be an advantage in wet summers, when planting may be held up due to unfavourable ground conditions. Crucially, for organic systems they give seedlings a perfect start in biologically active soil and can be much more robust and resilient than modular-grown plants. Counter-intuitively, they can establish more quickly than modules, with less 'transplant shock'.

A seedbed is prepared either in a greenhouse or outside, preferably with fleece or mesh protection, and rows are drilled with a seed drill. An area of 0.1ha with rows 25cm apart should produce around 40,000 brassica plants, targeting plants at 2–2.5cm apart. Be aware of the importance of a long rotation for brassicas – this can be particularly important if using polytunnel space and growing a lot of brassica salad crops over winter. Leeks can be sown much thicker, aiming for 10,000 plants per 120m of row length. Getting the seed rate right is crucial – the plants need to be stocky and if grown too close together they will become leggy. If possible, use a precision drill; alternatively, weigh the correct amount of seed for the row length.

It is advisable to prepare seedbeds well in advance and to allow time for a stale seed bed in order to reduce weed pressure (see Chapter 8). Brassicas will need six to eight weeks to grow six true leaves, which is the ideal stage for transplanting. Leeks should ideally be at pencil thickness for transplanting, which will take around twelve weeks from sowing.

Pulling by hand (not digging) will remove a lot of excess roots and make planting easier. Leek tops should be trimmed by about half to reduce wilting on planting. Grade according to size and sort into bunches of 25 to 50 with an elastic band.

Growing media

What do we expect from a growing medium? It should have enough nutrients to see it through until planting time, hold moisture well, be free from weeds and be light to handle. It should be made from sustainable resources, preferably local, that are cost-effective and available.

Most of the propagation systems used by growers over the past 50 0r 60 years have been based on the use of peat. The popularity of peat arises from its low bulk density for transportation, ease of handling, low pH, high buffer capacity (ability to resist changes in pH) and low or negligible levels of nutrients – meaning that it can be tailored to the requirements of the plants by adding nutrients or liquid feeds. However, there has been a growing recognition of the environmental damage caused by peat use and after many aborted Government targets, as well as a horticultural industry with its head in the sand, it looks like progress might be being made towards a ban for sale of peat to commercial horticultural businesses by 2028. The organic control bodies might ban peat use for organic growers earlier than that, closing the shameful anomaly that peat is allowed to be used in organic systems.

There are a number of commercially available organic peat-free growing media available, but the market is relatively small and the quality has been variable. A 2021 survey showed that half of organic growers who responded had no difficulties with the peat-free products available. The options include products based on coir (shipped across the globe), wood fibre and bark-based products. Survey respondents made it clear that there is a need for more locally sourced media using by-products from UK forestry, other wood-based products, or UK-grown biomass.

Making your own

Growers can be conservative. However, there are good reasons for caution: the growing medium must work, or seed, time, space and energy are wasted and you have a hole in your cropping schedule! The best approach is probably to use a bagged product from a reliable supplier – if in doubt, ask other growers – and alongside that, experiment

Growing media based on woodchip compost compared well with commercial standards in trials as part of an Innovative Farmers field lab.

Hand-sowing in modules at Troed y Rhiw.

with recipes, building confidence along the way. Many recipes are available online. Iain Tolhurst has been making his own for years and progressed from using green-waste compost to his own composted woodchip, which is matured for at least eighteen months. Iain's recipe for growing media for modules is as follows:

- 4 parts 10mm woodchip compost (4 × 15ltr bucket)
- 1.5 parts vermiculite (1.5 × 15ltr bucket)
- for alliums, add 1ltr organic fertilizer 5:5:5 (plant-based).

Blocking

It is not easy to find a replacement for peat to use as blocks, when planting mechanically. Defra/AHDB trials over five years using coir, wood fibre, bark, green-waste compost and digestate failed to come up with a reliable alternative. On a small scale, some

growers have had some success using mixes based on woodchip compost, but for blocks that hold together enough to survive mechanical planting, the search goes on.

Sowing

Good-quality seed, with high percentage germination and high vigour, is essential, as every module cell without a plant is a waste of growing media, space and energy. Some growers sow more than one seed per cell and pinch out the weaker seed in each cell, but this is time-consuming, expensive on seed and should not be necessary. It also risks disturbing the remaining seedling and providing an entry point for disease. Some crops, however, are intentionally multi-sown, for example onions, beetroot and leeks.

Hand sowing is fiddly work and best done by using a folded piece of smooth paper or foil seed

Table 2: Charles Dowding's recommendations for multi-sowing vegetables *

Charles' multi-sow veg	Seeds per clump	Desired plants per clump
Basil	3 or 4	2 or 3
Beetroot	4	4
Chard to cook	3	3
Chervil, coriander, dill, parsley	3	2
Fennel, Florence	3	1 or 2
Kale for salad	4	3
Leek	5 or 6	2 to 4
Onion for bulbs	6 or 7	4 or 5
Onion for salad	8 or 10	6 or 8
Oriental leaves to cook	2	1
Oriental leaves for salad	4	3
Peas for pods	2 or 3	1 or 2
Peas for shoots	4 or 5	3 or 4
Radish	5 or 6	4 or 5
Rocket, salad and wild	3 or 4	2 or 3
Spinach for salad	4	3 or 4
Turnip	5	3 or 4

* *See* Chapter 2 for further information about Charles Dowding.

Paul Izod of Arkstone Mill made this vacuum plate seeder, designed to sow complete trays in one go.

packet, with a knife or plant label to knock seeds into the cells. Precision vacuum seeders are an option for small to medium sized holdings; they can be purchased, but it is also possible to make your own. There are other small-scale tools such as vibrating spatulas, which some may find useful, but there's a lot to be said for the virtues of a steady hand and a good eye! Proprietary filling lines and automatic seeders are available for large operations.

As a final step, most seed needs to be covered thinly with growing media. Exceptions are seed that requires light to germinate, such as celery. After excess growing media is brushed off by hand, the trays can be placed in a germination room or hotbed (*see* below), or on a propagation bench.

Table 3: Germination and seed life of common vegetables

Crop	Optimum temperature for germination (C)	Days to germinate (under optimum conditions)	Seed life (from harvest, under optimum conditions)
Onions	10–35	6–12	Up to 3 yrs
Leeks	18–30	6–14	Up to 3 yrs
Beetroot/leaf beet/chard	10–30	4–14	2 to 3 yrs
Spinach	18–30	7–21	Up to 5 yrs
Chicory/endive	15–24	5–14	Up to 5 yrs
Lettuce	4–27	4–7	2 to 5 yrs
Cabbage family	7–30	5–10	3 to 7 yrs
Courgettes/squash	21–35	4–8	2 to 4 yrs
Cucumbers	16–35	4–8	Up to 10 yrs
Peas	4–24	5–8	3 to 5 yrs+
Broad beans	8–15	5–14	Up to 3 yrs
Runner/French beans	16–30	5–9	3 to 5 yrs+
Aubergines	24–32	7–14	Up to 5 yrs
Peppers	18–35	7–14	Up to 5 yrs
Tomatoes	16–30	5–14	Up to 8 yrs
Carrots	7–30	7–14	Up to 3 yrs
Celery/celeriac	16–21	10–21	Up to 5 yrs
Fennel	15–32	7–14	Up to 4 yrs
Parsnips	10–21	6–28	2 yrs max
Sweetcorn	16–32	4–7	Up to 3 yrs

Source: *Including Real Seeds*, ISTA. For guidance only.

Seedling care

Once blocks and modules, or whatever system you have settled on, have been prepared and germinated in a germination cabinet or on a propagation bench, they need moving to benches in a greenhouse or polytunnel. Although pots and trays *can* be placed on woven plastic (for example, mypex) on the floor of a tunnel or greenhouse, it is best to raise them above ground on benches to keep them away from rodents, as these will chew off seedlings and eat seeds out of pots. Some growers suspend shelves from crop support bars to keep the rodents away.

Plants will need access to full sunlight, so make sure that tunnel covers or glass panes are as clean as they can be. Ventilate as much as possible, as that will help to make the seedlings more robust, while keeping an eye on temperatures. Fleeces can be used at night when necessary. Supplementary lights may be useful for parts of the UK that have very short days in winter: for example, probably not necessary in Sussex, but essential in Shetland! Some crops, such as tomatoes, peppers and aubergines, may benefit from grow lights if aiming for early crops, for example when starting them off in January/February.

Watering is an art and is probably best done with a hose and spray wand, so that the water can be directed where it is needed. It is important not to overwater, but also not to let plants dry out. This is a matter of experience, but it is worth lifting trays to check how heavy they are, as sometimes they can appear dry on the surface while being wet underneath. You should also check closely for signs of stress/wilting. While the aim should be to avoid feeding anything, sometimes a little liquid feed of seaweed or other soluble organic fertilizer can be necessary if plants are held up for any reason.

On a small scale, an old freezer can be adapted as a germination cabinet, as here at Pitney Farm Market Garden.

Heated propagation benches apply heat from below via electric cables in sand or heated mats. Additional lighting and a protective plastic-covered frame keeps seedlings cosy at night.

Hotbeds

The off-grid alternative to germination rooms and heated benches is to provide heat from decomposing organic matter by making a hotbed. Traditionally, these have been created with large quantities of fresh horse manure, contained in a wooden framework (commonly pallets). Large quantities are needed. The temperatures can't be as easily regulated as with heated benches – only through ventilation, so the danger is that the temperatures can get too high, with the hot, humid atmosphere making seedlings leggy in low-light conditions. Making hotbeds with fresh woodchips is an alternative that has worked well for Gloucestershire organic grower Fred Bonestroo.

Fred Bonestroo of Close Farm, near Tetbury, with his hotbed made from pallets filled with freshly chipped woodchip – relatively small diameter branches work best. Fred observed that though it did not get as hot as a traditional manure hotbed, it did not cool as quickly and provided a more even heat for longer. He keeps his hotbed going from February to April and has a plastic cover over hoops to keep moisture in.

Chapter Eight

Living with Weeds

This chapter could be called 'Weed Control', but the true agroecological grower needs to take a different approach to weeds, accepting the need to live with them, acknowledging their benefits and learning to love them! Weeds are often defined as 'plants in the wrong place'. The language of weed control is all about battling or fighting the enemy. However, often, we weed purely for aesthetics or peer pressure.

My father was a farmer and as we drove across Salisbury Plain in my youth, he would 'tut-tut' about cereal fields full of poppies. To him, they were an abomination, a demonstration of poor farming. I have become more relaxed about weeds than my father and I don't like to see growers' holdings that appear too sterile with no weeds in sight!

Sure, weeds can have a negative impact on crop yields through competition for light, nutrients and water. They can hinder management, slow harvest and contaminate crops. They can also incur significant costs, in terms of the labour needed to remove them. The effect on the grower's psyche when weeds gain the upper hand should not be underestimated. Growers have been known to give up completely, when their holdings have become overrun by weeds.

The benefits of weeds

Weeds have many benefits. They cover the ground, preventing erosion and leaching, and act as hosts for mycorrhizal fungi or other beneficial soil micro-organisms. Deep-rooting weeds can penetrate the subsoil, busting through plough pans and improving soil structure, lifting nutrients from below and making them available to crops as they die and decompose.

Weeds are mostly native plants and act as hosts and food sources for many beneficial insects. At the same time, weeds can also help to keep pests away from your crop, by confusing them, or providing a physical obstacle to a pest seeing or landing on a crop. Many agroecological practices, such as planting flower strips or nectar plants within crops, are acting in a way that replicates the functions that can be provided by weeds.

The benefits of weeds were recognised by a study at the University of Sussex, which found that the abundance and diversity of pollinators visiting 'injurious' weed species – ragwort (*Jacobaea vulgaris*) and two thistles (*Cirsium arvense, C. vulgare*) – were far higher than plant species recommended by Defra for pollinator-targeted agri-environmental options.

OPPOSITE: Adam York of Glebelands Market Garden in Wales trialled the Terrateck wheel hoe with Bio-Discs as part of a Farming Connect study. A single pass with the Terrateck saved 47 per cent labour time, compared to using a stirrup hoe for intra-row, followed by a wheel hoe between the rows.

Thistles are great for biodiversity. However, not all biodiversity is great for the grower – here the dreaded cabbage white butterfly!

Research has shown that as organic farms mature, the volume of weeds does not increase, but the number of species present does. Weeds are biodiversity and that is a 'public good'! Weeds also tell you a lot about your soils. As 'bioindicators', they can highlight areas of soil compaction, high or low nutrient levels, pH and more.

Getting the balance right

The main aim of organic weed management should be to create environmental conditions that tip the balance in favour of the crop rather than the weed. To achieve that, you need to get to know your weeds and their ecology. What is the life cycle of the weed? What makes it 'tick'? How competitive is it? Why is a weed a problem? What are the weed's weak points and how can you tip the balance back in your favour?

To an extent, growers, especially those starting off, are dealt a certain hand: the seed bank and populations of perennial weeds present are partly a legacy of previous management of the land. It is up to the grower to reduce the burden of weeds that are there and limit further weeds coming in from outside, for example in imported manure (*see* Chapter 5).

In that context, rotations are also vital (*see* Chapter 6), with the fertility-building period playing a role in breaking the cycle of weed growth. Different crops will suppress weeds to varying extents, while cultivation times also influence the range of weed species present. The spacing of crops is an equally important factor. As a young grower, I was obsessed with planting crops at the optimum spacing, so that they covered the ground in order to outcompete weeds, while making the best possible use of light and nutrients for high yields. This may be easily achievable on bed systems, particularly when planting through mulches. But for row crops in the field, it may actually be more worthwhile to space crops more widely in order to allow for quick and efficient mechanical weeding, even if this means less yield. More airflow may also reduce diseases. Generally, the best defence against weeds is a well-grown crop.

However, you need constantly to ask yourself one question. Does the weeding actually need to be done, either to save the crop and/or to prevent build-up of seeds in the seed bank? Resist the tidying impulse – weeding may have little benefit to the crop and resources could be better spent elsewhere. Some weeds, such as dead nettle or speedwell, for example, have very low competitive indices. Equally, crops, such as carrots and onions, can be extremely sensitive to weed competition early on, but later the presence of weeds has little impact on their yield. At other times, weeding may be a lost cause. As a young grower, I spent too much time and money trying to rescue crops, which would have been better cultivated in, meanwhile missing opportunities to weed other crops at the optimum time.

Weed-management techniques

Tarps or tillage?

Tarpaulins (tarps) are opaque heavy-duty plastic sheets that are impermeable to water and are the 'go to' tool of the no-till grower. Renowned Canadian organic grower Jean-Martin Fortier wrote in *The Market Gardener*: 'Soil-covering tarps are about as effective at fighting weeds as a short cover crop in a conventional vegetable rotation, but they can be set up in one go. They work immediately and quickly and are the perfect fit for the intensive market gardening model.' They can be used to bring new patches of land into production by smothering weedy ground or pasture, covering unused beds to prevent nutrients leaching and stopping weeds establishing.

Tarpaulins come in a range of sizes – normally sold as black silage sheets – so you need to choose the size that best fits your system, bearing in mind that the larger the sheet, the heavier it will be. They can be rolled or folded when not in use and can last for several years if handled carefully. Tarps are held in place with sandbags or stones placed around the edges. They can be left down for any length of time, but most beneficial effects (weed control) need at least three weeks. If the aim is to rid an area of perennial weeds, it is best to leave down for a whole season.

Research trials at Cornell University in the US on the short-term use of tarps suggested that three weeks of tarping prior to planting should be enough to suppress weeds in the following crop. The researchers also found that soil nitrate levels increased significantly with tarp use, compared to the control,

possibly through increased temperatures promoting microbial activity and reducing leaching. Unlike tillage, tarp usage is not dependent on weather conditions and savings can be made on fuel use and labour. Soil is left undisturbed, moisture and organic matter are conserved, while leaching and waterlogging are prevented.

Tarps are, however, made from petroleum, which brings into play questions about sustainability, plus prices are likely to rise. There is also growing evidence that soils are acting as reservoirs of microplastic contamination – do we as growers want to contribute to that? There are also issues of phthalates, often added to polyethylene plastics, including silage sheets, to aid flexibility, which have been linked to several negative human health impacts. It has been suggested that woven polypropylene sheets are less likely to contain phthalates, but the microplastic problem remains. There are also aesthetic considerations – large areas of black plastic do not look pretty in the landscape.

Could there be alternatives out there, such as waxed cotton or sailcloth? Possibly, but expense and practicalities might preclude their use. Tillage is the traditional way of managing weeds, either as primary tillage, where weeds and weed seeds are buried or mixed into the soil, or secondary or tertiary tillage, where weeds emerge, then are killed by mechanical cultivation.

Primary tillage

The plough is the traditional tool for the first cultivations, inverting the soil so that the surface layer, which may contain weed seeds that have been shed on the surface, as well as weed and crop residues, are buried at the depth to which the plough share is set. To an extent this buries the problem rather than solving it. While many small-seeded and annual grass weeds are often short-lived, others have evolved mechanisms to lie dormant in the soil at depth for many years and if the soil is ploughed to the same depth in subsequent years these seeds will be brought back to the surface, ready to emerge if the conditions are right. In contrast, the no-till or minimum tillage systems leave the weed seeds at or near the surface, where they can be depleted by predation or shallow cultivations. Perennial weeds, on the other hand, can be reduced by ploughing, but often thrive under reduced tillage systems.

Secondary tillage

Rotavators, power harrows and disc harrows used to prepare seedbeds are referred to as secondary tillage, though many growers bypass the plough and use them for primary tillage. Implements will impact on the weed flora in different ways. Spring tines tend to move seeds upwards in the soil profile, while rotavators have the net effect of moving seeds further down. Therefore, tines can be used to retain freshly shed weeds near the surface for flushing out, rather than incorporating them into the weed seed bank.

Rotavators can increase problems by chopping up perennial weed roots and rhizomes into small pieces that will regrow, but can work for weed control as part of a sequence of cultivations that weaken the weed.

False and stale seedbeds

False and stale seedbeds are extremely important techniques for reducing weed pressure in crops. While the terms are often used interchangeably, there is a difference; false seedbeds use tillage or cultivation to kill the weeds, while stale seedbeds use thermal weeding for weed control.

Charles Merfield in his excellent guide on *False and Stale Seedbeds*, identified three key pieces of scientific theory, or 'golden rules', that underpin them:

1. Only 85–95 per cent of weed seeds are dormant at any given time, but of the 5–15 per cent that are non-dormant, most germinate (very) quickly.

2. Tillage is the most effective means of getting weed seeds to germinate.
3. Most weeds only emerge from the top 5cm.

The principle of the false seedbed is to create the ideal conditions for germination, a perfect seedbed, as if you were growing the crop; that may entail irrigation if the conditions are dry. False seedbeds need around two weeks between tillage and re-tillage; it is important to cultivate as shallowly as possible (ideally 2cm), so as not to bring up too many new weed seeds. On a small scale, this can be done with a wheel hoe.

For a stale seedbed, thermal or flame-weeding is used. This entails using heat to 'flash' the weeds, rupturing their cells and causing them to die. It is most effective on young broad-leafed weeds, but less so on grass weeds. The crop is sown into the seedbed and, for maximum effectiveness, flamed off just before the crop emerges. This can be a risky business; if the weather is wet, the window can be missed and the weeds get ahead of the crop.

There is, however, a way to ensure that you carry out the process in time. Lay a pane of glass over the crop row immediately after drilling, or following irrigation. The crop under the glass pane will emerge faster than in the open, which gives you a very short window (24 hours maximum, depending on species and time of year) to get out and flame off those weeds. So, make sure you inspect regularly and be prepared to go earlier if there is a wet period of weather approaching.

In some crops, such as sweetcorn and onions, it is possible to flame-weed post-emergence. In onions, for example, following a pre-emergence flame-weeding, two post-emergence passes with a flame-weeder at the three- and five-leaf stage can give economic control.

Mulches

The principle of mulching is to provide a physical barrier to the soil surface through which light cannot penetrate, thus preventing weed-seed germination and suppressing emerging seedlings.

Sheeted mulches

The off-the-shelf solution using rolls of black plastic, woven polypropylene or biodegradable alternatives like paper mulches, laid down by hand or by machine. Rolls of woven plastic can be re-used over many seasons - growers often burn holes in them at correct spacings for particular crops. Biodegradable sheet mulches are available, but they need to be free of GM-ingredients.

Organic mulching materials

Organic mulching materials can serve a dual purpose, feeding the soil and building organic matter (*see* Chapter 5 for discussion). The rates at which they need to be applied to exclude weeds (10–15cm) does mean that very large volumes are required, so care needs to be taken to avoid overfeeding and perhaps it is best to target mulches to crops that are not weed-competitive. Options include home-made compost, green-waste compost, woodchip compost, straw, hay/old silage and wool, depending on the scale required and local availability. Beware of the dangers of aminopyralid or clopyralid contamination and of bringing in weed seeds on imported hay and silage.

Another option is transfer mulch – a crop that is grown in one part of the holding and cut to use as a mulch or weed control in another part (*see* Chapter 5).

Flame-weeding overwintering onions at Strawberry Fields. The windows for flame-weeding can be short, especially in the autumn. Conditions should be calm and the ground dry.

Alternatives to plastic mulches

Due to issues of microplastic contamination and general overuse of plastic, we need to be moving away from plastic mulches, especially plastics used for only one season, even if they can be recycled. A trial led by Coventry University's Centre for Agroecology, Water and Resilience (CAWR), in conjunction with the Organic-PLUS project, explored a range of commercially available non-degradable and biodegradable alternatives to plastic mulches, including starch-based film mulches, woodchip, green-waste compost, cardboard and hay and grass clippings.

All of the black mulches effectively suppressed weeds while the crops were growing and even mulches that broke down before the end of the growing season could be worthwhile, depending on the crop. The best performing out of the loose mulches was hay, though there is a real danger of introducing weed seeds into the system. Lower application rates of loose mulches did not work as well and they proved more effective against annual rather than perennial weeds. Some will also add nutrients and impact on soil biology.

Onions planted through a range of mulches – woven polypropylene, polythene, biodegradable (commercial and innovative) with weeded and unweeded controls.

Cabbages planted through a range of mulches – early.

Loose mulch trial – green-waste compost, hay, grass mowings, woodchip and extruded wood.

Cabbages planted through a range of mulches – late.

Mulch systems and rotational no-till

Johannes Storch's system of rotational no-till at Bio-Gemüsehof Dickendorf in Germany has perfected the art of growing cover crops and mulch crops for planting into with a specially developed machine – the MulchTec Planter. On average, 3ha of grass, clover or cover crops are needed to mulch 1ha of crop.

* **Step one:** Mechanical loosening of the soil to break up compaction and deal with perennial weeds.
* **Step two:** Sow a winter annual cover crop (rye/triticale/vetch/peas).
* **Step three:** Flail-mow the cover crop, leaving a short stubble.
* **Step four:** Harvest mulch from other fields with a forage harvester, which chops it into 5–10cm pieces.
* **Step five:** Spread transfer mulch on to stubble, aiming to mulch to a depth of 8–10cm, around 12tonnes of dry matter per hectare.
* **Step six:** Transplant through the mulch.

The MulchTec Planter slices through the mulch with a cutting unit driven at high speed. The planting share follows in the slit created, finger wheels grab the leaves of the transplants and keep them upright so that they are not covered by the mulch, then press wheels close the slit of the mulch layer.

Living mulches

These are low-growing species, often legumes, grown as an understorey to tall crops, or as paths between beds. They can be sown prior to the crop as a green manure and a narrow strip cultivated into it for sowing or planting (strip-till or strip-plant). They can also be established by undersowing.

Strip-till systems are not always easy to manage and there have been unsuccessful projects, involving machines designed to cut clovers (roots and/or leaves) to minimise competition with the crop. They have been successful in arable crops and research is ongoing in this area.

The living mulch can benefit from a false seedbed before sowing; it is best if the crop can be hoed at least once before the undersow is broadcast, or drilled under the crop. For some crops (squashes, especially), there can be a very narrow window for establishment of the living mulch before the crop canopy closes in. In dry years, an undersow may compete with the crop for water.

Table 1: Undersowing vegetable crops

Crop	Suitable species for living mulch	Sowing rate	Notes
Squashes/pumpkins	Red/white clover	7kg/ha	Sow when squashes start to 'run'.
Kale, Brussels sprouts	Red/white clover/trefoil	7kg/ha	Sow around 20 days after planting. Best drilled or hand broadcast low under plants.
Runner beans/climbing French beans	Red clover	7kg/ha	Sow when beans 50cm high.
Leeks	Rye or oats	120–150kg/ha	Sown in late autumn to overwinter.
Tomatoes/cucumbers	Kent wild white clover/trefoil	7kg/ha	Sow when tomatoes 50cm high.
Sweetcorn	Red/white clover/lucerne (for long-term green manure)	7kg/ha 12kg/ha	Sow around 20 days after planting.

Mechanical weeding

In order to enable efficient mechanical weeding of crops, from wheel hoes, steerage hoes up to robotic weeders, it is necessary to have parallel rows. Everything stems from this and the simpler the system, the better. Not every row has to be straight, but it needs to be parallel to the adjacent rows. On a tractor-bed system, this is set by the spacing of the seed drill, or planting shares on the toolbar. On a smaller scale, the seed drill will have a row marker that marks the next row. For planting out, the seed drill can also be used to mark rows, or row markers can be pulled along or drawn across the bed.

The best time to tackle weeds is when they are small – the 'white thread' stage, when they are just emerging and may not even be visible – as they are at their most vulnerable stage and easily killed. At this stage, weeding can be fast and even pleasurable! A wheel hoe can be literally run through the rows with minimal effort, while very shallow cultivations with inter-row hoes will be similarly quick. In any case, you should try to cultivate before weeds get more than 2.5cm tall; beyond this, some weeds develop an incredible ability to re-root and survive cultivations. Taller weeds will take a lot more energy, time and money to weed, even mechanically. Hoe blades will need to go deeper, which means more soil disturbance and more weed seeds brought to the surface – and so, more weeds.

Inter-row weeding

Drilled crops need to be big enough to be visible, either by the naked eye or by a camera-guided system, before inter-row weeding can begin. For some slow-emerging crops like parsnips, a marker crop such as radish can be sown in the same drill, to enable easy detection of the row and early weeding.

For any inter-row weeding operation, it is important to get as close as possible to the row without disturbing the crop, as the weeds emerging closest to crop plants compete the most. Some inter-row weeders also throw soil into the crop row to bury small weeds, which works for brassicas and sweetcorn, but not lettuce and other salads. Growing potatoes and roots, such as carrots and parsnips, on ridges requires more space, but can enable effective mechanical weeding. Ridging after the crop has emerged both removes and covers up weeds at the same time. Ridging should be carried out when the soil is neither too wet nor too dry – around 40–50 per cent water content.

Intra-row weeding

Inter-row weeding is the easy bit, but the tricky thing is to control the weeds within the crop row mechanically, minimising hand-hoeing or hand-weeding. Finger weeders operate as two discs with flexible polyurethane 'fingers', which are angled down into the crop, either side of the crop row. They are ground-driven (that is, not powered) and attached to a toolbar. They can work the soil between the row, flicking the weeds away from the crop. The crop plant needs to be well-anchored to avoid uprooting. If your soil is prone to capping, finger weeders can be mounted behind hoe blade, which break the soil crust, as fingers work best on loose, dry soils. Harder fingers are recommended for heavier soils. The distance between the fingers can be adjusted to reduce or increase the aggressiveness of the action, depending on the size of the weeds and establishment of the crop.

Torsion weeders consist of two spring tines angled backwards and downward, either side of the crop row, the tips flexing around the established crop plants, uprooting small weeds within the row. Harrows can also be useful. Commonly used in arable crops, they consist of flexible spring-mounted tines on a frame, which vibrate through the soil, uprooting small weeds but gliding around the crop. Running harrows through crops can be nerve-wracking – the usual advice is 'Don't look back!'

These tools are not just the preserve of the field-scale grower. French company Terrateck has been revolutionising tools for organic farming and has produced tined harrows, torsion weeders and finger weeders to attach to wheel hoes. Treffler also produces a 'tiny harrow', which can be hand-pulled through greenhouse or intensive market garden plots.

Remedial action

For many reasons, things may not always go to plan and some hand-weeding might be needed. This is best done as a group activity – there is nothing more soul-destroying than weeding a large field or plot on your own. Whether hoeing or hand-pulling weeds, it is a skilled activity and it is best to give instructions, or to lead by example, both for efficiency and to reduce back problems. Using two hands rather than one is much more efficient for hand-pulling weeds and also allows for protection of the crop plant to prevent it from uprooting. As soon as the weeder sits (or even lies) down, weeding will take much longer. Frequent stretching is needed and, if hoeing, changing sides regularly can help.

For the field-scale operator, 'bed weeders' are available – tractor-mounted platforms with stretchers that workers lie on to remove weeds, while being pulled very slowly through the field. There are also self-propelled models (diesel or solar-powered) available as single- or double-row options.

On some occasions, topping, weed-surfing (mowing above the crop canopy), or strimming can be sensible remedial actions. If the topper or mower is set correctly, most of the weeds can be taken out and the balance restored in favour of the crop. It is important to avoid weeds setting seed (one year's seeds equals seven years' weeds, as they say), but also to know the biology of your weeds, as some seeds may continue to ripen after cutting, so may need removal for hot composting. On a final note, if you have not been able to avoid a significant weed seed drop, it is better to leave the land fallow over winter for birds to feed on than to cultivate.

Brush-weeding at Strawberry Fields.

Tractor-mounted finger weeder.

Wheel hoe with finger weeder for inter- and intra-row weeding in carrots at Pitney Farm Market Garden.

Tractor-mounted finger weeder.

Ridging up should be the only weed control needed in potatoes.

Hoe blades need to get as close to the crop row as possible.

Tractor-pulled lay-flat weeder.

Solar-powered, electric self-propelled lay-flat weeder, at a trade show in Germany.

Table 2: Annual weeds and their characteristics: competitiveness, emergence, seed count and longevity, bioindicators and biodiversity value

| Weed | Competitive in | | Peak emergence | Seed count/plant | Seed longevity | Germination depth | Bioindicator | Biodiversity value |
	Winter crops	Spring crops						
Annual meadow grass (*Poa annua*)		✓	April to October	10–500	4–5 years		Compaction, fertile	✓
Black bindweed (*Fallopia convolvulus*)		✓	May	100–1,000	>5 years	6cm	Acid soil, fertile	✓
Black nightshade (*Solanum nigrum*)			June	500	>5 years	5.5cm		✓
Charlock (*Sinapis arvensis*)	✓		March	16–25,000	60 years	4.3cm	High pH, high organic matter	✓
Cleavers (*Galium aparine*)	✓		October and April	300–400	1–5 years	7cm	High fertility, humus-rich, compaction, surplus N at surface	
Common chickweed (*Stellaria media*)	✓	✓	October and April	2,500	25 years	3.6cm	High fertility/humus	✓
Common fumitory (*Fumaria officinalis*)			October and March/April	1,600	>5 years	5.5cm	High pH, nutrient-rich, high K	✓
Corn spurrey (*Spergula arvensis*)			October and April	1–10,000	>170 years	3cm	Low pH	✓
Fat hen (*Chenopodium album*)		✓	September and April	3–20,000	6–20 years	4.8cm	High fertility/humus, excess uncomposted animal manure	✓
Gallant soldiers (*Galinsoga parviflora*)		✓	March to October	2–400,000	2–5 years	2cm		

Weed	Competitive in		Peak emergence	Seed count/plant	Seed longevity	Germination depth	Bioindicator	Biodiversity value
	Winter crops	Spring crops						
Groundsel (*Senecio vulgaris*)			October and May	2–3,500	1–5 years	2cm	High fertility, humus, excess N	✓
Knotgrass (*Polygonum aviculare*)		✓	April to May	<1,000	20 years	3cm	Acid, compaction, fertile	✓
Redshank (*Persicaria maculosa/Polygonum persicaria*)		✓	April to May	200–800	>5 years	1.5cm	Acid, high fertility/humus, poor drainage	✓
Scented mayweed (*Matricaria recutita*)	✓	✓	April/May and August/September	5,000	>5 years	0.5cm		✓
Scentless mayweed (*Tripleurospermum inodorum*)	✓	✓	October and April	10–200,000	>5 years	5cm		✓
Small nettle (*Urtica urens*)			May	100–1,000	>5 years			✓
Wild pansy (*Viola tricolor*)			November and May					✓
Pineapple weed (*Matricaria discoidea*)			September and April	0–6,000	>5 years	5cm	Nutrient rich, compaction	✓
Common poppy (*Papaver rhoeas*)	✓		October and April	20,000	Up to 100 years	0.5cm		✓
Prickly sow-thistle (*Sonchus asper*)			October and May	5,000	1–2 years	5cm		✓
Smooth sow thistle (*Sonchus oleraceus*)			October and May	Up to 100,000	1 year	2cm	Nutrient rich, excess N	✓
Common field speedwell (*Veronica persica*)	✓		October and May	50–10,000	3–4 years	6cm	Nutrient rich, compaction	
Ivy-leaved speedwell (*Veronica hederifolia*)	✓		November	40–100	3–4 years	11cm	Nutrient rich	
Wall speedwell (*Veronica arvensis*)			September	0–17,000	1–5 years	1cm		
Wild radish (*Raphanus raphanistrum*)	✓		September and April	160	>5 years	5cm	Low pH, anaerobic conditions	✓

Sources: Table draws on information from AHDB (2018); Maughan & Amos (2021); Davies *et al.* (2008).

Perennial weeds

Most of the chapter refers to the management of annual or seedling weeds. Some perennial weeds can increase over time in organic market gardens and may need special strategies to keep them in check. An understanding of the biology of the individual species will help to identify potential weak points in their life cycle. A range of control options are available, including cutting and mowing, cultivations and cover crops, with new technologies such as electrical weeding also coming on to the scene. Combining various weed-control tactics can have a powerful cumulative effect – the use of 'many little hammers', as Matt Liebman and Eric Gallandt have described.

It should be noted that there is a downside to some of the techniques below that involve multiple cultivations. They can cause damage to the soil structure, especially on sandy or silty/sandy soils with low organic matter levels.

Docks (Rumex spp.)

If you are on heavy land, or have taken over tired horse pastures, you may well have inherited a dock problem. Docks thrive on soils that are low in potassium and rich in nitrogen. Seed numbers in soil have been estimated to average twelve million per hectare! Mowing of fertility-building leys will stop them seeding at least, while every effort should be made to prevent docks from seeding in growing crops. In grassland, the roots can be dug out during early spring using a spade or purpose-made tool such as a 'lazy dog'. In potatoes, docks can be relatively easy to pull out because of the use of deep cultivations and ridging.

Docks can be dealt with by 'bastard fallowing' – taking land out of production for a season, or part of a season, so as to allow time for tillage to remove perennial weeds. Ploughing followed by repeated cultivations during spring and summer can exhaust the older roots and control young seedlings. Another approach to control established docks is through a series of three or four passes with a rotavator in April to June. Starting shallowly and cultivating progressively deeper each time to around 15cm can be effective, provided that the soil is moist.

Couch grass (Elytrigia repens)

Couch grass is a very common weed on cultivated land, occurring on most soils except those with a low pH. Although couch grass prefers heavier soils,

Dock gang at Glebelands Market Garden near Cardigan. The docks can be 'hot composted' successfully, or put in silage bags to rot down anaerobically before composting.

it can also spread rapidly on lighter soils. I once took on a walled garden that was covered in couch grass, with an almost impenetrable mat of rhizomes in the top 10cm of soil. After digging out mountains of roots with little impact, I got the whole area ploughed and, following a couple of passes with the rotavator, the couch was pretty much gone. Rotavating couch into lots of small pieces, all of which could regrow, sounds like a potential disaster, but provided that it is repeated it seems to work. Bastard fallowing, with repeated cultivations, can be effective. Starting in spring, harrowing should be repeated when regrowth has reached the three- to four-leaf stage, bringing the rhizomes to the surface to desiccate. Innovative Farmer trials using a buckwheat green manure as an alternative to bastard fallowing showed it to be reasonably effective at controlling couch, with other soil benefits, too (*see* Chapter 5).

Creeping thistle (Cirsium arvense)

Creeping thistle is another aggressive perennial weed that can increase in organic farming systems, so needs to be managed carefully. It occurs on almost all soil types, but favours deep, well-aerated soils. It thrives in vegetable holdings because many vegetable crops are weakly competitive. Longer periods of fertility-building therefore tend to reduce its dominance. Plough pans and compaction can cause creeping-thistle problems, so incorporating deep-rooting crops such as lucerne or fodder radish into the rotation can help, especially on heavy soils.

Creeping thistle can spread and be introduced by seed, or in manure as pieces of roots. Thistles can regenerate from fragments as small as 2.5cm long. Hoeing is effective in controlling seedlings during their first few weeks, but they can survive cultivations with tined weeders. When thistles are more mature,

it is better to pull them at the flower-bud stage, rather than cutting, to avoid new shoots developing. The old rhyme goes: 'Cut thistles in May, they'll grow in a day; Cut them in June, that is too soon; Cut them in July, then they will die.' The reason for this is that they are dependent on building up reserves during this period to survive the winter. A bastard fallowing can be effective for creeping thistle and is best carried out from the end of June to the beginning of August.

Pigs will also root out and consume couch rhizomes if confined in relatively small areas, moving regularly to maintain soil health. Breed is important; pigs with long noses like Tamworths tend to be good diggers, with young pigs (three to six months old) seeming to be the most effective.

Chapter Nine

Managing Pests and Diseases Agroecologically

Books on pests and diseases can be like medical textbooks – before long, you imagine you have the symptoms of many life-threatening conditions. It is better to focus on health, because most of the pests and diseases that your crops *could* get, you will never see, or at least not at levels that endanger crops or livelihoods. So, this chapter is about plant health care, using a systems approach to manage agroecological processes, while minimising the use of off-farm inputs.

Achieving good farm health with a biologically active soil (*see* Chapter 5), plus a highly diverse farm agroecosystem, does not happen overnight. Patience is needed, as there may be pest or disease problems, as well as crop failures, in the early years. A figure of seven years to achieve a balance of predators and pests is sometimes quoted, though this may be more anecdotal than evidence-based. It will be a continuous learning process; with every failure you will emerge with a better understanding of why the pest or disease has become a problem and what to do better in the future. Sometimes, it may be simply a case of holding your nerve, while waiting for the predators to build up and keep the pest in check, instead of reaching for a solution off the shelf.

So much depends on diversity; systems with higher diversity can be more productive and more stable. Numbers of crops and varieties grown are one aspect, but how those crops are arranged spatially is also important – intercropping and mixing varieties within plantings can slow the spread of pests and diseases, as can the biodiversity of non-cropping areas. Rotations build in diversity in time and space (*see* Chapter 6) to help prevent pest and disease build-up by breaking their life cycles.

Crop monitoring and forecasting

Regular crop walking is essential to keep on top of any potential problems. Field crops should be walked at least once, if not two to three times a week. Train yourself to recognise pests, but also the beneficials. Look for telltale signs – a slight yellowing or distortion on the leaf surface may mean a pest colony under the leaf, or it could be a disease. Correct identification of the damage is also key. I remember a Devon grower who was informed by a neighbour that: 'Those rabbits of yours, Mike – them be flying in!' The rabbits turned out to be geese!

Allied with the powers of human observation are trapping and forecasting systems. Traps can take the form of vision-guided traps attracting insects through colour (for example, yellow sticky traps used for monitoring carrot fly), water traps, smell-guided pheromone traps, or suction traps whereby insects are 'hoovered' out of the air. Traps can be part of a grower's own monitoring system, or be fed into forecasting systems. Beneficials can be monitored in the same way and some field-scale

OPPOSITE: Cornflowers in brassica fields attract beneficial insects to the crop and provide food for insects travelling from flower strips or hedgerows.

growers use pitfall traps to monitor ground beetles to see how far into the field they are penetrating. It is useful to subscribe to pest forecasting services, so that you are aware of what is around and what to look for. Pest forecasting can help with decisions as to when to put on and when to remove crop covers.

Agroecological approaches to pest management

The agroecological approach to pest management is best illustrated by the agroecological pest-regulation pyramid. The base of the strategy is the promotion of biodiversity in and around the crop fields. Building on this is site selection, varietal choice, rotational practices and so on. Targeted promotion of beneficial insects through beetle banks, companion plants and flower strips builds on this, with biopesticides, pheromones and physical control methods acting as the last resort.

Flower strips to promote beneficials in brassicas

FiBL Switzerland has done a lot of work on increasing the performance of predatory insects (spiders, ladybird larvae and so on) and parasitic insects (for example, parasitic wasps) in brassicas by improving their food base and overwintering opportunities. The presence of vetch, buckwheat and cornflower has been shown to extend the lifespan of parasitoid wasps, and thus the parasitisation of caterpillars and eggs. Planted together as flowering strips, they can double the biodiversity compared to the brassica field, with increases in bees, ground beetles and spiders.

The agroecological pest regulation pyramid. Source: Luka, 2021.

Encouraging natural enemies

The excellent *AHDB Encyclopaedia of pests and natural enemies* in field crops describes the 'SAFE' approach to provide appropriate resources for natural enemies of crop pests.

S is for shelter

Mixed hedges with several different species provide structure for shelter. Hedge bases or margins can be sown with flower-rich grass mixes and beetle banks can be created within fields using tussocky grasses.

A is for alternative prey

Other food sources are needed to maintain natural enemy populations. This can be provided by weeds, organic manures, crop debris and other crops. Predators can feed on aphids on old brassicas, ready to transfer to new plantings when they go in.

F is for flower-rich habitat

Pollen and nectar are essential food for many natural enemies like hoverflies and parasitic wasps. Special 'pollen and nectar' seed mixes can be bought and grown, with hedge margins or meadows allowed to flower. Coriander is great for attracting hoverflies.

E is for environment

Make sure that the whole holding has a sufficient spread of diverse habitats and vegetation. Some natural enemies don't stray far from the margins. Don't be too tidy. Weeds can be valuable, too.

Following is the flower-strip mixture for beneficials for cabbage production:

- **Vetch:** *Vicia sativa* – 44.8kg/ha
- **Buckwheat:** *Fagopyrum esculentum* – 11kg/ha
- **Cornflower:** *Centaurea cyanus* – 4.1kg/ha
- **Common poppy:** *Papaver rhoeas* – 0.1kg/ha.

FiBL advises the following strategies:

- **Crop rotation:** Avoid brassica species as green manures.
- **Plot selection:** Avoid proximity to other cabbage crops and rape-seed fields (including previous year's crops).

- **Establish the flower strip:** Sow or plant a flower strip of at least 3m wide, or the width of two beds, along the edges of the field or through the middle of the field. This width is sufficient to establish a beneficial insect population in a 40–50m wide field. On plots with low to medium weed pressure, the flower strip mixture can be sown. On plots with high weed pressure, it can be advantageous to raise the flower plants in modules and transplant into a biodegradable mulch film.
- **Planting companion plants:** If fleece or mesh covers are not used, cornflowers can be planted in the crop rows to increase beneficial insect efficiency.

Flower strips near cabbage fields make an essential contribution to the successful regulation of cabbage moth (*Mamestra brassicae*). They complement the effect of beneficial *Bacillus thuringiensis* preparations, which are only effective against very young larvae of the moth. This photo shows a flower strip planted in a biodegradable cornstarch mulch.

- **Monitoring pests:** Monitor and count all pests on cabbage plants twice a week during June to August. Use pheromone traps to monitor the swede midge (*Contarinia nasturtii*), especially if the occurrence is known to be high in your area.
- **Biopesticide use:** If the damage threshold is exceeded, use bioinsecticides that are gentle on beneficial insects.

Biological controls

Biological control, the specific use of targeted natural enemies, is mostly confined to the enclosed environments of protected cropping. There are many companies supplying predatory insects for all the major glasshouse pests. Decisions need to be taken early to introduce controls, as soon as the pest is spotted, as populations may take time to catch up.

Biopesticides

Biopesticides, as the name implies, are biologically based pesticides. They are usually microbial, but can also include nematodes and biochemicals – formulations of naturally occurring substances including plant extracts and pheromones. With the withdrawal of many conventional chemical pesticides, biopesticides are a growth industry. Though they have many advantages, including being less hazardous and having reduced environmental impact, they should neither be considered a 'silver bullet', nor as a like for like replacement for synthetic pesticides. The first commercially available product based on the bacterium *Bacillus thuringiensis* (Bt), now widely used to control caterpillars in brassicas, was developed in 1938.

Spinosad is an insecticide based on products derived from the soil bacterial species *Saccharopolyspora spinosa*. It is used to control a wide variety of pests, including caterpillars, spider mites, thrips and leaf miners. Its use does, however, entail some risk to key parasitoids.

Biopesticides for insect control are mainly based on bacterial, nematode, viral and fungal agents. For disease control, they are sometimes referred to as 'bioprotectants' and are mostly plant or microbial extracts. The use of these products in the field can be variable and the persistence of the product on its target and the microclimatic conditions encountered need to be taken into account. A lot of effort is being put into improving efficacy in the field. A growing number of products are likely to become available and approved for use; caution needs to be taken, however, as there is ongoing research to develop biopesticides through means of genetic modification, the use of which is not compatible with organic farming. In any case, you should check with the organic standards and with your organic control body before purchase and use of any of these products.

Trap cropping

Trap crops are crops that are grown to attract pests or pathogens away from the maincrop. Some examples are:

- Sticky nightshade (*Solanum sisymbriifolium*) and African nightshade (*Solanum scabrum*). These are used to clean up potato cyst nematode before planting potatoes. The plants produce a root exudate that stimulates the eggs of the nematode to hatch, but the pest is unable to feed and cannot complete its life cycle. They can be effective, but crops can still be difficult to establish. Research is ongoing with an Innovative Farmers' field lab on the topic.
- Chinese southern giant mustard (*Brassica juncea* var. *crispifolia*) and other mustards and rapes have been used in the USA as trap crops for flea beetle to protect broccoli plants. The trap crop needs to be planted ahead of the crop that is being protected. Around 10 per cent of the crop area is needed for the trap crop, which is usually planted around the perimeter of the field. Flea beetles can be removed by using a vacuum cleaner and placed in a freezer (!) and the trap crop is tilled in.
- Sacrificial crop. Carrot fly is usually more damaging around the edge of the field, so damage can be accepted in crops grown around the perimeter and used for stockfeed. Use cheap or old seed.

Biofumigation

Biofumigation refers to plants, mainly brassicas, being grown as a cover crop in order to be incorporated into the ground to reduce soil borne pests, pathogens and weeds. Brassicas contain glucosinolates which, when the plant tissues are damaged, combine with an enzyme (Myrosinase) and water to produce isothiocyanate (ICT). The cover crop is allowed to grow to 100–150cm high in order to maximise the biomass produced. It is then chopped with a flail mower and immediately cultivated to a depth of no more than 15cm. The ICT is released as a gas and is lost very quickly to the air, so rolling will help to seal the surface and trap the gas for best impact. Breeders, such as Tozer Seeds, have bred mustards that are high in glucosinolates and the enzyme, and thus especially suitable for the process. In addition to improving soil health, biofumigation can be used to suppress a range of nematode species, wireworm and soil borne pathogens such as *Verticilium dahliae*, *Pythium* spp., *Sclerotinia* spp., *Fusarium* spp., *Rhizoctonia* spp., and others.

The great cover-up

Floating crop covers are a popular tool for organic growers for excluding pests, both large and small. Fleece is a lightweight, non-woven polypropylene material that is used as a floating mulch, supported by the crop. It is also used for season extension. Different grades are available, offering varying degrees of frost protection. Fleeces normally last a couple of seasons, but can be easily damaged by deer and raptors trying to catch rodents underneath.

Mesh is made from UV-stabilised polyethylene and is much more expensive than fleece, but can last many years. Although mesh does create a microclimate and provides some frost protection, its primary use is to exclude insect pests from crops. Different mesh sizes are available according to the pests you wish to exclude:

- 1.3mm mesh will exclude cabbage root fly, carrot fly, aphids and most caterpillars apart from diamond back moth
- 0.8mm mesh will exclude flea beetle, whitefly, leaf miner and leek moth
- 0.37mm mesh is needed to keep out thrips.

Both fleece and mesh need to be in place before the pest infestation has taken place, which usually means straight after planting, though they can also be used in association with pest forecasting services. Edges need to be secured with pegs, sandbags or dug in, especially on the windward side, but bear in mind that you will need regular access for weed control and crop inspection.

Fleeces and meshes also exclude predators as well as pests, so if the pest has managed to get under the cover, it can multiply unchecked. Check transplants for eggs before planting and avoid using fleeces or meshes that are damaged. Sometimes the edges can be pushed up by weeds, allowing insects to enter, or eggs may be laid directly on to leaves through the mesh, by the pest.

Crop covers may be effective, but they are plastic-based, with the issue of carbon footprint and microplastic contamination of the soil. Many growers are now trying to reduce their use of crop covers. For brassicas, crop covers may be most useful at establishment stage to keep out cabbage root fly, flea beetle and birds, but they can be removed after two to four weeks to allow the predators and parasitic insects to keep the caterpillars in check.

The generalist pests

Some of the larger pests are less easily dealt with agroecologically – we're talking pigeons, rabbits, deer, badgers and the like. Rabbit fencing can be expensive, but effective. Electric fencing netting is a temporary solution – you will need it if you grow sweetcorn and have badgers in the vicinity! Humming lines, kites, 'scary man' scarecrows, bird scarers or bangers can be used to keep birds away, though you may need to keep changing strategy, so that the birds don't get used to them. I was once interrupted during a crop-monitoring walk on an organic farm by a loud electronic voice telling me 'You do not belong here!' I soon realised it was intended for the birds rather than me.

Enviromesh covering brassicas at Bennison Farm CSA in Essex. In the winter, crop covers are often used to exclude larger pests like pigeons.

Scarecrows can be creative projects, but the birds will soon get used to them!

Indian runner ducks are great consumers of slugs.

Managing diseases

As with pests, it is important to understand the biology of the major diseases that you might encounter, as well as the environmental and agronomic factors that allow them to thrive. The basis of disease management is good crop husbandry and soil management. Plants that are growing under adverse conditions, such as poor drainage or lack of nutrients or water, will be under stress and vulnerable to diseases.

Soil, manures and composts contain microorganisms that help directly to protect plants against disease. A healthy soil food web is important; interactions among soil organisms and plant roots can protect plants from attack by pathogens.

Diversity through variety selection

The choice of appropriate, locally adapted, robust species and varieties that are less susceptible to

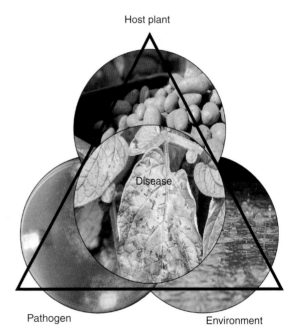

The disease triangle. There are three factors that must be present for a plant disease to develop: a susceptible host; the pathogen; and a favourable environment. If one of the three is missing, the disease does not occur.

diseases is important. The choice of varieties might not entirely be in your control and is to some extent dependent on your market. The supermarkets and packers have for a long time driven varietal choice in some sectors, particularly potatoes. That is starting to change and in 2022 the launch of the 'Robust Potato Pledge' followed the path trailblazed by the Dutch to ensure that retailers and breeders move to the use of blight-resistant varieties.

Some varieties have been bred to be resistant, or tolerant, to specific diseases. The resistance is not always durable, however. Lettuce breeders, for example, must keep up with the evolution of new mildew strains. Plant architecture of varieties comes into play, allowing airflow or minimising leaf contact with the soil, or in the case of cauliflowers with leaves arranged to protect the curd from pest attack.

Leek rust. Many diseases are present on organic vegetable farms, but normally at low levels. Often damage, such as leek rust, can be trimmed off and does not significantly affect yields.

Cultural practices to manage diseases

Cultural practices that can help to manage specific pathogens include:

- **Rotation:** Increasing the gap between crops of the same family, especially where there are known problems. The sequences of crops, for example alliums after brassicas, can also be important.
- **Mulching:** Can act as a barrier to entry for disease spores.
- **Row spacing:** Wider spacing allows more airflow and reduces humidity.
- **Polyculture:** Intercropping and varietal mixtures (at least three) can slow the spread of diseases.
- **Good hygiene and sanitation:** Avoid dumps of waste crop – feed to stock, or compost properly.

Plant biostimulants

Regulation (EU) No. 2019/1009, Article 47, states that a 'plant biostimulant' is a product that stimulates the nutritional processes of plants independently of the nutrients it contains, with the sole aim of improving one or more of the following characteristics of plants or their rhizosphere:

- the efficiency of nutrient use
- tolerance to abiotic stress
- qualitative characteristics
- the availability of nutrients confined in the soil or rhizosphere.

Surendra Dara of the University of California compares the use of biostimulants in agriculture to humans taking probiotics and vitamins, whereas pesticides are comparable to medicines. Extending this analogy further, a focus on soil health promoting healthy plants could be likened to a balanced diet.

As part of the EU-funded OSCAR project (Optimising Subsidiary Crop Applications in Rotations), the University of Kassel carried out trials on non-inversion tillage. They applied freshly cut grass/clover to potatoes as a mulch in mid-May with a manure spreader to 8–10cm depth.

The mulched potatoes in June. Spread of potato blight was about two weeks slower than the control plots. This was likely to be due to the reflection of light by the dried mulch creating an unfavourable environment for the blight sporangia.

There is considerable overlap between biostimulatory and biopesticidal properties; for some products, naming them a 'plant biostimulant' may be a way of getting round the pesticide regulations.

Examples of biostimulants include arbuscular mycorrhizal fungi and other microorganisms that are applied as compost teas, protein hydrolysates, humic substances, algal and botanical extracts, silicates and phosphites, and chitosan. Currently approved biostimulants for use in organic systems are dominated by seaweed-derived products. There is, however, an ever-growing range available, including ones based on beetle droppings, amino and fulvic acids, and other plant extracts, such as aloe, grape skins and more. Garlic extracts claim to have pest-deterrent effects, as well as improving the natural defences of plants against parasites.

Do they have a place in organic farming, or is it all marketing? There may be benefits when plants are subject to stresses from heat or salts, and for poor soils. However, they may have less effect when used on well-established organic farms that are using grass/clover leys, composts and manures to keep the soils biologically active.

Compost tea

Compost teas are liquids derived from compost to extract nutrients and beneficial microorganisms, including bacteria, fungi, protozoa and nematodes. They are applied as soil drenches or foliar sprays, or incorporated into irrigation systems. On a small scale, compost tea can be made by steeping a bag of compost in a bucket of water; more complex systems involve aerating the water by way of an aquarium pump, or use of specialist 'compost tea brewers', which are available from garden to industrial sizes.

The principal steps for brewing an aerated composted tea are:

1. Use rainwater, or allow mains water to stand overnight to dissipate any chlorine, or aerate for 20–30 minutes to achieve the same effect.
2. Add sieved mature compost in a porous sack, or loose according to brewer recommendations; some recipes say 1 part compost to 6 parts water. Symbio, which manufactures the BioBrewer, suggests 166ml, or one standard mug, for a 15ltr brewer.
3. Add activating ingredients: molasses or proprietary starter.
4. Turn on the pump to aerate and brew the tea for 18–48 hours, by which time there should be a sweet, earthy smell; allow to settle for 10 minutes.
5. Decant or filter the compost tea and dilute from 1 to 9 up to 1 in 30 with rainwater or dechlorinated water.
6. Spray pressure should not exceed 2.5bar (1–2bar is preferable) and nozzle size should not be too fine, as this would damage the fungi in the brew.
7. If you can't apply the tea immediately, keep it aerated and add small quantities of molasses or seaweed to keep the microbes alive for several days.

Source: Symbio.

Opinions of compost tea range from it being a miracle product to on a par with snake oil. There does appear to be, however, a growing body of evidence that compost-tea application helps to build healthy soils, which can lead to benefits for the crop, including improved crop health and nutrition, improved crop quality, as well as growth promotion and plant protection through pathogen suppression. It may also help crops to cope better with stresses such as drought (Amos, 2017). It is a living product and the quality of the compost you start with may vary, so it can be difficult to achieve consistent and replicable results. It seems to have most impact on poor or denuded, biologically inactive soils. The production of good-quality compost is key and compost feedstocks can be adapted to give the right balance of fungi and bacteria for specific crops.

For disease control, compost teas work by boosting plant defences and/or stimulating microbial leaf communities, protecting the plant from pathogen attack (Davies *et al.*, 2010). Rick Carr writes in his how-to guide on the Rodale Institute website: 'Compost extracts have been used for centuries because they work. While extracts can be variable and unpredictable, they will promote plant growth.'

Compost-tea brewer in action at Hemsworth Farm in Dorset, as part of an Innovative Farmers' field lab on 'Compost teas in arable cropping'.

The last resort

Organically approved pesticides and fungicides

There are some pesticides that are approved for use in organic systems, but it may be possible to manage without these, if your ecological infrastructure and cultural methods are functioning well. The EU Organic Regulation authorises the use of certain products and substances for pest and disease control where 'their use is essential for the control of a pest for which other biological, physical or breeding alternatives, cultivation practices or other effective management practices are not available'. There have been some horrific chemicals approved for organic use in the past, for example nicotine and rotenone, and some, like copper- and sulphur-based fungicides, are slowly being phased out.

Pesticides can have impacts on non-target organisms, so they need to be used sparingly and with caution, if at all. However, there may be occasions when things get out of balance, especially during the lag period when a pest population is exploding but the beneficials have not yet caught up, when you might be tempted to reach for the canned solution. It is essential to check with your organic control body before using any of these products.

The landscape of product approvals shifts constantly, so always search online for the permitted actives on the Health and Safety Executive website, as even if a product is authorised for use in organic systems under the EU Regulation, it may not be approved for use in the UK and the crops it can be used on may also be restricted.

Soft (fatty acid) soap

Soft soap is a physical agent derived from natural plant oils, which works by disrupting the waxy cuticle of insects and can also affect insect cell membranes. It is commonly used on soft-bodied insects such as aphids, thrips, whitefly and spider mites. It works by contact and breaks down very quickly, especially in sunlight, and is therefore not persistent in the environment. However, soft soap can also harm beneficial insects, such as predatory mites.

Potassium bicarbonate

Potassium bicarbonate occurs naturally and is also used in food products. It can be used as a contact fungicide as an alternative to copper- and sulphur-based fungicides, for the control of many powdery mildew species.

Copper

The use of copper in organic farming as a fungicide has long been a contentious issue. Copper is a trace element and an essential micronutrient, but its use to control bacterial and fungal diseases has been a stick used to beat organic farmers, as it can be toxic to earthworms and other soil microflora. It is also likely to be disruptive of natural antagonistic microbial communities on leaves, depriving plants of this natural biological control. In vegetable production, the primary use has been to control late blight in potatoes. Although progress has been made towards developing more efficient copper sprays, so that less active substance is used, I strongly believe that copper has no place in organic farming and that cultural techniques and the use of robust varieties can make its use redundant.

Sulphur

Sulphur is another controversial input that deserves a brief mention due to its historical and continued allowance for use in organic farming. It is, of course, also an important trace element, but has been used on some field vegetable crops as a fungicide. Though it may have less of a negative impact on soil life than copper, it has been shown to harm some natural enemies, such as parasitic wasps and predatory mites.

Table 1: Major pests of field crops: natural enemies, cultural, biological, chemical and physical control methods

Pest	Natural predators/ enemies	Rotation	Varietal choice	Cultural	Crop covers	Trapping M=Monitoring only	Biocontrol	Organic pesticides
Aphids	Parasitic wasps, ladybirds, hoverflies, lacewings and insect-pathogenic fungi		Limited. Some lettuces varietal resistance to Nasanovia root aphid.	Mulching. E.g. straw, living mulches. Avoid dark-coloured mulches.	✓	M	✓	Fatty acids (Flipper, Savona), natural pyrethrins
Cabbage root fly (*Delia radicum*)	Parasitic wasps, spiders, ground and rove beetles, and predatory flies (Muscidae)			Sowing bird's-foot trefoil in module. 'Collars' on small scale.	✓	M		
Cabbage white butterflies (*Pieris rapae/Pieris brassicae*) /cabbage moth (*Mamestra brassicae*) / Diamond back moth (*Plutella xylostella*)	Birds, large beetles, para-sitic wasp, viruses				✓	M		Bacillus thurungiensis (Bt), Spinosad, natural pyrethrins
Cabbage whitefly (*Aleyrodes proletella*)	Parasitic wasps, ladybirds							Natural pyrethrins
Carrot fly (*Psila rosae*)	Parasitic wasps, rove beetles	✓	Limited	Sowing times. Bigger fields less affected	✓	M Sacrificial trap cropping	Limited (Nematodes) Onion oil (repellent)	
Cutworms (*Agrotis segetum etc.*)	Ground and rove beetles, spiders, parasitic wasps, toads, nematodes and birds.			Irrigation			Nematodes	

Pest	Natural predators/ enemies	Rotation	Varietal choice	Cultural	Crop covers	Trapping M=Monitoring only	Biocontrol	Organic pesticides
Flea beetles	Parasitic wasps, lacewing larvae			Mulches. irrigation	✓	M Flea beetle trolleys Mustard trap crops	Nematodes	
Leatherjackets (*Tipula paludosa* and *Tipula oleracea*)		✓		Cultivations. Planting after mid-June				
Leek moth (*Acrolepiopsis assectella*)	Parasitic wasps	✓			✓	M	Nematodes	Bt
Onion thrips (*Thrips tabaci*)	Parasitic wasps, predatory mites, bugs and thrips, lacewings, ladybirds			Irrigation, undersowing leeks with clover				Spinosad
Pea moth (*Cydia nigricana*)	Parasitic wasps, pathogenic fungus			Sowing times		M		
Potato cyst nematode (*Globodera pallida* and *G. rostochiensis*)		At least 8 years	✓	Control volunteer potatoes – rogueing, mowing, pigs		*Solanum sisymbriifolium* and *Solanum scabrum* trap crops		Garlic granules
Silver Y moth (*Autographa gamma*)	Bats, birds, parasitic wasp and flies.					M		Bt
Slugs	Ground and rove beetles, parasitoids, birds, amphibians and hedgehogs			Cultivations, hand picking		Beer traps	Nematodes	Ferric phosphate (iron (III) orthophosphate)
Wireworm (*Agriotes* spp.)	Fungi, parasitic wasps, ground beetles, birds	✓ (Mustard cover crops)		Cultivation		M Trap crop: Research ongoing	Naturally occurring pathogenic fungus *Metarhizium brunneum* (no product available yet in UK)	

Note: It is important to check with organic control bodies and product approvals for crops with the Health and Safety Executive (UK) before purchase and use of pest control products.

Table 2: The most important diseases of organic vegetables

Disease	Source	Favoured environment/Spread	Rotation	Resistant varieties	Cultural controls	Fire-brigade treatments (active ingredients)
Potatoes						
Blackleg (*Erwinia carotovora*)	Seed	Damp tubers/poorly ventilated stores		Charlotte, Pixie, Saxon and Vales Sovereign		
Black scurf (*Rhizoctonia solani*)	Seed and soil		✓			
Common scab (*Streptomyces scabies*)	Soil mainly	Alkaline soils, dry conditions	✓	Ambo, Nicola, Pentland Javelin, Saturna, Symphonia	Irrigation.	
Late blight (*Phytophthora infestans*)	Airborne. Dumps of infected tubers	Warm humid weather	✓	Sarpo varieties, Alouette, Carolus	Chitting. Mulching. Burning off, flailing infected foliage.	Copper
Spraing	Seed. Mainly Tobacco rattle virus, transmitted by nematodes	Damp soil	✓		Avoid irrigation. Caliente mustard to reduce nematodes.	
Brassicas						
Club root (*Plasmodiophora brassicae*)	Soil	Low pH. Transplants, compost, manure, machinery	✓	Brussel sprouts – crispus Cabbage – Cordesa, Kilaton, lodero Calabrese – monciano, Cauliflower –clapton, Swede – gowrie, marian	Good hygiene and preventing infection vital. Liming to pH 7.2. Good drainage and soil health. Remove and burn (or compost off site) infected plants. Remove brassica weeds e.g. bittercress, shepherd's purse, charlock. Avoid summer planting. Irrigation and earthing up may help.	

Disease	Source	Favoured environment/ Spread	Rotation	Resistant varieties	Cultural controls	Fire-brigade treatments (active ingredients)
Downy mildew (*Hyaloperonospora brassicae* – formerly *Peronospora parasitica*)	Soil-borne, also airborne			Some varieties less susceptible	Mainly in propagation. Avoid overwatering. Good ventilation. Only plant healthy transplants. Harden off well.	
Dark leaf spot (*Alternaria brassicae*)	Seed-borne		✓	Some varieties less susceptible	Avoid overlap between overwintered and spring crops. Plough in crop residues promptly after harvest. Site crops away from oil-seed rape.	
Ring spot (*Mycosphaerella brassicicola*)	Airborne	Wet weather		Some varieties less susceptible Roscoff type cauliflowers have some resistance.	Avoid year-round production. Overwintered crops at highest risk. Plough in crop residues promptly after harvest. Separate blocks of brassicas from each other.	
Broad beans						
Rust (*Uromyces fabae*)	Seed and airborne	Warm, wet weather			Plough in or compost crop residues at end of season. Good potash levels in soil help. Remove volunteer plants. Avoid summer cropping (worse in July and August).	

(continued)

Disease	Source	Favoured environment/ Spread	Rotation	Resistant varieties	Cultural controls	Fire-brigade treatments (active ingredients)
Carrots						
Alternaria blight (*Alternaria dauci*)	Seed-borne	Warm, wet weather		Some resistance e.g. Maestro	Use healthy certified seed.	
Cavity spot (*Pythium violae & Pythium sulcatum*)	Soil-borne	Wet weather	✓	Some: Nerac, Narbonne, Navarre, Valor, Bolero, Boston	Early lifting helps. Select fields with no history of problems. Improve soil aeration and drainage. Add lime: (lowest impact at pH 8). Increasing exchangeable calcium in the soil changes soil microbiota.	
Celery						
Leaf spot (*Septoria apiicola*)	Seed-borne	Warm, wet weather	✓		Healthy seed (heat-treated) and transplants. Harvest early. Separate plantings spatially. Prevent spread via crop covers, mulches, machinery, footwear.	
Cucurbits						
Powdery mildew (*Erysiphe cichoracearum*)	Overwinter on plant debris	Prefers drier conditions		Some varieties less susceptible	Rogue badly infected plants. Successional plantings help with courgettes, as affects older plants, but separate spatially and take care with picking (pick younger plantings first).	Cerevisane (yeast-based), potassium and sodium hydrogen carbonate (aka potassium/sodium bicarbonate), sulphur
Alliums						
White rot (*Sclerotium cepivorum*)	Soil-borne	Active between 10–20°C	✓ Place onions after brassicas		Good hygiene to avoid transfer on machinery, footwear, manures and composts	

Disease	Source	Favoured environment/Spread	Rotation	Resistant varieties	Cultural controls	Fire-brigade treatments (active ingredients)
Leeks – rust (*Puccinia allii*)	Crop-borne	Occurs from mid-summer to late autumn	✓	Some varieties less susceptible e.g. Bandit, Conora	Remove badly infected plants. Separate successional plantings spatially. Avoid excess N or low K. Allow airflow between plants.	
Onion downy mildew (*Peronospora destructor*)		Warm, wet weather		Hylander, Promotion	Separate successional plantings spatially. Break cycle of cropping (e.g no overwinter crop).	
Onion neck rot (*Botrytis allii*)	Seed-borne	Infect through wounds			Use healthy seed and sets. Minimise damage to bulbs during weeding and harvesting. Leave at least 80mm neck if topping. Ensure dry before storage.	
Lettuce						
Downy mildew (*Bremia lactucae*)	Airborne mainly, but can survive in soil	Cool moist conditions		Yes, but new races evolve and new resistances needed	Mixing varieties in plantings slows spread. Late plantings most vulnerable.	Cerevisane
Grey mould (*Botrytis cinerea*)	Airborne	Occurs throughout the year			Avoid deep planting and wet/poorly drained sites. Minimise damage during weeding operations.	Cerevisane

Note: It is important to check with organic control bodies and product approvals for crops with (UK) the Health and Safety Executive before purchase and use of pest control products.

Chapter Ten

Protected Cropping

For the intensive market garden, and especially when direct marketing, polytunnels or greenhouses are pretty much essential to extend the season and maximise potential and income from a small patch of land. The range of crops that can be grown increases dramatically, with the added premium of freshness that substituting imports with local produce provides. Another attraction of protected growing is the degree of control it gives over the environment in which you are growing. Keeping the rain off can mean applying only the optimum water needed for crop growth and minimising leaching and crop losses due to disease. The quality of crops can thus be increased.

days. Fleece comes in various widths from bed (2m) to plot size (10–12m) and different weights (18g/m^2 to 30g/m^2), according to the degree of frost protection needed. Fleeces are supported by the crop itself, but can be easily damaged by deer and other animals, so can't be expected to last for more than one or two seasons, especially if also needed for pest exclusion. Make sure to roll up and store when dry and hang from a roof to avoid mice nesting in the rolls! One disadvantage of fleece is that you can't easily see through it to monitor the crop underneath, while weeds that grow well in the protected environment can easily get away.

Protected cropping structures and systems

Floating crop covers

Fleeces are the cheapest way to extend the season for field crops, advancing maturity by ten to fourteen

Polytunnels and multi-spans

The polytunnel comes in many shapes and sizes and is simply a metal-hooped structure covered with plastic. It is best to get the biggest and best that you can afford, for they will surely repay your investment. At the lower budget end of the spectrum, it is possible to

Crop covers for season advancement at Trill Farm Garden at the end of April.

OPPOSITE: Hankham Organics in Sussex is a great example of a diverse agroecological system under cover. A wide range of crops, green manures and flowers for attracting predators is grown.

pick up second-hand tunnel frames on online auction sites relatively cheaply, though you may need to pay for transport to bring them home. Straight-sided tunnels allow more flexibility of cropping and for easier use of machinery inside. Avoid tunnels over 30m in length, as they can get too hot in the middle, unless additional venting is in place. Wide and high tunnels will maximise space for tall-growing profitable crops like tomatoes, cucumbers and climbing beans. Siting is important: avoid frost pockets; locate on a slight slope, if possible, to allow airflow; orientate north–south (less important for propagation tunnels); and choose a sheltered, but not shaded, spot. Windbreaks can be erected, or, for longer-term protection, planted. For large new tunnels and multi-spans, it may be sensible to get professionals to put them up. If you do, watch them in action in case you need to recover or repair the tunnels another time.

For larger tunnels, the foundation tubes may need to be concreted in and covers secured to side rails, which can be combined with ventilation netting. Tunnels provide a large surface area, so you need to think about catching the water through gutters for irrigation, or at least ensuring that there are adequate soakaways.

The technology of polytunnel plastic has improved over recent years, with additives preventing degradation due to ultraviolet (UV) light and extending the lifespan of the cover to eight or ten years. Some covers have anti-fog properties, which reduce condensation and minimise the risk of water dripping on to plants.

Movable tunnels

Eliot Coleman, in his seminal work, *The New Organic Grower*, came up with the concept of the movable tunnel. The advantages are that the soil is exposed to nature for part of the year and green manures or fertility-building leys are grown outside without giving up valuable cropping area 'inside'. Tunnels are moved on rails, which can be either on the ground, or fixed to the tunnel.

A single-span polytunnel with diverse cropping at Cotesbach Gardens.

Multi-span tunnel at Trill Farm Garden with winter salad crops (taken in January).

Caterpillar tunnels

Caterpillar tunnels are a cheap and flexible form of protected cropping. They are temporary structures made of steel pipe hoops or PVC water pipe, with ropes criss-crossing over the top, to give the appearance of an oversized cloche … or caterpillar. Hoops are pushed directly into the ground, or placed over rebar (steel reinforcement bar) ground stakes, placed 1.8–3m apart, depending on how exposed the site is. A pipe or rope (purlin) runs from end to end, tying all the bows together to give stability, and is tied to stakes at either end of the tunnel run. The covering is pulled over and held down by sandbags, bricks or pegs. Stakes between the hoops on each side hold

Caterpillar tunnels are becoming an attractive option for small growers.

the ropes, which go over the top to hold the plastic in place. This allows full ventilation when needed in order to reduce humidity and disease problems, as well as relatively easy removal.

Spanish tunnels

Spanish tunnels are similar to caterpillar tunnels, being made of lightweight construction without permanently fixed foundations. They can be opened at the sides to improve airflow, reduce humidity and disease risk. Both their popularity and notoriety have spread, with huge uptake by the soft-fruit industry in Hertfordshire and Kent in particular, where farm-scale adoption of Spanish tunnels has created public outrage, so that they are often now subject to planning restrictions.

Large enough to allow tractor access, Spanish tunnels can be single span or multi-span and are adaptable to the ground, following the contours of the field. Their design has become more sophisticated, with options including guttering, venting and telescopic feet that can be raised or lowered during the season. The strength and stability of the structures have also improved, with gothic-style hoops now available for snowy areas.

Greenhouses

Greenhouses are the most expensive structures for protected cropping, but are long-lasting and the most efficient for heat retention. Traditionally, they have been heated and provided with supplementary lighting to grow out of season crops. The capital investment for new glass is high and the commercial greenhouse world is very high-tech, with sophisticated ventilation and climate-control systems. New-generation commercial glasshouses are taller and have wider bays, as, counter-intuitively, it is more efficient to keep a larger air mass heated and the temperature is also more stable. Wider bays mean less obstructions for cultivations, while fewer gutters and posts mean less shade. The gutter height of modern tomato greenhouses may be as much as 6m high.

You may be lucky enough to have a site that contains existing glasshouses, such as an old plant nursery or walled kitchen garden. You may even have, or be able to create, a solar greenhouse, which can take many forms, but an easy example is the 'lean-to' greenhouse built against a south-facing wall, which absorbs the heart and radiates it at night. Insurance may be high and they will need maintaining, but they can be rewarding growing spaces.

Organic tomato production at Wight Salads.

Growing under cover

Soil management

There has been a debate, over many years, around organic standards and the need for growing in the soil. In Scandinavia, until recently, demarcated beds – growing in large containers or growing bags – was permitted. In the USA, hydroponic systems have been certified as organic. The overriding organic principles still hold – and are supported by EU Organic Regulations – that production should be rooted in the soil and the soil fed, rather than the plant. Fertility should therefore be primarily supplied from slow-release organic fertilizers, such as manures and composts.

Green manures are seldom used in intensive greenhouse production of long-season crops, such as tomatoes, cucumbers, peppers and aubergines, because there is often only a short break between crops from November to January. Organic amendments, such as composts and composted animal manures, are applied as a base dressing prior to planting, with top dressings of rapidly mineralising fertilizers through the season. Some larger commercial growers like Wight Salads have their own composting operations, giving them greater control of the feedstock and the ability to incorporate their own crop residues. The turnover of nutrients in these systems is high and liquid fertilizers are applied via a diluter, a process called fertigation. The use of additional fertilizers will need to be justified to the organic control body through nutrient budgets and/or soil analysis.

Although no-till techniques are becoming increasingly popular and feasible, most tunnels and glasshouses are still managed with cultivations. Due to the scale, pedestrian rotavators or compact tractors are often used. In unheated glasshouses and tunnels, nutrient requirements are less, so high-quality, home-produced compost from crop wastes can be utilised. On a small scale, liquid manures can be made using diluted fermented extracts from nettles and/or comfrey.

Green manures in tunnels/glasshouses

It is a long-held conception that protected cropping space is too valuable to include crops that have no direct cash value, but in fact it is both possible and advisable. There are a few approaches:

- Movable tunnels/caterpillar tunnels: grow the green manure outside and move the tunnel to follow the cultivation or termination of the cover crop.
- Undersow tall crops with green manure.
- Lay living mulches as pathways.
- Grow your green manure elsewhere on the farm and cut and spread on tunnel beds as a transfer mulch (*see* below).
- Use any available gaps in cropping to fit in a fast-growing green manure or cover crop.

Your market will to some extent influence which approaches are appropriate. For the wholesale grower, where the focus is on summer cash crops like tomatoes and cucumbers, undersowing of low-growing clovers and/or the use of living mulches as paths may be the best options. The clover may not contribute much nitrogen during the growing season, but if

Compost tea? Paul van Midden of Lembas Organics with a dilutor, which can be used to apply plant tonics such as seaweed solution to the crops through the overhead spray line.

The Seed Co-operative bought Gosberton Bank Nursery in Lincolnshire with 1ha of glasshouses in 2016. They entered into a two-year organic conversion period and sowed lucerne (alfalfa) in the glasshouses to kickstart the fertility-building process.

left over the winter until the following spring, it can contribute a lot more. This depends on the need or demand for winter crops. They will also require a lot of water, probably best through overhead irrigation, especially if clover is being grown in the paths. Be aware that increased watering from above could lead to diseases, such as late blight and *Botrytis* through the increased humidity within the crop.

Crop diversity and rotations in polytunnels/ greenhouses

Large-scale, even organically certified, greenhouse production can be high-tech monocultures. Focused on hygiene with hairnets, lab coats and handwipes, they can seem more akin to food factories than organic farms. In contrast, Hankham Organics in Sussex is a revelation, consisting of 6,000m² of glasshouse with a highly diverse, intensive vegetable cropping rotation, growing for its box scheme. Glasshouse growers often concentrate on tomatoes, peppers and aubergines, which are all in the Solanaceae family, as well as cucumbers, while casting aside the principles of rotation and agroecology. Hankham Organics demonstrates that it doesn't have to be like that. There are so many crops that can be grown under cover, giving lots of possibilities for extending the season and variety of crops for direct marketing.

Mixed-salad bags have become a very profitable crop for growers, with salad brassicas making up a big proportion of the winter mixed-salad bag. There is an ever-increasing range of leaf shapes, colours, textures and flavours (rockets, mustards, pak chois and so on), all of which grow well under cover in winter. The temptation is to fill the tunnels with brassicas in the winter months, but this increases the risk of running into disease problems. There are many frost-hardy vegetable and salad crops that can be grown in unheated tunnels or greenhouses overwinter. Lettuce can stand temperatures down to −11°C and there are varieties that are adapted to short-day production.

There can be conflicts at the start and end of the summer season. Winter crops need to be removed early enough to get summer crops established, so may need to be ripped out while they are still cropping, which can be difficult during the hungry gap (the period between the end of the winter crops and before the new season's plantings are ready to harvest, when there are few UK crops available – normally from April to mid-June). In the autumn, the tomatoes, peppers and so on may still be producing, but the winter salads need to establish before the days get too dark. There are two ways of easing that transition:

- **Intercropping:** Many tall-growing summer crops can be inter-planted into standing winter crops. Tomatoes, for example, can be

Growing glasshouse fertility at Hankham Organics

Following are three green manures that Hankham Organics have had good results with.

Quick mix for summer (two to three months)

This consists of a non-hardy non-leguminous, fast-growing, weed suppressive and reasonably drought tolerant mix of three species:

* **buckwheat:** $4g/m^2$
* **amaranth:** $0.3g/m^2$
* **phacelia:** $1.2g/m^2$.

Sow anytime from April to August and incorporate from six weeks onwards. Broadcast the small amaranth/phacelia seed mixed with sand, then the large buckwheat separately.

Summer N-fix (two to three months)

This consists of a half-hardy mix of sweet and crimson clover, 50:50. It requires weed control and inoculant. It has good potential for fixing nitrogen and organic matter building with a deep root system. It is usually sown in June and incorporated in early September and can be cut to regrow if weeds become a problem.

Sow in rows 25cm apart with an Earthway seed drill, using the radish/leek disc ($2g/m^2$). Be sure to roll the seed in, especially on light soils. A wheel hoe is then used when the clover is 7–10cm tall. Flail-mow and incorporate at ten weeks, or cut to allow regrowth. It can be undersown with the quick mix above when hoed so as to increase bulk.

Winter N-fix

This consists of a fully hardy mix of vetch and grazing rye (*Secale cereale*), 80:20. It is particularly good before hungry summer crops, but may require weed control, so is best sown in rows at $20g/m^2$ using the Earthway seed drill with the disc for beans/small peas. The rye helps as a row marker and support for the vetch. It can also be undersown with phacelia in late February, to add volume. Hoe just before vetch start to 'wander'.

Source: Dollimore, P. (2011).

Quick mix: buckwheat, phacelia and amaranth.

Summer N-fix: sweet, crimson and alsike clover.

Table 1: Protected crop planning

Crop	Unit size	Quantity for 50 customers	Frequency	Sales period	Average weekly requirement	No. of weeks	Total requirement	Yield per plant	Number of plants	Plants per sq m	Total area in sq m
Tomatoes	0.5kg	25kg	weekly	Jun–Oct	25kg	20	500kg	2.5kg	200	2	100
Aubergine	400kg	20kg	monthly	Jun–Oct	5kg	18	90kg	1kg	90	3	30
Cucumbers	1no	50no	weekly	Jun–Oct	50no	20	1.000no	20	50	1	50
Peppers	300g	15kg	fortnightly	Jun–Oct	7.5kg	18	135kg	1.5kg	90	4	22.5
Cl French beans	400g	20kg	weekly	May–Jul	20kg	8	160kg	2.5kg	64	10	6.4
Onions	500g	25kg	weekly	Jul–Sep	25kg	12	300kg	0.25kg	1,200	30	40
Courgettes	500g	25kg	fortnightly	Jul–Jul	12.5kg	4	100kg	2.5kg	40	1	40
Parsley	50g	2.5kg	weekly	Jan–May	2.5kg	16	40kg	0.4kg	100	20	5
Basil	60g	3kg	fortnightly	Jun–Oct	1.5kg	11	16.5kg	0.27kg	60	20	3
Salad leaves(a)	100g	5kg	weekly	Sep–Mar	5kg	26	130kg	0.5kg	260	10	26
Salad leaves(b)	100g	5kg	weekly	Sep–Mar	5kg	26	130kg	0.5kg	260	10	26
Salad onions	bunch	50no	weekly	Feb–Jun	50no	16	800no	0.2no	4.000	400	10
Spinach	200g	10kg	fortnightly	Mar–Jun	5kg	10	50kg	0.5kg	100	16	6.25
Early beetroot	bunch	50no	fortnightly	May–Jun	25no	5	125no	0.07kg	625	80	7.8
Early carrots	bunch	50no	weekly	Apr–Jun	50no	10	500no	0.05kg	4.000	250	16
Total											388.95m^3*

(a) Brassicas: rocket, mizuna, tatsoi, mibuna, red mustard, green mustard.

(b) Non brassicas: Claytonia, chrysanthemum greens, Chinese celery, corn salad.

*This is not the total tunnel area required because of double and sometimes triple cropping.

Source: Hitchings, R. (2009)

planted into beds of winter salads, strategically harvested to allow space for tomatoes to be planted. Other options include garlic in the middle of a bed of winter lettuce, which could transition to tomatoes; and growing celeriac, celery, onions or dwarf beans under tomatoes.

- **Relay cropping:** Get crops ready in advance by pre-sowing in modules. This works on the principle that the day one crop comes out, another goes in.

Weed control

Weeds can grow fast under cover and many growers use ground-cover fabrics or polythene mulches to exclude weeds and also retain moisture. Ground covers can, at least, be reused many times, but can also transmit diseases between crops, if not cleaned, dried in sunlight and stored in a dry place between crops.

No-dig systems work well under cover, as, without disturbance of the soil, the weed seed bank is

Intercropped celery and cucumber at Pitney Farm Market Garden. Four rows of celery were planted on a 1.2m bed, with a single row of cucumbers planted a couple of weeks later. The cucumber side shoots and fruits were removed up to 60cm stem height. Later leaves were removed to 1m to allow light in for the celery.

One problem area can be the edges of tunnels, where weeds can encroach from the outside. Deep mulching or plastic mulches between tunnels can be useful to prevent this happening. On the other hand, a few weeds encroaching can be beneficial from an agroecological standpoint, as nettles, speedwell, red deadnettle and chickweed can all be hosts or food sources for beneficial insects.

Irrigation

Watering tunnel crops is a skill. Underwatering or uneven watering can lead to stresses, splitting of fruit or bolting. Overwatering can cause excessive humidity, which may lead to disease. Watering regularly and often is best.

Watering by hand, even with a hosepipe, is too labour-intensive for anything but the smallest tunnel or greenhouse. The choice, for commercial polytunnels or greenhouses, is between overhead irrigation using sprinkler lines, or drip/trickle irrigation. It can be useful to have both. Drip lines are more targeted and efficient, with the water applied directly to the root zone of crops, and they can operate at lower pressures. They will need to be monitored carefully for leaks (rodents may chew through them for a pastime) and blockages.

gradually depleted. Material mulches such as compost should also prevent weeds emerging. Drip irrigation will result in fewer weeds than when watering with overhead spray lines, as weeds mostly emerge in the 'wet zone' and mulches can be targeted in this area.

Table 2: An example polytunnel rotation

Year 1	Summer	Tomatoes
Year 1	Winter	Second planting brassica leaves
Year 2	Summer	Climbing French beans, early courgettes
Year 2	Autumn	First planting non-brassica leaves
Year 2	Winter	Early beetroot, carrots, etc.
Year 3	Summer	Fertility crop or catch crops - salad onions, herbs, etc.
Year 3	Winter	First planting brassica leaves
Year 4	Summer	Cucumbers, peppers
Year 4	Winter	Second planting non-brassica leaves

Source: Hitchings, R. (2009).

Lettuce, kohlrabi and fennel growing at Lembas Organic, near Aberdeen.

End of March salad harvest at Trill Farm Garden.

Aubergine harvest at Teign Greens CSA.

Tomatoes at Pitney Farm Market Garden.

Wall-to-wall Mangetout peas in June at Bennison Farm CSA.

Overhead irrigation can be handy when the soil needs a proper soaking, for example with drilled crops and green manures. You either require good mains pressure, or a pump. Overhead irrigation can also increase humidity for crops that need it, such as cucumbers, and it also helps to avoid problems such as red spider mite, populations of which can expand rapidly in hot, dry conditions.

Summer relay cropping

For some box schemes and CSAs, summer can be a quiet time – customers are away on holiday and box numbers dip. When grower Dom van Marsh started working at Canalside CSA in Warwickshire, three out of seven polytunnels were empty for two to three months during the summer months. So, he set about finding alternatives to fill the gaps. The gap in question was usually after early crops of potatoes, carrots, beetroot and leek nursery beds had finished and before winter crops are planted during September. He found that the following crops worked well:

- **New Zealand spinach:** Module-sown five weeks before planting, this drought-tolerant crop proved very popular with members, planted in June and out by the end of September.
- **Basil:** Multi-sown in modules five weeks before planting at the end of June, following harvesting of early beetroot. Replaced by overwinter spinach in September.
- **Huauzontle:** A rapid-growing, weed-smothering crop in the fat hen family, this strange delight was grown for its sprouts; module-sown four weeks before planting.
- **Celery and fennel:** Provided that they are given enough water, both are excellent summer crops, following early carrots. Fennel was module-sown five weeks before planting and celery was grown in a tray for pricking out into modules about six weeks before planting.
- **Direct-drilled herbs:** Coriander and dill both grow rapidly, but keep an eye on them as they are quick to bolt.

Source: van Marsh, D. (2020)

New Zealand spinach. A good crop for the heat of a polytunnel in summer.

Wherever possible, collect rainwater from buildings and from the tunnels or glasshouses themselves. Polytunnels can be retrofitted with gutters that feed into storage containers such as IBCs (intermediate bulk containers), or storage reservoirs.

Climate control

Alongside watering, the grower can regulate the climate inside the tunnels and greenhouses through ventilation. This can be as basic as opening and shutting tunnel doors; larger tunnels are often fitted with side vents that can be rolled up to increase airflow. This can be important to prevent extreme

Polytunnel guttering can be attached to side rails of polytunnels where there is side ventilation, or retrofitted.

temperatures and plant stresses, as well as pest explosions (the aforementioned red spider mite). In glasshouses, sophisticated climate control systems can be installed. Every crop has its own ideal climate, so, if possible, group crops according to their heat and humidity requirements – for example, grow tomatoes and aubergines in the same tunnel. Of course, there is also value in diversity, so compromises may be needed.

Agroecology under cover

There has been a divergence of organic protected cropping systems between large-scale, high-tech commercial growers, whose emphasis is on biosecurity and biological controls, and smaller growers, who tend to concentrate on multiple crops and more biodiversity. Science is now supporting the smaller growers' agroecological approaches, with advice and guidance as to the best plants to accompany crops in order to encourage beneficial insects.

I used to plant a few English marigolds (*Calendula*) around the ends of beds in my tunnels to 'keep the whitefly away' without understanding

Drip irrigation can be run at low pressure, is efficient and keeps the humidity low.

the science. It is now known that marigolds are attractive to *Macrolophus pygmaeus*, a predatory bug, both as a food source and for egg laying; the bug predates on spider mites, which can be a real problem in tunnels, as well as *Tuta* (tomato leaf miner) and whiteflies. As an added benefit, the flowers are edible and can be included in salad bags. As another example, I planted perennial fennel in the awkward to crop corners of tunnels as an early source of nectar for hoverflies.

It's not just about nectar and pollen – plants can provide alternative prey, shelter or somewhere for natural enemies to lay eggs. Good biodiversity outside can also benefit the ecology inside. If there is no pressure to remove a crop to make space for the next one, flowering crops such as brassicas can support and build up natural enemy populations. Consider harvesting and relocating ladybird larvae off spent crops before removing them to the compost heap. The table looks at beneficial plant species in greater detail.

A good location for flower strips to support natural enemies is the outermost bed (edge) of the tunnel or greenhouse, as this is often less productive or left uncropped. The strips should contain a mix of easy-growing species that will not compete with crops and can withstand neglect! Perennials are preferred as they will flower earlier, but there are also many suitable annuals.

Many growers have found that by encouraging natural predators and 'holding their nerve', they have managed to cut out the use of sprays completely when occasionally things have got out of balance. There may be times when 'off the shelf' biological controls need to be used for specific pests, so careful monitoring is essential for timely interventions. Examples include various parasitic wasps and gall midges for aphids, predatory mites for red spider mite and nematodes for vine weevil.

Table 3: Families and examples of easily grown species that can provide effective resources for various groups of natural enemies

Plant family	Example species (A = annual, P = perennial)	Natural enemies supported	Main pests regulated
Apiaceae	Coriander (*Coriandrum sativum*, A), dill (*Anethum graveolens*, A), Bishop's weed (*Ammi majus*, A), fennel (*Foeniculum vulgare*, P)	Hoverflies, lacewings, parasitoid wasps	Aphids, moths
Brassicaceae	Sweet alyssum (*Lobularia maritima*, A)	Hoverflies, parasitoid wasps	Aphids
Polygonaceae	Buckwheat (*Fagopyrum esculentum*, A)	Hoverflies, parasitoid wasps	Aphids
Asteraceae (shallow florets)	Yarrow (*Achillea millefolium*, P), oxeye daisy (*Leucanthemum vulgare*, P), golden marguerite (*Anthemis tinctoria*, P), corn marigold (*Glebionis segetum*, A), cornflower (*Centaurea cyanus*, A)	Hoverflies, lacewings, ladybirds, parasitoid wasps	Aphids, moths
Asteraceae (deeper florets)	Marigold (*Calendula officinalis*, A/P), brown knapweed (*Centaurea jacea*, P)	Predatory bugs (*Macrolophus, Orius*), ladybirds	Whitefly, moths, incl. *Tuta absoluta*
Fabaceae	Bird's-foot trefoil (*Lotus corniculatus*, P), common vetch (*Vicia sativa*, P)	Ladybirds (*Scymnus*), parasitoid wasps	Aphids
Other	Annual baby's breath (*Gypsophila elegans*, A)	Hoverflies, lacewings	Aphids

Source: Lambion and van Rijn (2021).

Flower strip in a side bed of a polytunnel at Northdown Orchard, taken at the end of September.

The predator and nectar strip at Hankham Organics includes golden rod, yarrow, sneezewort, dill, borage, calendula, poached-egg plant, oregano, marjoram and thyme.

Jayne Arnold at Oxton Organics in the Vale of Evesham grows a mix of tagetes, alyssum, resunda, ageratum, nigella, trefoil, dwarf calendula, linaria, convolvulus, candy turf, purple oxalis, parsley, Greek basil, leaf celery and summer savory under her tomatoes.

Jayne Arnold grows a mix of linseed, crimson clover, trefoil, Californian poppy, nigella and alyssum under her cucumbers. She aims for a high diversity of crops to improve the soil, but they are all flowering species that will also be attractive to beneficial insects.

Chapter Eleven

Harvesting, Storage, Selling and Marketing

Growing the crops is only part of the job. The other crucial aspect of growing is selling those crops. As a jack of all trades, the successful grower needs to be able to do both well, or have access to the skills of marketing within the wider team. The grower needs to understand the market and the organic consumer, providing consumer requirements when wanted and as efficiently as possible.

Harvesting

Each vegetable will have its optimum period for harvesting, so it is essential to keep a close eye on your crops. Over-mature crops will not last long, while immature crops may last longer and travel better, but lack taste. Unusual weather, such as hot periods, can play havoc with expected harvesting dates and continuity. Anticipating when the crop will be ready and in what quantities takes experience. Retail outlets will need to know at least a week in advance when a new crop is coming on stream, so that they can stop wholesale orders from elsewhere. Some crops, such as courgettes, cucumbers and green beans, will need to be harvested regularly when they are at the right stage, regardless of market sales, in order for the crop to continue producing.

Harvesting is a skilled job; care is needed to ensure that your produce arrives at the shop, or in the customers' hands, in peak condition. As soon as vegetables have been picked, they start to deteriorate, so keeping them cool and reducing moisture losses through respiration is important. Short-term storage at 1–2°C or above (cool ambient storage is acceptable if refrigeration is not available) and a relative humidity above 85 per cent is ideal for most crops.

In the summer, you will need to harvest early in the morning, making sure that crates don't stand in the sun. Conversely, harvesting in wet weather can affect quality and storage ability. If you have set picking days, a degree of flexibility may be required. Keep an eye on weather forecasts in case you need to get crops in before a big freeze or wet spell.

Having the right tools for harvesting, such as sharp knives, will help (plus a first-aid kit handy). It takes skill to direct the cuts needed to top and tail leeks, or trim a cauliflower with the minimum strikes. Knowing your crop is key; if harvesting over a period, think about how best to ensure regrowth. This may mean picking out a growing point to encourage bushiness of leafy crops, or cutting to allow growing points and leaves to regrow from the base.

If hand-harvesting, pulling leeks and roots may be possible if beds are loose, but in some cases a fork may be needed; inserting it at the right angle will avoid 'steel worm' (piercing of the roots by the digging implement). Simple mechanised harvesting may assist the process for field crops, for example the use of bed lifters that ease the crop out of the soil.

OPPOSITE: An August harvest of baby Patty Pan summer squash at Southern Roots Organics in Pembrokeshire provides a tasty delicacy for their customers. Summer squash needs regular picking – daily, or at least every other day – for optimum size.

Minimising the handling of crops is necessary, as vegetables can be easily bruised. 'Treat them like eggs' was a refrain I often heard when harvesting potatoes or apples as a teenager. Grading and packing in the field directly into marketing crates can reduce handling when conditions allow. Ensuring that crops are free of damage will reduce later losses from rots.

Washing vegetables before sale is common in North America and for supermarket sales, but can reduce storage life drastically. Also, it may be considered a 'processing activity' by the organic control body. There are times when washing is necessary, for example when harvesting leeks from a very wet field and the produce is caked with soil (you don't want to give your soil away to your customers!), but if you can avoid it, do.

Food processing and packing areas are technically subject to food-safety legislation. Although vegetables carry a lot less risk than animal products, problems can occur, especially when dealing with salads and fruit intended for direct consumption. Growers should be mindful of their duty of care to customers and consumers, with personal hygiene being a most important aspect to consider.

Transport in stackable crates with clear identification of origin is necessary for sale to intermediaries. Take care to avoid high temperatures in vehicles in the summer. Consider refrigerated vans, or at least insulated boxes, time of travel and avoid parking in the sun, if possible.

Storage

Aside from short-term storage of harvested crops prior to sales, general storage will extend the season. Produce grown in optimal conditions will store best. Immaturely harvested crops, those that have experienced drought stress, or have pest and disease damage will not keep well. Nutrient over-supply, especially nitrogen, will also have a negative impact on storage. Careful selection of varieties that will store well is recommended, as is choosing which varieties to sell first. Some potato varieties, for example Sarpo Mira, have long dormancy, which means they will take longer to sprout and thus will store well.

Field storage

It is possible to store some crops in the field. Frost-hardy crops, such as parsnips, can remain in place until they start to go to seed in March or April. Many brassicas are winter-hardy and the flavour of Brussels sprouts and kale will be improved with frost. Some cabbages, such as savoys, will stand through the winter, while white and red cabbages are best cut and stored in November or early December. Leeks are another crop that will stand well, with the blue-green types being the hardiest, until they bolt in April. While the climate is changing, with winters tending to get milder, you will still need to be able to react quickly if crops are left in the field and a cold snap is forecast.

Crops such as beetroot, celeriac and carrots can be stored in the field in mild areas with straw for protection, but very cold weather can cause damage. Storing carrots in situ by covering with a plastic sheet and a thick layer of straw is common practice. However, removing the straw in the spring is necessary, as, if incorporated, it might cause nitrogen lock-up in subsequent crops. Carrots with strong tops (for example, Chantenay Red Cored and Oxhella) make for easier hand-pulling.

Field-stored crops can also be vulnerable to pests, such as slugs, wireworm and rodents. Crops can rot in the field, too, particularly in heavier, colder soils and from secondary infection after pest damage. Harvesting during wet conditions can be difficult and potentially damaging to soil structure.

Root vegetables in crates at Sandy Lane Farm. Washing may be necessary if produce is caked with mud, but will reduce shelf life.

Adam Beer picking beetroot at Pitney Farm Market Garden.

Potato harvesting at Southern Roots Organics.

Harvesting kale at Sandy Lane Farm.

Celery harvesting at Strawberry Fields. Celery is cut, trimmed, bagged and boxed in the field.

Leek packing into nets at Strawberry Fields.

Harvesting onions at Bennison Farm CSA.

Squash harvest at Sandy Lane Farm.

Bringing home the harvest with quad bike and trailer at Teign Greens CSA.

Fennel harvest at Strawberry Fields.

Squashes in boxes at Strawberry Fields. It is best to keep single varieties in boxes, as they deteriorate at different rates.

An HDC (Horticultural Development Council) trial in 2008 on the use of biodegradable mulches for field storage of carrots found that sugar levels, dry matter and marketability of carrots under biodegradable mulches were not significantly different than the industry standard (40micron, 2m wide black plastic), but none of the brands trialled were strong enough to be used to hold the weight of straw to remove from the bed in April.

Clamps

Clamps are the traditional method of bulk storage of root vegetables and can be made outside, in pits or in barns. Potatoes will store in clamps without sprouting until January or February. Beyond this, the sprouts will need to be knocked off the potatoes before sale. Swedes, celeriac and beetroot can be stored until March.

Clamping can be simply covering a heap with soil or straw, or structures built with straw bales as walls and roof. The humidity levels in clamps should be monitored and managed carefully to prevent drying out, but also to avoid them being too damp. One option for clamping in barns is to use pallet boxes inside straw walls, with the pallet base providing some ventilation. Wire mesh can be used to keep rodents out. Some growers use old duvets or mattresses to top clamps for ease of access. Bigger roots will store longer, so sell smaller ones first.

Barn storage

Crops such as onions, garlic and squash need to be properly dried or cured before storage, either in the field, if conditions allow, or in a polytunnel or glasshouse. They can then be stored stacked in boxes in a barn. White and red cabbages can also be stored in this way. Cool ambient temperatures are best for most crops (7–8°C), though squash will store better at warmer temperatures (15–18°C). Adapting existing buildings or rooms that are north-facing can be as effective as a cold store. Insulate and lower the floor, if possible, to keep cooler. For larger growers, barns can be purpose-built or adapted with insulation for box storage with fan-assisted ventilation.

Refrigerated storage

Refrigeration can be useful for short-term storage of crops in order to extend sales, as well as when buying in produce for selling on. Bear in mind, though, that some crops can be subject to chilling injury (for example, tomatoes, aubergines, courgettes and green beans) and need to be handled with care. Cold storage can also be used for long-term storage of crops beyond March and April and into the hungry gap, but this can be expensive. Cold stores can be retrofitted into buildings close to packing and retail areas, or acquired as refrigerated lorry containers in various sizes.

Selling

There are many routes to market and the routes chosen will partly depend on the resources, skills and desires of the grower. It is essential to take a hard look at the economics of the different outlets, including fuel for the van and everybody's time. The direct approach, with as short a supply chain as possible, has many benefits to the grower, not least retaining the full value of the crop. It can also be very rewarding, given the direct contact with consumers. However, it can be a huge amount of work. The more diverse the system, the more complex marketing becomes. It is of course possible, and indeed advisable, to operate a number of the models below simultaneously. Don't keep all your egg plants in one basket …

Farm stands and vending machines

Perhaps the simplest form of direct marketing is to have a self-service farm stand by the roadside, with an honesty box. It needs to be protected from the sun and the rain and should be regularly replenished. Produce needs to be ready bagged or sold by the unit, with prices clearly marked in easy denominations. It

Cold store at Trill Farm Garden.

is a flexible option, as you can only sell what you have, with no obligation to have a full range of produce. It also doesn't tie up much staff time. In the US, these farm stands sometimes take creative forms, with trailers and canopies. In the UK, you are more likely to see a table with a cover, or a small kiosk or shed. To reduce the risk of theft, make the money box secure and empty it regularly, particularly overnight. Security cameras may also help, or, more simply, a picture with eyes overlooking the honesty box is said to keep people … honest.

Vending machines are a notch up and take more investment, but they can be refrigerated, take card payments and give change. They may also have flexible locker sizes to accommodate anything from a bunch of radishes to a 25kg sack of potatoes.

Salad bags

Charles Dowding cites the salad bag in the very first *Organic Grower* magazine in summer 2007 as 'saving his existence as a grower', when he started selling them in 2003. Mixed-salad leaves in a bag are now so ubiquitous that it is hard to imagine a time when the supermarket shelves weren't packed high with them and growers struggled through the winter to grow lettuce in tunnels, which mostly limped through and finally succumbed to mildew.

In the 1980s and 1990s, Joy Larkcom (1984, 1991) opened up growers to a new world of oriental mustards and the huge range of other salad leaves of different textures, colours and flavours that can be grown throughout the year. A cook's eye and palate are needed for blending different leaves that work well on the plate. A few edible flowers (nasturtiums, marigolds and so on) and herbs such as Greek basil can elevate the bag to the sublime, when available.

Mixing salad leaves at Pitney Farm Market Garden.

May salad-leaf selection at Trill Farm Garden.

A lettuce harvesting technique, popularised by Charles Dowding, is to pick the outside leaves regularly, thus prolonging the harvesting period.

November salad-leaf selection at Trill Farm Garden.

The Veg Hut at Westmill Organics, near Swindon.

Glebelands Market Garden farm shop.

Scilly Organics' idyllic roadside stall on St Martins, Isles of Scilly. The stall has an honesty box and sells a wide range of vegetables to holidaymakers, from potatoes and carrots to tomatoes and salad.

Farm shops

The mantra 'location, location, location' holds true for farm shops. If your farm is accessible (no gates or long muddy farm tracks), you have a suitable building to convert, or space for a new one, then you might consider starting a farm shop. The farm should be the draw and you need to make your offer different to other outlets and your produce the star. If you are only selling your own produce, you may not require planning permission. In any case, you will need investment (grants may be available), a business plan and a long-term vision. Farm shops can be hard work and full-time retail may require new skills, but also provide employment for family members and/ or locals. There may be opportunities to broaden the offer, including cafés, restaurants, or experiences such as farm tours.

Farmers' markets

Farmers' markets, where the emphasis is on local produce, would seem an ideal outlet for the grower. They don't require much investment (tables and a gazebo, scales and so on) and fees are usually small. However, while some markets are thriving, others wax and wane. Ideally, support your local market – they can be great for getting your name known and building sales through other outlets you may have. The best ones operate weekly, but in smaller towns they may be once a month. This is not so great for vegetable sales, as customers will not be able to buy a month's supply from you. You may be able to attend markets further afield on other weekends (usually stallholders need to be within a 30–50-mile radius of the market, but rules vary). In some areas, where there are a lot of producers, the market organisers might not have space for another vegetable stall. Although farmers' markets are usually shorter in duration than regular town markets (which can also be worth considering), they do entail giving up a substantial amount of time at the weekend – picking, setting up and packing away at the end, then back at the farm. They can be fun and social events, but do consider how well they fit into your family routines and lifestyle.

School farmers' markets, targeted at the hour or two after schools close, have been promoted by the Food for Life programme. They are attractive to the producer, as they are short and intense, so not too much time away from the farm, and good for building community relations. Great for the school kids, too. Another option, if you have a large farmyard, is to bring the market to you, especially if you already have a farm shop.

Nathan Richards of Troed y Rhiw was a founder member of the Monday Market in Newport, Pembrokeshire. Nathan said: 'The market runs between Easter and New Year officially, but during the other winter months, or when the market is cancelled due to high winds and the danger of stalls blowing over (we are right on the Irish Sea), we turn up anyway and sell directly from the back of the van. For me, to make it successful it has to be all about reliability – our customers know that whatever the weather, we will be there with top-quality organic veg. Our customers eat veg 52 weeks of the year and I produce it 52 weeks of the year – it's a good match. It's the reason we only do weekly markets, no food festivals, no monthly or fortnightly markets, as that makes food exclusive and "special" in the wrong way. It is definitely worthwhile, but it is hard work. I have a very loyal customer base who buy most of their weekly vegetables from me.'

The author's market stall at Lutterworth Farmers' Market in August 2010. It took place once a month, so we used it to raise awareness of where to buy our produce regularly.

Trill Farm Garden market stall in Lyme Regis.

Would your mum buy it?

Producing good-quality organic fruit and vegetables for sale is about much more than just presentation. Soil health is vital, as is avoiding pest and disease damage through good management of rotations and biodiversity. But being organic is not enough on its own. Correct spacing through precision drilling or careful plant spacing should help to ensure uniformity of size and reduce misshapes. Good training of cucumbers will reduce the number of bent cucumbers. Irrigation will prevent the bitterness in lettuce or pithiness in celery caused by drought stress.

Most food purchases are bought on impulse, based on appearance. You should grade out damaged or under/oversized vegetables. Outgrades can be used for catering, if you have an on-farm café or restaurant, or offered at a reduced price in nets or bags. At worst, they can be composted or fed to livestock. Following are some tips for retail to boost sales:

- **Elbow to eye level is best:** Ideally display your produce at a height between 45–175cm.
- **Appearance of bounty:** Stack up produce to make it more visible from a distance ('Stack it high and watch it fly'). Tilt the crates towards the customer to make the produce more visible and inviting. Keep crates regularly topped up.
- **Be consistent and logical:** Arrange produce in groups, with roots at one end and salads at the other.
- **Contrast colours to break up blocks of green and brown:** Do this either with the produce itself, or with the display materials. Turn the colourful side of the produce towards the customer.
- **Smell:** Brush the basil whenever you walk past it!
- **Clean and uniform display boxes and baskets:** Natural materials such as baskets can enhance the appearance of displays.
- **Weigh in advance:** 'Grab and go' bags or punnets can save time on the day.
- **Mist:** Do this regularly to keep the produce fresh.
- **Remove sad/wilted produce:** Trim or peel back yellowing leaves.
- **Clearly label your prices:** Otherwise people think you have something to hide! Keep prices simple and round for busy markets.
- **Be enthusiastic about your produce:** Give people recipe tips or ideas for crops they may not be familiar with. Offer samples.
- **Keep smiling and friendly:** This is important, no matter how stressed you might be feeling.

Mobile store

Instead of (or in addition to) taking your produce to a market, you can kit out a van with shelves and bring the market directly to the consumer by visiting set locations at set times each week. A mobile store can provide a valuable community service in rural areas, or get you directly to where your customers are, for example the car park of large employers.

Pick your own

Pick your own (PYO) seems to be making a comeback, due to increasing problems around sourcing labour for harvesting. While PYO is suitable for some crops, such as pumpkins/squash, for others it would probably result in too much crop wastage. For it to work, you need good road access, sufficient hardstanding for car parking, toilet facilities, good signage and

The Cultivate Oxford Veg Van is a roving ethical food truck supplying locally grown produce from a farm near Didcot to various locations around Oxford.

strong social-media campaigns or local advertising. Somebody needs to be present to take money and explain how it works, so PYO would work best as an 'added attraction' to a farm shop.

Box schemes

The vegetable box scheme is a simple and effective method of marketing and distributing vegetables to customers and is used by many growers. Box schemes can be farm-based or not farm-based, and on a regional or national scale. For a farm-based box scheme, the attraction is that you decide what the customer gets and can tailor the offer according to what you have. The heyday of the no-choice box may be over, however. Box schemes offering more choice to their customer, either in terms of opting in or out of certain lines, or a more bespoke ordering service, appear to be doing better.

While the box scheme bypasses much of the costs associated with longer supply chains, it also adds costs to the producer in terms of labour, packing, materials and delivery. Running a box scheme can be very complex and time-consuming. There are, however, platforms and software to assist with improving the shopping experience for the consumer, as well as simplifying administration, logistics and financial management. Examples include Ooooby and Growing Good. There are several options for delivery/pick-up that can be considered:

- **Customer pick-up from the farm:** This works best if close to an urban area or busy road.
- **Individual deliveries.**
- **Drop off at hub points:** For example, a customer's garage or a retail outlet; this usually involves a discount or free box for the host, or some other incentive.

The other decision you need to take is whether to provide only your own produce, combine with other local producers, or buy in from wholesalers. If the former, you may decide to operate seasonally and close during the hungry-gap period. As most consumers choose box schemes for freshness and to support local producers, it can be a risk to buy in produce. However, this has to be weighed up against the chance that customers won't return when you reopen as they have found alternative sources for their weekly shop.

Creating a vegetable box or bag is like assembling musicians for an orchestra; they all need to work harmoniously together. It is not just a case of chucking in a bit of everything you have available. Put yourselves in the shoes, or the apron, of the customer and think about what your reaction would be and what you would do with the contents. Are the quantities of each item appropriate? Some producers design their boxes around recipes and include them in the box.

There is a temptation to stuff your boxes with produce that it is glutting. Resist this, as one of the major reasons for customers leaving box schemes is that they can't keep up with the produce and hate having to throw food away. It is therefore better to deal with gluts by offering optional extras – boxes of tomatoes for freezing, peppers for dehydrating and so on.

To maintain your customers' loyalty, keep them engaged and informed with regular communications, which can be through newsletters, emails or social media. Hold open days and festivals and be transparent. Provide both customers and non-customers with price comparisons with the supermarkets – they may be surprised!

Community Supported Agriculture (CSA)

Community Supported Agriculture (CSA) schemes are on the rise – membership of the CSA Network UK has doubled in the last couple of years. They are proving to be a resilient farming model, providing comparatively easy access for new entrants. CSA schemes are a form of agriculture in which customers or members share the risks and rewards of farming with the farmer or grower. Members commit to buying a share of the harvest for the whole season and may also volunteer, often with the actual work of farming, but also with things like finance, administration and marketing. The commitment often entails upfront payment, or payment throughout the year, which improves cash flow, increases financial stability and hugely reduces waste, as the grower knows exactly how much produce (and what type) they need to grow for the whole season before it has even started.

George Bennett packing veg boxes at Sandy Lane Farm.

Vegetable boxes at Troed y Rhiw.

CSAs generally start as either 'community-led' (where the community sees a need for good local food, forms an entity and employs a grower), or 'grower-led,' where one or more growers follow a desire to produce good local food in tandem with a community, find land and recruit members. Despite differences in the way they begin, CSAs often end up looking quite similar, the main differences generally being, firstly, that in grower-led CSAs the growers do all the tasks associated with running the CSA, not just the growing, but also administration, finance and marketing, whereas in a community-led CSA these are shared. Secondly, they vary in terms of the number of people involved in decision-making (more in a community-led scheme).

There are clear similarities between a veg-box scheme and a grower-led CSA and there are some good examples of farms that have transitioned from a box scheme to a CSA. Waterland Organics in Cambridgeshire converted from a vegetable box scheme to a CSA in 2015 after twenty years of organic growing. They say that it has made accounting a lot less complicated, by now asking for one payment in advance for the whole season, which avoids tracking small transactions and chasing small payments. The CSA model is part of a wider global network of solidarity agriculture and many CSAs are looking for ways to increase equity and justice in the work they do. Frameworks for CSAs include:

- **Bidding-round CSA:** In this model, which operates in many European countries, CSA members come together at the beginning of the year to offer anonymous contributions that make up the annual farm budget. If the required amount is not reached, subsequent bidding rounds are instigated until costs are covered.
- **Sliding-scale CSA:** CSAs ask you to self-select whether you are high, medium or low income or unwaged, with the share price varying accordingly.

- **Wage-based CSA:** If it takes the CSA an hour to create your weekly share (including all the additional tasks like finance, administration and so on), you pay the CSA the equivalent of your hourly wage for your share.
- **Self-pack CSA:** Members pack their own selection from bulk boxes, with the amounts suggested, but can leave and sometimes swap produce they don't want.
- **Self-harvest CSA:** Customers harvest what they need from lists provided with advice/assistance from growers when needed.
- **Full-farm or full-diet CSA:** This model usually consists of a cooperative of producers covering meat, fruit, vegetables, dairy, bread, flour, pulses and so on, so that members can do their full weekly shop through CSA shares.

Medium share at Bennison Farm CSA.

Van packed with vegetable shares, Bennison Farm CSA.

Smart alternatives

Various initiatives have sprung up that aim to create online food hubs or virtual farmers' markets. The concept of the REKO (which means 'fair consumption' in Finnish) originated in Finland in 2013 and brings together growers and producers through closed Facebook groups. Within the groups, growers list what they have for sale and customers order what they want. Then the delivery takes place at an agreed location, where customers collect their orders. REKO is a quick and efficient way of connecting growers, and especially new businesses, to consumers without a retail partner. They have spread rapidly through Europe, including the UK. While some may have misgivings about using Facebook, REKOs have the potential to reach a lot of people quickly. REKO may be more suited to urban and peri-urban areas, with shorter travel distances and larger customer bases.

The Open Food Network is a global, not-for-profit movement 'focused on building the tools and resources needed to create a new food system that is fair, local and transparent'. It uses open-source software for managing online farmers' markets and provision of free resources for producers and community food enterprises. Through its platform, you can set up your own shop, add products from other producers and plan deliveries and payments.

Selling to retail

It can be simpler, in theory, to sell in larger quantities to retail outlets, essentially becoming a wholesaler, though the prices you receive will be lower. Local shops and post offices, community shops, garages, campsite shops, farm shops, garden centres, box schemes and health food shops may all be potential outlets. Some might grow their own, or be buying from other growers or wholesalers, so you will need to have the conversations as to what produce they would be interested in and when. The attraction for the retailer to buy from you should be the premium of freshness that comes from being local, but you will need to be competitive on quality and price, too. Some outlets may not be used to selling and displaying vegetables, so you may need to assist on stock rotation, perhaps offering a display stand for use inside or out, with produce on a sale or return basis. Nothing destroys sales more than tired, limp produce.

Selling to the catering trade

Many pubs, cafés and restaurants proudly proclaim to be sourcing 'local food' or 'seasonal produce'. It is your job to keep them honest! Salad leaves can be a good way in, but talking to chefs might open lots more possibilities beyond the garnishes. Unusual and heritage crops can provide a point of difference. Be aware, though, that such outlets can be fickle and demanding customers and there is often a high turnover of chefs and cooks. The chef doesn't always have a free hand with ordering and price and cash flow can be an issue; chef proprietors can be the best customers, as they order the produce and pay the bills.

If you are in a tourist area, you have the advantage that the demand from cafés, pubs and restaurants will mirror your produce availability from April to October, peaking in the summer holidays. Caterers also offer potential – while they are not always so transparent as to where they are sourcing their food, they may be open to local, seasonal produce.

Public procurement is another ball game. The Danish experience shows that organic public procurement – supplying hospitals, old people's homes, schools, works canteens, town halls and the like – can be done, if the will is there. In Denmark, the growth in this sector has been a significant driver in the increase in the organically farmed area. With public procurement, there will normally be a bidding process, with scoring on a set of criteria, including reliability of supply but also sustainability issues. This market can be difficult to break into but not impossible, especially if you combine a bid with other growers. In some areas, away from the obvious vegetable and salad production, there can be a lack of local competition from conventional growers, as many no longer exist.

Wholesale

The organic wholesale sector plays an important role in supplying independent retailers, farm shops and box schemes to supplement their own produce. National box schemes such as Riverford or Able & Cole, while not wholesalers as such, act in a similar way from a grower's perspective. If you are buying in from an organic wholesaler, there may also be possibilities of selling produce to them. It is wise to talk to them early in the year about growing crops specifically for their requirements, rather than panic call when you have courgettes coming out of your ears in late July! Prices will be less than for selling directly to retailers or customers, but the wholesale sector can be a good option for field growers, enabling bulk sales with minimal hassle. Quality, consistency of supply and price will be the key issues. Facilities for on-farm grading and packing will be needed, plus there may be additional transport costs and marketing commissions.

The Better Food Shed in London, set up by Growing Communities in 2018, works with growers in East Anglia and the south-east of England, supplying community-led box schemes, shops, food projects and local authorities. Growers let the Better Food Shed know what they have and an amalgamated price list is sent out to customers once a week. A 15–20 per cent mark-up is added to the price from farmers to cover overheads. It works well for smaller growers, allowing them to concentrate on higher-value crops suited to their farms and giving them a guaranteed market. There is some cooperation amongst growers to develop coordinated cropping plans and pricing.

Wholesale boxes of bunched beetroot at Strawberry Fields.

Supermarkets

The largest quantities of organic produce are marketed through supermarkets and handled by packers. Contracts need to be in place prior to growing crops. Prices received will be lower than for wholesale, plus quality requirements, such as chilling, size, shape and freedom from imperfections, can be exacting. Some crops, like cabbages and cauliflowers, are often packed on harvesting rigs in the field. Supplying packers generally requires less on-farm storage and packing facilities and entails lower grading costs than growing for wholesale.

Processing

While there may be small-scale artisan processors, who will take small quantities of excess and grade-out produce, most processors require high volumes of quality produce grown under contract. Examples are frozen food, baby foods and preserves.

Adding value by on-farm processing can seem a good option to deal with gluts and as a rainy day activity, but it entails a lot of work and returns may not always justify it. Chutneys, pickles, pestos, relishes, spreads and fermented foods such as sauerkraut are all possible and can be a great draw for customers. A kitchen processing area requires approval by the local authority, which may be easier and less painful than you may think. If you are buying in for a box scheme, you should be covered under the processing licence, but check with your certification officer. Ingredients used need to be tracked and declared, leaving less scope for improvisation. Advice and training are available on food safety, allergens and labelling.

Working together

The UK has a reputation of being a country where cooperatives, especially with farmers, do not work. There may be opportunities, however, to work together. The Mach Vegbox in Machynlleth, west Wales, comprises four small market gardens and a micro-dairy, with two non-grower members taking care of the admin and packing. A small charge is added to each vegetable bag sold to cover admin, with one of the growers (on rotation) helping with the packing. While planning together what to grow can take time, the social aspects of working together and mutual support are invaluable. Groups of growers can collaborate informally or formally to run market stalls or farm shops, freeing up individual growers and enabling some specialisation in crop growing.

Marketing

In addition to finding a market, you will need to promote yourself continuously, particularly if selling directly. This is not a one-off activity – in times of austerity and cost of living crises, you may need to keep working hard to stay afloat. Having a strong brand and logo will help, emphasising your point of difference – why choose you over a supermarket or national box scheme? A good website and an active social-media presence is necessary to engage with your customers. However, not all potential customers will be on social media, so ads in local papers and leaflet drops can prove worthwhile. Attracting the public with themed open days such as pumpkin or harvest festivals and farm to fork dinners can also help to get you known.

Some may prefer to emphasise the local over the organic. You may need to challenge the preconception that organic food is elitist and expensive. The important thing is to communicate your values, ad the value of your products, and be proud of it. The Soil Association has produced a reference document, *Marketing Organic – what you can say in marketing & advertising*, which contains statements about organic food and farming that have been assessed against the UK Advertising Standards Authority's code.

Packaging

One of the concerns of the organic consumer is the use and abuse of plastic, often exacerbated by supermarkets packaging organic products in plastic to differentiate the products from conventional. Some products, such as salads and greens, will lose moisture quickly if not packed in plastic. Alternatives are available, but these need to be ethical and cost-effective, as well as truly compostable at a garden level (not just 'degradable'). They also have to be transparent, look and feel good and not suck moisture out of the product! Prices at present are considerably higher than for 'normal' plastic bags, so a premium may need to be charged.

It is a complex issue and single-use paper bags also have a carbon footprint. A fairly recent development is the marking of fruit and vegetable plastic packaging as recyclable through the bins at most of the major supermarket chains.

Pricing

Pricing is a delicate issue. Not many growers set their prices according to the cost of production to give themselves or their employees a fair wage. Prices charged by wholesalers, other retailers, or farm shops will be a useful indicator for your own pricing. The Soil Association provides a weekly price service, listing prices (range and average) from UK organic wholesalers and retail/farm shops. This does not currently include supermarket prices, but these can be obtained online. Can you compete at these prices? Are you comparing like with like?

You should be able to charge more for some lines that can be sold at a premium for taste or uniqueness, such as heritage tomatoes. They will cost more to grow, as they will yield less than 'standard' varieties. The other common mistake is to price too low when you have a glut. Customers may not buy any more at the lower price, as they just buy what they need (unless they can freeze or preserve the excess), so the end result is less return and profit for you.

As a rule, at least 30 per cent can be added on to the wholesale price for retail through direct routes, though some shops may add 90–100 per cent to account for the perishability (wastage) of produce.

When selling unusual products to restaurants, it can be difficult to find any information on prices. If you develop a good relationship with chefs, you could ask them what they would expect to pay.

Chapter Twelve

Managing Labour, Time and Complexity

Growing vegetables is very labour-intensive and seasonal, so most growers will need extra help at some point. Many smaller-scale and community-oriented holdings rely on volunteers. When I was a grower in the 1990s, my father said to me: 'If you can't afford to pay people proper wages you shouldn't be in business.' I was shocked, but he had a point. We relied too much on WWOOFers and locals working a morning a week in exchange for a vegetable box.

One of the core organic principles is fairness, which means respect and support for all should be integral to your operation. There are practices commonplace on organic farms that may not stand up to legal scrutiny. Although there is a role for volunteers in certain situations, they should not be used to prop up unviable businesses. Organic production needs to be professional, which means setting out clear arrangements and proper Human Resources (HR) policies.

Staff, volunteers and interns

The use of volunteers forms part of the contract with the community that is integral to the CSA model. The social and educational element of volunteering also shouldn't be ignored.

Being a WWOOF host (*see* Chapter 3) can be an enriching experience, meeting people from all walks of life; an opportunity to receive physical and moral support for your project, to exchange ideas, values and knowledge. For the WWOOFer, it is an education and an act of solidarity. It should never be an exploitative relationship. WWOOFers are expected to work around half of each day's stay, sharing in the daily routine and receiving room and board.

Employing seasonal staff for horticulture, especially from abroad, has become increasingly difficult since Brexit. A Defra survey in the second quarter of 2022 showed an average shortfall of 8 per cent for survey respondents who required seasonal labour.

If there is enough work throughout the season, you may decide to take on full or part-time employees. At present, there is a skills gap, with many businesses unable to fill vacancies. As an alternative, you could take on an intern or trainee on a short- or medium-term placement. As with volunteers, it is an exchange and you must be prepared to train and educate the intern in all aspects of the business. There are farms that do this on an informal basis for board and lodging and a small stipend, but this may not be legal. This training is also not as accessible to those from less advantaged backgrounds, without savings or family support. You have to ask yourself if you are sufficiently experienced to be able to train an intern or apprentice, or are you just looking for cheap labour? The Biodynamic Apprenticeship scheme rightly insists on paying a full salary to trainees over its two-year period.

OPPOSITE: Rita Oldenbourg at Pitney Farm Market Garden.

Workshare Wednesday (10am to 1pm) at Bennison Farm CSA. Great for teamwork, such as bringing in the onion harvest.

Whiteboard at Teign Greens CSA with weekly tasks and responsibilities.

Work dynamics

Employing people can be daunting, but also liberating if you are prepared to relinquish some control and allow your staff to become growers. There is a need for clear communication, defined roles and responsibilities. This will entail regular meetings, standard operating procedures and task lists. Ben Hartman, author of *The Lean Farm,* suggests breaking down tasks into steps, key points and reasons. Standard Operating Procedures condense these into instructional sheets with pictures. These can help to ensure that repetitive tasks are performed the same way by all workers and can be reviewed and improved. Hartman recommends laminated sheets, placed near where the job is carried out.

Working with a partner/family

Many growing enterprises are family- or couple-run. This is often not easy, particularly in the early stages of establishing a business. Raising a family can be lonely and isolating on a farm, but they can be great places to bring up kids. Following are some pointers gained from grower experiences:

- Communication is crucial, but don't talk about work all the time!
- Be clear about your roles and value the work of the other person. Childcare is as important as weeding the carrots.
- Be adaptable: during pregnancy, appropriate jobs will need to be found. Scything, strimming and harvesting tall crops are pregnancy-friendly jobs. Ask for help, or offer help, with lifting.
- Slings may work for some mothers and babies, but not all.
- Make use of childcare opportunities when you can.
- Don't feel guilty about shipping the kids off to clubs and the like; sustaining yourself will benefit your kids.
- Make life simpler – hiring skilled workers may be less stressful than managing volunteers.
- Give your partner freedom and space to develop their independent interests and skills. Take time off separately and together; external interests help!

The youngest member of the Teign Greens CSA team catches some rest while the rest of the team picks salad.

Work alongside your staff, noting both the positives and areas for improvement. Simple economies of movement can make big differences, for example using two hands for hand-weeding and filling both hands when picking before transferring produce to the harvest box. Be relaxed and encouraging. From my own experience, and with the benefit of hindsight, demonstrating a super-fast pace may not always motivate others!

White boards with daily, weekly or monthly tasks in a central location can keep workers informed about what needs to happen and when. These can be ticked off or colour-coded according to status. Performance reviews and appraisals may seem the territory of *The Office*, but can be useful opportunities for people to be open and honest with each other. Taking set breaks together for tea and lunch can build relationships and nurture a sense of community.

Lean farming

The concept of lean production, which aims to eliminate waste, comes from the Japanese car industry and has been widely used in industry around the world. US grower Ben Hartman set out to apply these principles to his farm and wrote the book *The Lean Farm* in 2015. Agroecological farming with an emphasis on diversity tends to add complexity to a system. However, Hartman says that 'complexity is the enemy of lean'. Despite the seeming contradiction, Hartman argues that lean farming can be used to strengthen sustainability – that the spirit of lean farming is to 'farm better, not meaner'. The five core principles Hartman found to be of most benefit to his farm are:

1. **Keep only the tools that add value:** Don't hoard. If you have not used a tool in the last year, you don't need it.
2. **Let the customer define value:** Keep the customers and their wishes in mind by seeking to answer the questions: What do our customers want? When do they want it? What amount do they want?
3. **Identify the steps that add value:** Concentrate on actions that build value, such as seeding and harvesting.
4. **Cut out anything that doesn't add value:** This means trying to eliminate over-production, waiting, unnecessary driving, physical work that doesn't create value and damaged crops. It also involves creating smoother and more predictable workflows. Unused talent is also a waste.
5. **Continuous improvement:** Aim to align production with demand and to cut out waste.

Mental health and avoiding burnout

Behind the bucolic image of working in harmony with nature in idyllic surroundings, growing can be tough and stressful. Long hours, lone working, remoteness, unpredictability of weather, market volatility, bureaucracy, financial concerns and housing issues can all cause stress. The UK Government identified the following in *Five Ways to Wellbeing*:

1. **Connect:** Have good social connections and support networks. Family, friends, neighbours, church, the pub, clubs, grower networks and local groups are vital. Connecting with other local growers can be hugely important – social support is as crucial as technical support.
2. **Be active:** Most growers are very active creatures and remain physically fit. Even so, an evening cycle or activity beyond growing can be therapeutic. Any problems with physical health can impact on mental wellbeing.
3. **Take notice:** This means becoming more aware of our own feelings, sensations and thoughts and being attentive to what is taking place in the present. I remember a WWOOFer remarking to me 'This is such a beautiful place to

work, you're very lucky.' I had to blink away the stresses and take in the view, as if for the first time, and acknowledge it. Some may find that 'mindfulness' helps to focus on the present, concentrate better, aids creativity and helps with relaxation and sleep. It doesn't have to mean sitting in meditation – taking time at sunset to observe nature can work wonders.

4. **Keep learning:** Learning plays an important role in human social and cognitive development. Learning can help with self-esteem, adaptation to change and keeping the mind open. It could involve joining a grower discussion group, watching webinars, or doing a Masters in Organic Farming. Or you might want to learn something completely different, like a foreign language.

5. **Give:** Helping, sharing and team-oriented activities can increase a sense of self-worth and positive feelings.

The importance of rest and renewal is clear, but it does not always seem possible in the height of the season. Set boundaries so that you have proper breaks; consider not working on Sundays, or taking time off to go to the cricket or football (other events are available). Have hobbies and interests outside the farm. Structure your business to have a more balanced workflow throughout the year. Take a holiday. A good balanced diet can also help and should not be difficult on an organic farm – yet how many of us end up eating something fast at 10pm in the summer months?

Above all, be honest with yourself and others and just talk. There should be no shame in admitting if you are struggling. Open the conversation – you will be surprised by how many others will have been there, too. If you need to talk to someone outside your circle, the Royal Agricultural Benevolent Institution (RABI) operates a 24/7 helpline and mental-health counselling, with online and direct support available.

Teamwork can be empowering – even dock digging!

Chapter Thirteen

Crop by Crop Guide

Alliums

Garlic

Garlic is a high-value crop, especially when fresh, and, once dried, it stores well for direct marketing over a long season.

Fresh garlic at Trill Farm.

Garlic	
Varieties	Soft-necked varieties suitable for North European climate. Varieties for spring or autumn planting available.
Planting	Garlic is propagated vegetatively from cloves, bought as 'seed garlic', that need to be broken down. Own 'seed' can also be saved (choose the best). The really small cloves can be grown very close together and sold bunched as green garlic. Plant in October or November for overwintering or in early spring (ideally by end of February). **Distance in rows**: 15cm. **Distance between rows**: 30–50cm.
Soils/ fertility	Likes deep, well-drained loams with high organic matter content and good K levels. pH range 6–7.5. Needs early N in spring.
Irrigation	Not normally necessary, unless very dry spring/early summers.
Weed control	Not competitive. May need hand-hoeing in dry spells during winter, or use a mulch. Intercropping, e.g. with lettuce or mustard, keeps weeds down.
Pests	Leek moth, wireworm, allium leaf miner are increasingly a problem. Use mesh covers, where known problems.
Diseases	Rust, basal rot (*Fusarium*), white rot. Rotations, wider spacing for airflow.
Harvesting/ storage	Early crops can be harvested fresh from late June (earlier under protection) with a fork (avoid 'steel worm'!). Maincrop for storage can be lifted from mid–late July. Commercial garlic growers use machines, which undercut and pull the bulbs with the stalks. Drying can start in the field, or in trays in a tunnel or glasshouse. On a larger scale, hot air (30°C) can be blown through the boxes until the exiting air is the same temperature as the incoming air.

OPPOSITE: A selection of seasonal vegetables at Sandy Lane Farm.

Leeks

Another staple crop, which is often grown at a field scale. Breeding means it is possible to grow varieties that can be harvested from late June though to May. Box schemes and CSAs often choose to wait until the summer crops have tailed off before starting the leek harvest.

Leek Monstrueux de Carentan.

Leeks	
Varieties/ types	Green varieties for summer/autumn. Blue/green hardy varieties for overwintering. High-yielding hybrids increasing in availability.
Sowing/ planting	**Direct-drilling:** Only possible at low weed pressure and with good weeding kit/skills, e.g. flame weeders. Sow mid-March–May. **Sowing rate:** 12–25 seeds/m. **Distance between rows:** 40–60cm.
	Modules: Sow 1–2 per module from February for April planting, from March for maincrop June/July planting. *See* soil-assisted modules (Chapter 7). Machine-plant or hand-dib. **Distance in rows:** 8–15cm. **Distance between rows:** 40–60cm.
	Bare-root transplants: Best suited for open-pollinated varieties (hybrid seed is expensive). They can be planted deeper, establish quicker and produce a high-quality leek. Precision-drill in tunnels (from February), or outside once soil temperature reaches 10°C (from April). Allows flexibility of planting, as land becomes available (aim for pencil thickness). Machine-plant (trim tops and roots), or plant into formed furrows to allow for mechanical weeding. **Sowing rate:** 90–120/m, aiming for 85 plants/m. **Planting distance:** as modules.
Soils/ fertility	Can be grown on many soils, but deep fertile loams best. pH best above 6.5. Sensitive to compaction.
Irrigation	Necessary for establishment. Can be drought-tolerant, once well-rooted. Irrigation can help to reduce thrip and cutworm damage.
Weed control	Not competitive. Use stale/false seed beds, where possible. Inter-row weed or ridge up. Undersow with cover crops after 2 or 3 weedings, or in late August/September.
Pests	Thrips (mostly cosmetic), leek moth, wireworm, onion fly, allium leaf miner increasingly a problem, rabbits, birds. Use mesh covers, where known problems.
Diseases	Onion white rot, rust, downy mildew, white tip, *Botrytis*. Rotations, wider spacing for airflow.
Harvesting/ storage	Early varieties can be harvested from late June, later ones through to April/May. Big plants mean less labour trimming. On a small scale, lift by fork and trim in the field to avoid double handling. Sharp knives essential! On a larger scale, they can be undercut. If cold spell anticipated, they can be lifted with soil on roots and stored in a barn or cold store for a few weeks.

Onions

Onions are a popular crop, usually grown on a field scale. With the right choice of varieties and storage, they can be sold all year round. If you can't compete with the field growers, try specialising in overwintered onions or shallots.

Onions at Bennison Farm CSA.

Shallots: A useful crop for direct marketing. Can be sown as multi-sown modules, or bought as sets.

Spring onions: Very useful salad crop and catch crop, inside and out. Can be grown as multi-sown modules, or direct-drilled. Spring and overwintering varieties available.

Onions	
Varieties/types	Red and white varieties, for maincrop and overwintering. More choice as seed than sets. Some mildew-resistant varieties on market.
Sowing/planting	**Direct drilling**: Only possible where low weed pressures and with good weeding kit/skills, e.g. flame weeders. Sow in March for maincrop, or end of August/early September for overwintering. **Sowing rate**: 30–40 seeds/m. **Distance between rows**: 40–60cm.
	Modules: Sow 5–6 per module/block in February/March for April planting. Also sow in mid–late August for overwintering. **Distance in rows:** 20–25cm. **Distance between rows:** 40–60cm.
	Sets: Quicker to establish and earlier yields than module-grown. Plant March/April or September for overwintering. **Distance in rows:** 5–15cm, depending on required bulb size. **Distance between rows:** 40–60cm.
Soils/fertility	Can be grown on a range of soils, but do best on lighter sandy soils with good drainage. pH 6.2–7.5 on mineral soils; 5.4–7.5 on peat. Too much N late in the season can delay ripening and impede storage. Overwintering crop is N-demanding. Manure from previous crop. Overwintering crop may need extra N in spring.
Irrigation	Essential for establishment of transplants and on lighter soils.
Weed control	Very sensitive to weed competition in early stages. Thermal weeding and inter-row weeding with finger-weeders.
Pests	Wireworm, allium leaf miner, onion fly, rabbits, birds. Use mesh covers, where known problems.
Diseases	Onion white rot, downy mildew, *Botrytis*. Avoid irrigating in morning.
Harvesting/storage	Early crops can be harvested green for bunching when 15–25% of tops have fallen over. When >50% have fallen over, harvest for storage. Windrow and dry in field, then in trays or with hot air. Ambient storage to March in barns.

Chenopods (Beets)

Beetroot

I must confess, beetroot is not my favourite vegetable, but it is easy to grow and sell. It is one of those crops that you don't see much in the supermarkets – fresh anyway – so it offers a point of difference for the customer. It can have a long season of sales, starting with tunnel and glasshouse crops in May, through to the following spring (stored maincrop).

Bunched beetroot at Southern Roots Organic.

Beetroot	
Varieties	As well as the 'standard' red, round types, beetroot can come in white, yellow or stripy ('Chioggia') and cylindrical types. Fast-growing versions, which don't bolt, are needed for early sowings and late crops for bunching. Seed is multi-germ, a cluster of seeds, though monogerm seed is available for precision drilling.
Sowing/planting	Early crops are often started as multi-sown blocks or modules from early February and transplanted after 4–5 weeks. Direct drilling is possible, once soil temperature is above 7°C (April through to June outside), though they may bolt if temperatures are below 10°C for a prolonged period. Sow monthly for successional bunching. For storage, sow in second half of May. **Sowing rate:** 25–30 seeds/m. **Planting distance in rows:** 15–30cm. **Distance between rows:** 30–50 cm.
Soils/fertility	Prefers a rich loamy soil, but grows in most soils. pH neutral. Boron deficiency can cause lesions and heart rot.
Irrigation	Not too demanding, though can crack with irregular water supply. Excess watering leads to leaf, rather than root, growth.
Weed control	An easy crop for weed control, quick to establish. Flame-weed drilled crops. inter-row hoe twice a season.
Pests	Voles, mice, rats can be a problem for crops stored in a field or store. Leaf miners can make tops unsightly for bunching, then extra time for preparation required.
Diseases	Scab can be an issue on light, alkaline soils.
Harvesting/storage	Harvest for bunching from golf ball size. Ensure roots in bunches are of similar size. Can be field-stored in milder areas until around Christmas with some protection. Harvest for storage (clamps) in October and November before heavy frosts.

Leaf beet/chard

Leaf beet is often sold as 'spinach', but is also known as perpetual spinach or spinach beet. It is very robust and easy to grow and has a much longer season than true spinach, as it can overwinter and provide green leaf in the hungry gap. It is therefore a staple of many box schemes, despite the arguably less refined taste.

Swiss chard is a close relative and comes in green and coloured versions, which can make an impact on a market stall. It is a dual-purpose vegetable, as the broad midribs can be sauteed separately to the leaves. It is not quite as winter-hardy as leaf beet, but will survive to the spring in some areas. It is sometimes used as baby leaf in salad mixes, but is best used sparingly.

Chard leaves at Trill Farm Garden.

Leaf beet/chard	
Varieties	Few named varieties of leaf beet; offerings will vary between seed houses. Single colours, rainbow chard or 'Bright Lights' chard are attractive options.
Sowing/ planting	Early plantings can be module- or block-grown in February and March, with maincrops drilled directly, when the soil has warmed up in spring. Can also be sown in July/early August for autumn/early winter pickings and a spring pick, before they bolt. **Sowing rate:** 10–15g/m. **Planting distance in/between rows:** 30cm.
Soils/fertility	Prefers a rich loamy soil, but grows in most soils. pH neutral. Both crops are steady feeders and need more N than beetroot to sustain leaf growth over a long season. Good dressings of mature compost will be beneficial
Irrigation	May be needed in hot, dry spells.
Weed control	A competitive and fast-growing crop. Weeds easily controlled by inter-row weeding.
Pests	Few pests. Leaf miners can be a problem, increasing picking time. Pick off affected leaves and compost or feed to chickens. Plant flowering umbellifers to encourage parasitic wasps. Use mesh covers, where known problems.
Diseases	Leaf spot. Hot-water treatment of seed can be effective.
Harvesting/ storage	Several pickings possible; either hand-pick largest leaves, or cut and allow to regrow. Early morning picking with dew and while leaves are cool will prolong freshness.

Spinach

The 'true' spinach is beloved of chefs and foodies, but is more difficult to grow than leaf beet and chards and bolts readily, requiring regular sowings.

Freshly picked spinach at Southern Roots Organics.

Spinach	
Varieties	Hybrid varieties bred for downy mildew resistance tend to perform better than open-pollinated varieties.
Sowing/planting	Sow in modules/blocks from February for early plantings in tunnels. Sow directly, when soil is warm enough from early March to August for cropping through to autumn. Overwintering crops under cover can be sown or planted from September–October for April/May harvest. **Sowing rate**: 5–10g/m. **Distance between rows:** 15–30cm. **Planting distance:** 15–20cm.
Soils/fertility	Needs a very fertile, moist soil.
Irrigation	Regular and often to avoid bolting.
Weed control	A competitive and fast-growing crop. Weeds are easily controlled by inter-row weeding, but be careful as leaves are easily damaged.
Pests	Aphids can be a problem before predator populations have built up. Use mesh covers, where known problems.
Diseases	Downy mildew. Choose resistant varieties, or increase spacing around plants.
Harvesting/storage	Several pickings possible; either hand-pick largest leaves. or cut and allow to regrow. Early morning picking with dew and while leaves are cool will prolong freshness.

Compositae

Chicory/endive

Both chicory and endive are useful autumn crops for salads and great as a following crop for the 'second spring'. The English palate is perhaps taking a while to catch up with the Italian and French appreciation for bitter flavours, but a huge genetic diversity means that chicory and endive can add flavour and visual appeal to salads, balancing the hotness of the oriental mustards in mixed-salad bags. They are tasty cooked, too.

Forced chicory at Trill Farm Garden.

Chicory/endive	
Varieties	**Chicory:** Different shapes and heart densities and a wide range of leaf shape and colours for winter leaves are available. 'Witloof' and some other chicories (e.g., 'Rosso di Treviso') can be lifted and forced. **Endive:** Frizzy endive is great for salad bags. Broad-leaved endive produces large hearts, which may be more difficult to market.
Sowing/ planting	Sow ('Witloof') chicory for forcing in May to allow time for roots to develop. For whole heads (e.g., radicchio) sow early to mid-July. Chicories for winter leaf are best sown in late July/early August. Sow endives before the end of June for an autumn harvest. **Sowing rate:** 0.3 to 0.5g/m. **Planting distance in/between rows:** 30–35cm.
Soils/fertility	Can be grown on a range of soils. Not nutrient-demanding.
Irrigation	During establishment. Chicory is deep-rooting, so irrigation should only be necessary under extreme conditions.
Weed control	Easy to control weeds, as less weed emergence at typical sowing/planting times.
Pests	Slugs can be an issue in damp autumns, especially hiding in curly leaved endives.
Diseases	Usually trouble-free.
Harvesting/ storage	Chicory colours intensify with cold temperatures, but firm hearts can be damaged by hard frosts. Chicory for forcing needs to be dug up in late autumn and put in containers with compost in a dark, warm place; inspect regularly! Endive also will survive light frosts, but can be damaged by hard ones.

Lettuce

Lettuces are the ultimate summer salad crop. Demand varies according to the season – when people want it (in warm weather), it is hardest to grow! Generally, there is still a healthy demand for headed lettuce, though the trend for lettuce leaves as part of mixed-salad bags is increasing.

Lettuce at Southern Roots Organics.

Lettuce	
Varieties	Huge range of varieties and types. Butterheads and icebergs are losing ground in popularity, crispy cos/romaine types are ever popular and Batavian types are great for flavour. A range of colours and leaf shapes are available. Modern varieties are bred for mildew resistance, but some heritage varieties can have field resistance to rival them. Salanova types have been bred by Rijk Zwaan for ease of harvest and leaf separation for salads. Some growers swear by them, but personally I don't find their texture and taste that appealing.
Sowing/ planting	For headed lettuce, sow every 10–14 days for successional harvesting. Sow in large modules or blocks. Direct drilling possible for baby-leaf production. **Sowing rate**: 0.05–0.1g/m. **Planting distance in/between rows:** 15–30cm, depending on variety.
Soils/fertility	Good soil structure, high organic matter and drainage are important. Best grown using residual fertility from previous crop.
Irrigation	Essential for reliable crops and where cutworms are an issue. Trickle/drip irrigation keeps leaves dry, reducing disease risk.
Weed control	Keep inter-row weeding speeds low to avoid throwing soil on to the crop. Mulches keep the crop cleaner.
Pests	Slugs, cutworms, aphids, wireworm, rabbits, birds. Mulches reduce aphid attack, but avoid dark-coloured mulches.
Diseases	Downy mildew, especially late in the season. Mix varieties to slow disease spread.
Harvesting/ storage	Needs to be harvested early in the morning to avoid field heat, or cooled rapidly to about 3°C. Outer leaves can be harvested regularly, which prolongs their life until they eventually bolt. Alternatively, drilled rows can be cut to allow them to come again for subsequent harvests.

Salsify and scorzonera

Salsify and Scorzonera are not lettuce (though also in Compositae family); they are minority root crops for the specialists, suited to extend the winter seasonal offer. Direct sow (40 seeds/m) as early as conditions allow, up to mid-May. Can be left in the ground over-winter and harvested as needed.

Brassicas

Brussels sprouts and Kalettes®

Brussels sprouts are for life not just for Christmas! The butt of many jokes, there is a good demand for sprouts around Christmas, but you may need to work harder at marketing outside the festive season. Kalettes® are a relatively new vegetable, developed by Tozer Seeds and launched in 2010. Previously called flower sprouts, they are a cross between Brussels sprouts and kale, with a mild, sweet and nutty flavour, gaining in popularity.

Brussels sprouts on the stalk at Sandy Lane Farm.

Brussels sprouts/Kalettes®	
Varieties	Hybrids are best for ease of growing, disease resistance, yield and taste. Choose varieties according to maturity time. Kalettes® are only available as (non-organic) F1 hybrids; use 3 varieties to spread the season from October–February.
Sowing/ planting	Sow under cover from mid-April for planting 5–6 weeks later. **Distance in rows:** ≥60cm apart. **Distance between rows:** ≥60cm apart.
Soils/fertility	Need good soils with manure/compost; benefit from lime (club root). Brussels sprouts prefer heavier loams and need a good supply of nutrients and a firm soil. Too much N can cause sprouts to 'blow'. Equally, Kalettes® don't like too much N and perform well on poorer soils.
Irrigation	Necessary for establishment until they are well-rooted.
Weed control	Easy with inter-row hoes. Can be undersown with clovers. Inter-row hoe twice a season.
Pests	Cabbage root fly, caterpillars of various types, aphids, flea beetles, aphids, whitefly, pigeons. Whitefly and aphids, in particular, can be problems in both crops until first frosts, especially where N is high. Promote beneficials. Use mesh cover for 2 weeks after planting against cabbage root fly.
Diseases	Apply lime against club root (dislikes alkaline conditions). Dark leaf spot and ring spot can be a problem on sprouts. Choose resistant varieties; increase spacings.
Harvesting/ storage	Yellowing of lower leaves can indicate maturity for Brussels sprouts. Flavour is better after first frosts. Can be sold on the stalk to save labour costs. Hand-picking on a freezing December morning is not a popular job – rubber gloves are recommended! Stalks also hard to cut when frozen. Kalettes® are fast to pick and can yield 700g/m².

Cabbage

This versatile and important, but under-sung, vegetable comes in a range of types and with the right choice of varieties, planting dates and storage, they can be available for much of the year.

Savoy cabbages can stand in the field in winter.

Cabbage	
Varieties	Cabbages can be grouped into: **Summer and autumn cabbage:** Fast-growing pointed or round non-hardy types for fresh sales from June. **Winter cabbage:** 'January King', Savoys and 'Tundra'; hardy types for cutting from November–February. **Winter storage cabbage:** Red and white cabbages. **Spring greens and spring cabbage:** Overwintered for hungry gap sales in April.
Sowing/ planting	First sowings of summer cabbages can be made in February in modules or seedbeds; sow storage cabbages from mid-April for June planting, hardy winter cabbages early to mid-June for planting by the end of July. Spring greens can be sown in late July–early August, directly to be thinned as greens or transplanted in September. Can be grown outside or under cover. **Sowing rate:** Bare-root transplants: 60 seeds/m. Spring greens: 40 seeds/m. **Planting distance in/between rows:** Summer varieties: 30–45cm. Winter cabbage: up to 70cm, depending on market needs.
Soils/fertility	Needs good soils with manure/compost; benefits from lime (club root). Getting a balance between fertility and spacing is important in achieving desired head size. Spring greens need light soils, which warm up quickly in the spring. May need additional N feeding.
Irrigation	Mostly during establishment.
Weed control	Easy with inter-row hoes. With spring greens, weeding windows may be few in wet winters.
Pests	Usual brassica pests (*see* Brussels sprouts). Aphids and whitefly can be a problem for crops standing in the field after September before first frosts. Pigeons can be a nuisance, especially in the spring. Use mesh cover for 2 weeks after planting against cabbage root fly.
Diseases	Many diseases may be present in small degrees. Ring spot and dark leaf spot can cause problems, usually on outer leaves, which can be trimmed off.
Harvesting/ storage	Harvested fresh in field for immediate sales. Red and white storage cabbages should be harvested by mid-November and stored in trays, then inspected regularly and outer leaves removed before sale; last to March or even June with cold storage.

Calabrese and purple sprouting broccoli (PSB)

Although grouped together, the ubiquitous calabrese and the traditional sprouting broccolis are quite different beasts. Calabrese – once known as Italian sprouting broccoli before the supermarket PR machines got on the case – is essentially a summer vegetable with cropping possible from early June to early November. Purple sprouting broccoli (white and gold also available) is less often found in the supermarkets, which gives the market grower an advantage, especially with freshness. It is easy to grow and relatively hardy, though it occupies the ground for a long time. New varieties allow for sales from December through to the hungry gap in May.

Purple sprouting broccoli at Southern Roots Organics.

Calabrese/sprouting broccoli	
Varieties	Calabrese production is dominated by 2 F1 varieties, 'Marathon' and 'Ironman'. Open-pollinated varieties are less consistent, but may produce over a longer period. Purple sprouting broccoli (PSB) varieties are available for summer, autumn and spring cropping from February–May. White sprouting types are available, but less popular. Asian broccoli or kale/Chinese broccoli crosses with small heads on tender stems are becoming very popular and useful for the grower (sticcoli, kaibroc, tenderstem).
Sowing/planting	Sow calabrese from January–June in modules/seedbed for March–July planting and successional harvest from spring–autumn. Sow PSB from January in modules/seedbed to May for late spring varieties. Successional sow Asian broccoli types every 2 weeks from January to June. Transplanting from March–July. **Distance in/between rows:** Calabrese: 30–60cm. PSB: 60–90cm. Asian broccoli: 45cm.
Soils/fertility	Need good soils with manure/compost; benefit from lime (club root).
Irrigation	Mostly during establishment.
Weed control	Easy with inter-row hoes.
Pests	Usual brassica pests (*see* Brussels sprouts). Aphids and whitefly can be a problem for crops standing in the field after September before first frosts. Pigeons can be a nuisance, especially in the spring. Use mesh cover for 2 weeks after planting against cabbage root fly.
Diseases	Not usually a problem.
Harvesting/ storage	Heads need to be harvested while beads are tight and compact. Subsequent smaller harvests possible, depending on variety and spacing. PSB is picked over a longer period, which is labour-demanding. Asian broccoli types need picking regularly.

Cauliflower

Cauliflowers are not the easiest brassicas to grow. They take up a lot of space and time in the ground, especially winter- or spring-headed types, which are the most valuable for the market garden, available in the hungry gap.

Purple cauliflowers and romanesco cauliflower at Sandy Lane Farm.

Cauliflower	
Varieties	Summer, autumn and winter (mostly Roscoff) as well as novelty types: orange, purple and green cauliflowers and Romanesco, a chartreuse spirally head, which blurs the lines between broccoli and cauliflower, are now available.
Sowing/planting	Succession is as much about variety as sowing date. Summer varieties are sown from February–May, planted from April–July for July–October harvest. Autumn varieties are planted in July for November harvest. Winter types are sown from April–June and planted in July for cutting from December–March in milder areas. Elsewhere, the Roscoff types will head from March–June from a July planting. **Planting distance in/between rows:** Summer types: 50cm. Winter types: up to 70cm.
Soils/fertility	The most nutrient-demanding brassica. Needs good, firm well-drained soils with manure/composts; benefits from lime. Can follow a grass/clover ley or a previously manured crop, such as early potatoes (for autumn/winter types).
Irrigation	May be needed for establishment and for summer crops. Winter cauliflowers are traditionally grown without irrigation.
Weed control	Easy with inter-row hoes.
Pests	Usual brassica pests (*see* Brussels sprouts). Especially cabbage root fly. Use mesh cover for 2 weeks after planting against cabbage root fly.
Diseases	Ring spot and *Alternaria* can cause problems, especially for overwintering crops. Allow airflow and keep weeds under control.
Harvesting/storage	On a field scale, harvest rigs are used. Harvests of 90–100 heads/man hour can be achieved. Check crops regularly and harvest as soon as any curd is showing. Harvesting early is better than too late. Achieving tight size specifications can be difficult, giving the direct marketer an advantage.

Kale

At one time considered cattle fodder, but now hailed as a superfood and with a market to match, kale is probably the easiest of brassica crops to grow.

Kale at Southern Roots Organics.

Kale	
Varieties	A range of leaf types and varieties exists. The coarse but traditional hardy, curly, green and red types are the mainstay, with 'Cavalo Nero' (aka Tuscan kale, black kale or palm kale) being useful for autumn and early winter. The superbly tender and mild 'Red Russian' kale belongs to the *Brassica napus* species, and thus is related to swedes rather than kales. Hence it needs to be treated slightly differently. 'Red Russian' and 'Cavalo Nero', when young, are tender enough to be used as baby leaf. Thousand-headed kale, marrow-stem and 'Hungry Gap' produce tender shoots that are good for the hungry gap.
Sowing/planting	For early production of baby leaf, kale can be drilled in tunnels from late January, sowing successively at 2- to 3-week intervals, moving outside when warm enough. For maincrop, sow in modules or seedbeds from May–July, transplanting from July onwards. **Distance in/between rows:** depends on variety. 'Red Russian': 17–45cm. Curly kale: 60cm.
Soils/fertility	Not as demanding as some brassicas, but benefits from good fertility and liming.
Irrigation	Mostly during establishment.
Weed control	Easy with inter-row hoes.
Pests	Usual brassica pests (*see* Brussels sprouts). Whitefly and aphids can cause problems in mild autumns. Pigeons can be a problem in cold winters. Swede midge can be a problem on 'Red Russian' kale. Use mesh cover for 2 weeks after planting against cabbage root fly.
Diseases	Usually relatively trouble-free.
Harvesting/Storage	Harvest individual leaves when hand-sized. 'Red Russian' kale can be cut like perpetual spinach.

Kohlrabi

Hugely popular in Germany and other parts of northern Europe, it has always been a minor vegetable in the UK. Kohlrabi is a fast-growing brassica, which deserves to be more widely grown.

Kohlrabi for the wholesale market. Strawberry Fields.

Kohlrabi	
Varieties	Purple and green/white types. Choose bolt-resistant types for early production (e.g., 'Azur Star').
Sowing/planting	For early crops, sow in modules successively from February and plant out under cover for cropping before summer crops, such as tomatoes. Outside crops planted from mid-March. Avoid temperatures below 10°C at night in early stages. For autumn crops sow by mid-July for August planting outside. Sow end of July for September planting under cover. Can also be direct-drilled from March–early August. **Sowing rate**: 50 seeds/m. **Distance in/between rows:** Inside: 25cm. Outside: 30cm. Strong-growing autumn types: up to 40cm.
Soils/fertility	Less demanding than other brassicas. Best to rely on fertility from previous crop.
Irrigation	Needs regular irrigation, splitting with uneven watering.
Weed control	Easy with inter-row hoes.
Pests	Usual brassica pests (*see* Brussels sprouts). Damage from cabbage root fly can cause distortion. Use mesh cover for 2 weeks after planting against cabbage root fly.
Diseases	Leaf spots and downy mildew, seldom serious.
Harvesting/storage	Best harvested at apple size, though some, e.g. Superschmelz, will grow to a much larger size while remaining tender.

Radishes

This fast-growing salad crop is the first vegetable of spring and bunches of red radishes add welcome colour and appeal to a vegetable box or market display. It can also be a great intercrop and used to mark rows of slow-growing vegetables like parsnips. Autumn and winter radishes also provide interest later in the season, plus there is a growing demand for use in kimchi. Radish flowers and pods also have their interests for chefs.

Trill Farm Garden radish.

Radishes	
Varieties	'Cherry Belle' and 'French Breakfast' types are standards for fast-growing catch crops. Different colours are available for mixed bunches. Mooli types are great for summer/autumn sales. 'Black Spanish Round' types and 'China Rose' are a bit hardier and add interest to winter boxes.
Sowing/planting	First sowings in tunnels in early February and then successively 7–14 days apart, moving to outside sowings when conditions allow. Bolt-resistant mooli varieties can be sown from spring, with maincrop sown in July. Some varieties, e.g. 'China Rose', can be sown in October/November in a tunnel for February cropping. **Sowing rate**: Salad radishes: 30–40 seeds/m. Mooli/winter radish: 10–20 seeds/m, thin to 10–25cm apart. **Distance between rows:** 15–20cm.
Soils/fertility	Grows well on most soils. Best to rely on fertility from previous crop.
Irrigation	Outdoor crops may need irrigation to delay bolting and reduce flea beetle pressure.
Weed control	Grows so fast, it barely needs weeding. Hand-hoe once, if necessary.
Pests	Usual brassica pests (*see* Brussels sprouts). Flea beetle is the biggest problem, especially for bunching as disfigures leaves. Cabbage root fly – problem for longer-season radish. Best avoid growing in height of summer. Use mesh cover if known problems.
Diseases	Leaf spots can be an issue. Increase planting/sowing distance to allow airflow.
Harvesting/ storage	In warm weather, pick early morning. Flavours/hotness increase with age. Mooli need care to lift, as they can be brittle. Can be cold-stored for up to 6 weeks. Some radishes are (relatively) hardy and can be left in the ground until around Christmas.

Salad brassicas

These cool-season, fast and easy growing leaves come in a range of different shapes, colours, textures and flavours – from mild to hot! Popularised by Joy Larkcom (1984, 1991) in the main, they have revolutionised the salad mix.

Mixed brassica salad leaves grown in Cotesbach Gardens.

Oriental brassica leaf	
Varieties	An ever-growing range is on offer: rockets, cresses, mustards – fiery green in snow to mild serrated mizuna leaf and even finer frilly types. Pak chois and tatsois offer texture and mildness.
Sowing/planting	Can be module-sown from February, or direct-sown under cover. Can be sown outside from March. Best in cool seasons, quickly running to seed in summer. Do well in tunnels overwinter and can be multi-sown in modules in September for relay cropping (= planting in October after summer crops have finished). **Sowing rate**: 120–200 seeds/m and pick small/thin for baby leaf. **(Planting) distance in/between rows:** 15cm or as practical.
Soils/fertility	Grows well on most soils. Best to rely on fertility from previous crop.
Irrigation	Outdoor crops may need irrigation to delay bolting and reduce flea beetle pressure.
Weed control	Grows so fast, barely needs weeding. Hand-hoe once, if necessary.
Pests	Usual brassica pests (*see* Brussels sprouts). Flea beetle is the biggest problem. Best avoid growing in height of summer; use mesh cover if known problems.
Diseases	Leaf spots can be an issue. Increase planting/sowing distances to allow airflow.
Harvesting/ storage	In warm weather, pick early morning. Cut and come again until they bolt. Flavours/hotness can increase with age.

Swedes/turnips

Swedes are unfashionable other than on Burns Night and outside of Scotland, but are a hardy cool-season crop. Turnips are also a minority crop, but are fast-growing and a good early vegetable for bunching, as well as for winter use.

Bunched turnips at Trill Farm Garden.

Swedes/turnips	
Varieties	Limited choice of swede varieties, with some different colours. Fast-maturing turnip varieties best for early use under cover and outside.
Sowing/planting	Swedes sown directly in May and June. Sow turnips directly from February to mid-August. **Sowing rate**: Swedes: 6–7 seeds/m (or to match desired head sizes). Turnips: 20–40 seeds/m. **Distance between rows:** 30–40cm.
Soils/fertility	Light, fertile soils with low N levels. Best to rely on fertility from previous crop.
Irrigation	Swedes may need irrigating for germination and to minimise flea beetle damage. Turnips need regular irrigation.
Weed control	Easy with inter-row hoes.
Pests	Usual brassica pests (*see* Brussels sprouts). Damage from cabbage root fly and swede midge can be high. Use mesh cover early for cabbage root fly and swede midge. Remove covers once crop well-established.
Diseases	Relatively disease-free. Powdery mildew can cause problems, exacerbated by crop covers. Remove covers once crop well-established.
Harvesting/storage	Swedes can be harvested from September, trimming roots to remove any cabbage root fly damage. Can be stored in ground in mild areas, or with straw cover or clamped until March. Turnips can be harvested 8 weeks after sowing for bunching, maincrop can be lifted from September. Less hardy than swedes; harvest before hard frosts and top; can store at 0–4°C and 90–95% humidity for 4–6 months.

Chinese cabbage

Quick-growing, cool-season salad vegetable for tunnel cropping and/or autumn use, growing best between 13–20°C. A February sowing, for tunnel planting (25–35cm apart), will be ready for harvest early to mid-May. Sow from mid-June to mid-August for autumn. Flea beetle and cabbage root fly can cause quality issues.

Pak choi

Some varieties of pak choi can be useful as salad leaves, but 'Joi Choi' F1 is unsurpassed for producing heads. A flexible crop, it can be grown over winter in a polytunnel from a September sowing, or from mid-February for a May harvest. Sow mid-March for April planting outside under fleece or mesh, ready for harvest in June. Needs to be protected with covers from flea beetle and cabbage root fly.

Cucurbits

Courgettes/summer squashes

Courgettes and other summer squashes (*Cucurbita pepo*) are prolific and easy to grow vegetables, which are generally harvested at an immature stage. They are well known for glutting, just as the majority of customers disappear on their summer holidays or are harvesting their own; the skill is to produce them early and late in the season, when prices are better.

Trill Farm Garden courgettes.

Courgettes/summer squashes	
Varieties	As well as the traditional long green types, there are also yellow, round and stripy varieties, such as 'Cocozelle von Tripolis', which has great flavour and holds its flowers well for stuffing. If intending to sell marrows, it is best to select varieties for that purpose. Of limited market but adding interest to displays or for chefs are patty pan, custard squashes and crookneck types.
Sowing/ planting	Summer squashes need warm temperatures to germinate (15–20°C), but can grow fast and don't like any stress caused by cold weather, being pot-bound, transplant shock, wind exposure, etc. Start early crops in large modules or pots. Early crops can be planted under cover in April, but pollination can be a problem, unless a parthenocarpic variety is used. Alternatively, grow flowers to attract pollinators in and open doors/sides of your tunnel/ greenhouse. Summer squashes grow bigger inside, so need sufficient space. Use fleece for protection outside for early plantings (May) and remove when plants are flowering and the risk of frost is gone. A late June or early July direct sowing (later in some areas) can provide crops into the autumn, depending on weather. **Distance in/between rows:** 60cm (90cm inside). Plant on beds or allow space for picking between double rows.
Soils/fertility	Summer squashes like well-drained sandy loams with good levels of organic matter. Rely on previous crop's fertility, when grown in tunnels to avoid excessive leaf growth.
Irrigation	Necessary for establishment and yield.
Weed control	Fast-growing and competitive, so mulching or a couple of hoeings usually suffices.
Pests	Slugs at planting time.
Diseases	Mosaic viruses; powdery mildew can reduce yields. Can be related to root water stress. Successional plantings help, as younger plants less affected.
Harvesting/ storage	Pick courgettes regularly and often to maintain consistent size, up to once a day in height of season. Marrows and other mature summer squashes can be stored until around Christmas, if skins are cured (left in the sun) for a few days.

Cucumbers

Although cucumbers can be grown outdoors, they are more reliably produced in tunnels/greenhouses. They can be very productive, so only grow as many as you need.

Cucumbers at Southern Roots Organics.

Cucumbers	
Varieties	Mini and midi types supplement the traditional 'long' cucumber and can be really useful for boxes and smaller households. All-female varieties (mostly F1) are best for commercial use.
Sowing/ planting	Sow with heat from December for heated glasshouse crops, planted January–February at 8–10 leaf stage. For growing under unheated glass or in tunnels, sow in March for April–May planting. Ensure the base of the stem is above ground when planting. Cucumbers need a higher humidity than tomatoes and are susceptible to cold draughts. Train up strings, which can be buried under the plant at planting and attached to the top wire. One system is to pinch out all side shoots and fruit until plants reach 1m height, then pinch out side shoots beyond 2 leaves, until they reach the top wire, when they are let loose. Another is the 'Y' system, which takes an early side shoot up a separate string as a second main stem. **Distance in/between rows:** 50cm.
Soils/fertility	Highly demanding, particularly of K; can abort fruits, if they run out of nutrients or become stressed. Incorporate or mulch with compost/composted manure.
Irrigation	Need lots of water, but avoid overwatering; water little and often. Useful to have overhead irrigation to increase humidity and to slow spread of red spider mite.
Weed control	Mulches or hand-hoeing.
Pests	Red spider mite is the scourge of cucumber crops. Encourage natural predators through flowering strips. Monitor closely; if problem is evident, introduce biological controls (predatory mites) early.
Diseases	Powdery mildew-resistant varieties available. Avoid root water stress. Increase ventilation, prune to increase spacing and allow airflow. If root diseases, such as *Fusarium* present, grafted varieties should be used. Compost may suppress disease problems.
Harvesting/ storage	Pick regularly every couple of days; store cold and cover boxes in plastic to prevent moisture loss.

Winter squashes/pumpkins

Winter squashes are growing in popularity. With the right choice of variety, careful harvesting and curing, they can be stored and sold through to the next harvest. They can be a profitable field crop. Pumpkins are in high demand at Hallowe'en, though many customers never eat them.

Squash at Troed y Rhiw.

Winter squashes/pumpkins	
Varieties	There are many types of winter squash available, starting with the reliable early cropping 'Red Kuri' (aka onion squash) to the superb 'Crown Prince', for roasting and long-term storage. *Cucurbita moschata* types include butternuts, which can be grown outside in southern England, but may not ripen in poor seasons. In the north, they are better grown in tunnels, planted mid-June for harvest by October. Many of the finest squashes are *Cucurbita maxima* types, which include 'Hubbard', 'Buttercup', 'Red Kuri' and 'Kabocha'. Then there are *Cucurbita pepo* types, such as 'Acorn', 'Delicata' and 'Spaghetti' squashes. The latter only reliably stores until Christmas. Pumpkins (mostly *Cucurbita pepo*) also come in a range of sizes, from smaller pie through to lantern types and monsters (usually *Cucurbita maxima*) for showing.
Sowing/ planting	Grow fast – sow into pots or large modules around 18 days before intended planting date (after last frosts). Harden off well and protect from frost/wind with fleece. **Distance in/between rows: 90–140cm.**
Soils/fertility	Prefer a well-drained sandy loam with high organic matter. Need good levels of compost, but too much N can cause excessive leaf growth at expense of fruits.
Irrigation	Needed for establishment of crop and possibly to help germination of an undersown green manure.
Weed control	If planted on the square, they can be harrowed both ways. For smaller scale, weed with wheel hoes. After a couple of weedings and once plants start to run (around 4 weeks after planting), they can be undersown with green manure.
Pests	Keep pots/modules above ground away from mice, which love the seeds. Slugs at young transplant stage.
Diseases	Powdery mildew late in the season, but can assist ripening of the fruit, as the foliage dies back.
Harvesting/ storage	Hardness of stalks and skin colour will help indicate ripeness. Handle with care; bruised fruits or ones that have lost their stalk will not store well. Pick in crates and leave in the sun or into a tunnel to cure, raised above ground. Make sure fruits go into store totally dry at 10–13°C, 60–70% humidity, checking regularly. Don't mix varieties in store.

Melons

Melons are a marginal crop, but satisfying to grow. Mostly grown in tunnels, they fit nicely after a spring-harvested crop for June planting. They can either be left to sprawl over the ground or trained like cucumbers, for which support will be needed. Purton House Organics, near Swindon, hit the tabloids when they appealed for donations of bras to support their melons!

Legumes

Broad beans

Broad beans are another cool-season vegetable that is great for the (normal) British climate. Overwintering or early sowings are harvested in time for a following crop to be grown and they can be sold when not much else is available.

Broad beans at Sandy Lane Farm.

Broad beans	
Varieties	Long-pod types contain 8–10 pods and tend to be hardier, with 'Aquadulce Claudia' the mainstay for overwintering. 'Windsor' types have shorter and wider pods, with 4–7 seeds per pod, are more suitable for spring sowing and have a fine taste.
Sowing/ planting	Sow overwintering crop in late October–November. Spring-sowing from end of February–March/April. Sowings can continue to June, if you have a market. Not much kit available for sowing; some growers adapt potato planters to sow into furrows. Can be grown in tunnels, though they get very tall and there may be more economic crops for the space. **Sowing distance**: 5–10cm apart, 7cm deep. **Distance between rows**: 45–75cm.
Soils/fertility	Need free-draining, fertile soil, but grow on a range of soils including clays; not N-demanding, so can follow a previously fertilised crop. High demand for K.
Irrigation	Only when very dry during flowering/pod formation.
Weed control	Inter-row weeding or use of comb-harrows. Overwintering crops may need hand-hoeing.
Pests	Blackfly, when beans have too much N. Usually the predators will clear them up, but if severe infestation tops can be pinched off.
Diseases	Chocolate spot in wet seasons on overwintering crops, affecting appearance of pods. Rust, particularly for later crops, as it develops quickly in warm weather.
Harvesting/ storage	Avoid letting the pods become over-mature. Picking windows 10–20 days from start of harvest, tending to go over more quickly in hot weather. In some seasons, the harvest periods of different plantings can merge together, causing gluts.

French beans/runner beans

Runner beans are a classic garden and allotment crop, which can impact on sales. French beans have perhaps more potential as a market garden crop, especially climbing types, which can be very productive in tunnels in the spring. French beans sold in supermarkets are often imported due to the amount of labour required for picking. Home-grown crops are a fresher and more sustainable alternative, which should make them attractive to your customers!

French beans at Trill Farm Garden.

French beans/runner beans	
Varieties	Though flower colour can vary, there isn't masses of variation in form or shape of runner-bean pods. French beans are more varied with dwarf and climbing types, with a range of colours and pod shapes. Climbing French beans make better use of space than dwarf types and are good for tunnels and intensive market gardens. 'Helda', 'Eva', 'Limka' and 'Cobra' are all reliable varieties for tunnels. Borlotti beans can be harvested and dried as a 'winter offer' for vegetable boxes or CSA share. Dwarf beans create less work and can be sown in succession. The variety 'Maxi' holds its beans above the plant for easy picking.
Sowing/ planting	Climbing French beans for tunnel use can be sown from late March in large modules, but must be protected from frost when planted in April. They can be grown up biodegradable twine, fixed under the module and attached to the top wire at planting, allowing for easy composting once the crop is finished. Both, French and runner beans can be sown from late April and planted outside from late May, with some protection to avoid wind damage and transplant shock. Can also be sown directly from June (when the ground is warm enough). For dwarf beans, sow every couple of weeks until mid-July. For climbing types, a couple of staggered plantings can extend the season. Various structures can be used for climbing beans outside. Long runs of wires and canes need to be strongly secured by posts and strainers. Alternatively, individual wigwams of four canes each on a square can be secured with wire tie at the top. **Sowing/planting distance in rows:** Climbing French and runner beans: 30cm. Dwarf beans: 15–24cm. **Distance between rows:** Climbing French and runner beans: in double rows 60cm apart. 90cm between as paths. Dwarf beans: 75cm.
Soils/fertility	Light loams, rich in organic matter. Ideally following a well-fertilised crop.
Irrigation	Essential. Trickle irrigation works well, but overhead irrigation can help with flower set.
Weed control	Installation of support structures can be delayed until the beans start to run, enabling inter-row cultivation or hoeing. Paths can be sown with living mulch after a couple of weedings.
Pests	Slugs and birds at establishment; cover with mesh/fleece until the plants get going. Red spider mite in tunnel crops; overhead irrigation will help, but biological controls may be needed.
Diseases	Not many problems; *Botrytis*, when plants overcrowded in humid conditions.
Harvesting/ storage	Climbing crops best picked every 2–3 days. For dwarf beans, a couple of hand-pickings or a single, destructive harvest possible (some varieties produce enough mature pods at once to make pulling the whole plant and harvesting in the shed worthwhile). At end of season, cut any ties and leave haulm in situ, as it's great for overwintering ladybirds.

Peas

Fresh peas are seldom seen in supermarkets and the required labour for hand-picking sugar snap/mangetout peas results in mainly imported produce, even during the UK season. Despite that, they can be a rewarding cool-season crop. Crops can be dual purpose – grown for pea shoots, which are a great addition to salad bags or for chefs, and then grown on for pods.

Peas: 'Kelvedon Wonder' for Seed Co-operative.

Peas	
Varieties	Round-seeded for overwintering, wrinkle-seeded less hardy. Dwarf and taller (often heritage) varieties. Mangetout and sugar snap peas possibly the most attractive for grower and customer.
Sowing/ planting	Sow round-seeded varieties like Feltham First in favoured locations outside in November, or in tunnels. Sow Mangetout and sugar snaps in tunnels in October–November and from January/February. Sow wrinkle-seeded varieties outside, as conditions allow followed by sugar snaps and mangetout. Tall varieties are good tunnel crops, as they make best use of space and can be trained up netting (old sheep flexi netting is great) or trellis of biodegradable twine, that can be composted at the end of the season. If you have hazel, you can fashion your own pea sticks. **Sowing rate**: 50–100 seeds/m. **Distance between rows:** grow on beds. Shorter varieties: 25cm. Taller varieties: 60–120cm.
Soils/fertility	Well-drained soils with good K levels. Fertility from previous crop.
Irrigation	Only necessary in very dry seasons and if growing throughout summer season.
Weed control	Due to early sowing, weed strikes prior to drilling unlikely, but if a problem, pre-emergence flame weeding possible. Once peas are 6cm tall, comb-harrows can be used. Ridging for taller varieties.
Pests	Mice: on a small scale, traps or holly leaves buried alongside seeds can help. Pea moth: main egg-laying season is June and July so early and late crops are less susceptible.
Diseases	A number of diseases affect peas, sometimes related to poor soil structure and intensive legume cropping. Spots on leaves, pods and stems can affect yield, quality and picking times. Downy mildew resistant varieties available. Powdery mildew in dry seasons.
Harvesting/ storage	Overwintering crops of fresh peas can be harvested in June–September. Dwarf crops can be cleared in one picking, while taller varieties are picked several times. Mangetout peas and sugar snaps can be harvested from late April/May in tunnels; to be picked regularly to ensure optimum size and encourage production.

Solanaceae

Aubergines

Aubergines divide growers as much as customers. While some do not consider them worth the effort or tunnel space, or have had problems with *Verticilium* wilt, others have found ways to produce good, viable crops. They can be too expensive an item to put in a set-value box – though small-fruited types might work well – but can be great for markets and shops.

Aubergines at Pitney Farm Market Garden.

Aubergines	
Varieties	Some growers swear by the F1 types like 'Falcon' and 'Black Pearl' for yield, earliness and reliability, but there are champions of the open-pollinated varieties, too, such as 'Black Beauty' and 'Long Purple'. Purple, green, yellow, white, stripy, mottled, egg-shaped and finger-shaped types available.
Sowing/ planting	Aubergines need a long season, so start in seed trays to prick out, or in modules at 24°C in January/early February. Keep warm and plant in late April–May in tunnels (fleece may be needed for cold nights). If you don't have heated propagation facilities, it may be better to buy in plants. Pinch out side shoots to allow three main stems, which can be supported by strings tied to the plant and to the top wire, or by a pair of bamboo canes crossed behind each plant and tied with a taping machine. **Planting distance in rows:** 45–65cm (in beds). **Distance between rows:** 1m (if grown in rows).
Soils/fertility	Heavy feeders, so need plentiful compost/manure; alternatively follow a green manure.
Irrigation	Drip lines under mulch is a common method, watering weekly. A drier environment helps to reduce *Botrytis*; high humidity can reduce fruit set.
Weed control	Use woven plastic, compost or living mulch.
Pests	Aphids and red spider mites. Encourage predators with flower strips. Use biological controls for spider mite such as *Phytoseiulus* at earliest opportunity.
Diseases	*Botrytis*: ventilate well, prune for airflow and increase spacing. *Verticillium* wilt: aubergines most affected crop. Use woodchip compost or other composts high in lignin to help suppress it. Use of grafted plants resistant/tolerant rootstocks can also help (and against *Botrytis*).
Harvesting/ storage	Harvest weekly from late June–late October, using secateurs. Fruits can mark easily. Yield 3–4.5kg/plant in good season.

Peppers

In the UK, peppers need to be grown under protection. They are relatively easy and are available in a range of shapes and colours. Growing them to the green stage is relatively straightforward, but there is a limited market for green peppers. It can take another month for them to ripen to their designated colour.

Troed y Rhiw farm grow some magnificent peppers.

Peppers	
Varieties	Sweet peppers range from the traditional blocky bell to the conical 'Bull's Horn' (*Corno de Torro*') types, which are gaining in popularity and can be easier to train. Speciality peppers like small round varieties for stuffing are also available. F1 types can be earlier to ripen, but there are some good open-pollinated varieties around, too. Chillies have their place, but don't overdo it – the market is small and plants can be very productive. Mild 'Padron' types for frying are also a good potential niche market.
Sowing/ planting	Peppers need a long season; sowing for heated glasshouse crops starts in November for planting in January–February. For tunnel crops, start in seed trays to prick out, or in modules at 24°C in February. Keep warm and plant in tunnels in late April–May (fleece may be needed for cold nights). Alternatively, buy in plants. After planting, allow for two main stems, which can be supported by strings tied to the plant. Alternatively, use strings either side of the bed to contain plants within. **Planting distance in rows:** 40–50cm (in beds). **Distance between rows:** 85cm (if grown in rows).
Soils/fertility	Needs plentiful compost/manure; alternatively follow a green manure. Too much fertility can cause soft growth attractive to aphids.
Irrigation	Drip lines under woven plastic is a common method, watering weekly. A drier environment helps to reduce *Botrytis*; high humidity can reduce fruit set.
Weed control	Use woven plastic, compost or living mulch.
Pests	Aphids: encourage predators with flower strips. Rodents have a knack of finding the ripening sweet peppers.
Diseases	*Botrytis:* ventilate well, prune for airflow and increase spacing. Grafted plants offer resistance to some viruses.
Harvesting/ storage	The first green peppers are ready around 8 weeks after planting in June/July. Pick the first central fruit from bell peppers before it gets jammed in. Pick a few as green, if you have a market; if left to ripen to colour, they will be ready from mid-August.

Potatoes

Potatoes are sometimes considered an arable crop rather than a vegetable, but they are essential for market sales and part of most growers' rotations. Supermarkets may only sell one or two varieties of 'multipurpose' organic potatoes (such as 'Lady Balfour'). As a market grower, you have the opportunity to offer a range of floury to waxy types for different culinary purposes. Potatoes are an easy crop to grow on a field scale, though only early crops are economic for smaller holdings. They are not so easy for no-dig systems, however.

'Sarpo' potato variety trials.

Potatoes	
Varieties	Early potatoes are the most valuable crop for the grower; when dug fresh, they are at a premium and another crop can follow them. For maincrops, blight-resistant varieties are crucial, becoming increasingly available, e.g. from Sarvari Research Trust ('Sarpo') and Continental breeding programmes, such as Agrico. Different colours offer visual appeal, but ensure that you have a range of floury, waxy and multipurpose varieties, too.
Sowing/ planting	Early potatoes can be chitted – the seed potatoes are laid out in trays with warmth and light to break dormancy. Potatoes are normally grown on ridges that are formed and planted in one pass. Planting machines can be bought cheaply second-hand, or borrowed from neighbours. On a larger scale, de-clodding and de-stoning will ensure more regular shapes and ease harvest. **Planting distance in rows:** Salad potatoes for punnets: 15cm. Early potatoes: 20–30cm. Maincrop: 25–40cm. **Distance between rows:** according to machinery used.
Soils/fertility	Nutrient-demanding and frequently grown after the fertility-building phase. In Continental Europe, they tend to avoid this due to wireworm risk. Well-composted manure should be applied to the fertility-building crop or incorporated before planting. Too much N can delay maturity of early crops.
Irrigation	Can be grown without irrigation, especially drought-tolerant varieties like some of the 'Sarpos'. However, irrigation will improve yields and quality, especially on lighter soils. Trickle irrigation can help to reduce the risk of blight to reduce scab (*see below*). Overhead irrigation through rain guns or sprinklers is simpler, but monitor moisture levels.
Weed control	Potatoes are a 'cleaning crop', as they grow fast and out-compete weeds. Weeds are best controlled with mechanical means by knocking down the ridges with harrows and then re-ridging when weeds are at 'white thread' stage. Occasional roguing of fat hen may be needed. Reduced tillage options include mulching with a thick layer of green material applied with a manure spreader.

Potatoes	
Pests	Wireworm can be very damaging. Keep well-watered. Harvest early to avoid damage and choose more tolerant varieties. Slugs, particularly on heavier soils. Some varietal differences – 'Romano' shows some resistance. Early harvesting reduces damage in the field, but remove any infested potatoes before storage. Nematodes, particularly in locations with a history of potato growing. Long rotations and resistant varieties together with good sanitation practices are the best tools. Trap crops (*see* Chapter 9).
Diseases	Late blight is the most significant disease. Apply cultural methods, such as chitting, wide spacing, trickle irrigation, mulches and early defoliation. Robust varieties, including ones acceptable to the consumer, are becoming more widely available. Common scab is favoured by high pH (apply lime after potatoes in rotation, if using) and dry conditions, so best to keep soil moist until 4 weeks after tuber initiation.
Harvesting/ storage	Early potatoes will need defoliating (topping) 2 weeks before harvest, if set skins are required. For harvesting on a small scale, a spinner can be used, which turns the potatoes out on to the surface of the ground for collection; alternatively trailed harvesters can be used. Can be bagged immediately for fresh sales. Alternatively put in trailers (avoid drops of more than 20cm to avoid bruising), where they can be cured for 2 weeks, reducing temperature gradually from 15°C for following barn or clamp storage in boxes.

Tomatoes

In the UK, tomatoes are most successfully grown in polytunnels or greenhouses, though with a changing climate it may be worth trying hardier blight-resistant varieties outside in some areas. Be sure of your market, as your crop will probably glut just as customers disappear on annual holidays, or harvest their own. Getting an early crop and selecting types that are not available in the supermarkets therefore is key. Your tomatoes will also have the added advantage of freshness and taste.

Mixed punnets of tomatoes at Daylesford Farm in the Cotswolds.

Tomatoes	
Varieties	Probably more choice of varieties than in any other crop. Standard round, cherries, cocktail, beefsteak, plum, wild, as well as red, green, striped, yellow, pink varieties available. Select for taste, robustness and yield. For yield, reliability and robustness to diseases and splitting, the F1 types are hard to beat ('Sakura', 'Sungold', 'Douglas', 'Velocity' etc.), with some good-tasting ones, too! But there are many great open-pollinated and heritage varieties, such as 'Brandywine', 'Black Russian' or 'Yellow Submarine'. Indeterminate (cordon) varieties make best use of space inside, but bush tomatoes such as 'Red Alert' can provide an early harvest in a tunnel.

(continued)

Tomatoes	
Sowing/ planting	For unheated polytunnel production, start sowing with heat from mid-February in seed trays for pricking out into pots or into modules for potting on. Plant into final destination in April/May, protecting with fleece as necessary. Strings can be buried under plants for attaching to top wire when fleece is no longer required. Side-shoot regularly to concentrate energies into fruiting. Can also be trained as double leaders.
	For heated glasshouse production, tomatoes can be sown in midsummer and transplanted in September to crop over winter and up to June. They need to be kept at around 25–30°C in the day and 15–20°C at night. **Planting distance in rows:** 45–60cm (2 rows/beds). **Distance between rows:** 85cm. Can also grow as single row on bed with 2 leaders per plant, especially when using grafted (expensive) plants.
Soils/fertility	Need plentiful compost/manure; alternatively follow a green manure. Intensive production needs high inputs of N and K.
Irrigation	Drip irrigation reduces humidity, discouraging *Botrytis* and late blight. Watering every couple of days encourages deeper rooting and prevents fruit splitting. Reduce watering towards end of season.
Weed control	Use mypex, compost or a living mulch.
Pests	Aphids, whiteflies, red spider mites; encourage predators with flower strips. Nematodes can be a problem, where no rotation or a long history of tomato growing.
Diseases	Late blight in damp summers/autumns. As with *Botrytis*, remove infections, ventilate well, prune for airflow and increase spacing. Soil-borne diseases such as *Verticillium*; using grafted plants and encouraging biological life through the use of woody-based composts helps. Viruses, often transmitted by aphids. Grafted plants offer resistances.
Harvesting/ storage	Ideally picked over every other day for uniformity. Fruits best harvested a few days before fully ripe. Pick with the calyx on, as then fruits will keep longer. Cold storage will impair flavour, so store at 10–15°C under high humidity for up to 2 weeks. Clear at end of season, when space is needed in October and allow green fruit to ripen in shallow trays, or sell for chutney making.

Umbellifers

Carrots

Carrots are one of the most ubiquitous of vegetables, always in demand but not necessarily the easiest crop. They are usually grown on a field scale on light sandy soils and it can be difficult for the market grower to compete. Early, bunched, coloured carrots or unusual shapes are a way to differentiate your offer from that of supermarkets.

Freshly pulled carrots at Trill Farm Garden.

Carrots	
Varieties	Short-rooted 'Nantes' types are generally used for early production. Short, stumpy, good-flavoured 'Chantenay' carrots, originally a summer crop, are undergoing a revival and now grown all year-round. Longer cylindrical 'Berlicum' types are the mainstay of production, often F1 hybrids. 'Autumn King' types can be large and tapered and store well. There are also coloured types, sometimes sold as 'heritage carrots', but often the result of modern breeding programmes.
Sowing/ planting	Seed can be natural, primed or pelleted for precision sowing. The first sowings can be made in January–February in tunnels, or outside under fleece in mild areas. Sow maincrop carrots end of May–early June to avoid first carrot fly generation. Early crops for bunching can be grown in tunnels from late summer through to November for overwintering. **Sowing distance:** with precision drill. Inside: 120 seeds/m. Outside: 33–45/m. **Distance between rows:** depending on system. Beds, or on flat: 25–38cm. Ridges: 60–70cm apart.
Soils/fertility	Light sandy to medium loams. Heavy clay soils, needing excessive cultivations to produce fine seedbeds, are best avoided. Carrots are not highly nutrient-demanding and it is best to rely on fertility applied to previous crop.
Irrigation	Possibly needed to flush weeds in stale seedbeds and for germination, if dry, but be careful to avoid capping. In dry seasons and light soils irrigate for yield.
Weed control	Stale seedbeds/thermal weeding essential, followed by inter-row weeding. Optimum time for hand-weeding is 4 weeks after 50% crop emergence. Crop covers can increase weed growth by 4 times, so regular monitoring is needed.
Pests	Carrot fly is the major pest. Sowing times and crop covers are the main tools, used together with forecasting services. Early harvest can avoid late damage. Cutworms can be managed by irrigation.
Diseases	*Alternaria* blight is seed-borne and can cause losses during germination/emergence. Cavity spot is more a problem in conventional production; long rotations reduce risk.
Harvesting/ storage	Harvesting is easiest on lighter soils. Can be machine-harvested, undercut and/or hand-lifted, depending on scale. Carrots store best and keep longer when not washed. Can be stored in ground until Christmas, but losses to slugs and carrot fly possible. For winter storage in ground, carrots can be covered with black plastic and a thick layer of straw.

Celeriac

Celeriac can be a useful addition to the winter box or shop display. It needs a long season to achieve a good size.

Celeriac at Bennison Farm CSA.

Celeriac	
Varieties	Limited choice of varieties/types.
Sowing/ planting	Start early with heat (15°C) from February in modules or blocks for planting (shallowly) from May to mid-June. Cold nights early on can cause bolting. **Distance in/between rows:** 30–40cm.
Soils/fertility	Celeriac is a marshland plant, so it likes fertile, deep, rich soil with plenty of organic matter. Doesn't tolerate compaction. Sensitive to low boron levels, especially on sandy soils.
Irrigation	Needs plentiful water throughout the season.
Weed control	Needs good early inter-row weed control or mulching, thereafter competitive against weeds.
Pests	Celery leaf miner is increasingly problematic. Encourage predators with flower strips. Carrot fly damage may need trimming off.
Diseases	Celery leaf spot (*Septoria*) usually less than with celery.
Harvesting/ storage	Bulks up most from September and can be harvested until October, but will need protection from frosts. When harvesting, use a sharp knife to trim mass of knobbly roots and tops. Can be clamped for winter use, trimming tops only; trim roots, when comes out of storage.

Celery

Celery is a flexible and useful crop, which can be grown successively, starting early in tunnels through to the autumn outside.

Celery at Pitney Farm Market Garden.

Celery	
Varieties	Self-blanching types are standard for summer to autumn cropping. Good-quality F1 varieties available. Trenching types, which are hardier, have more or less disappeared due to plentiful cheap imports, but are more work. Leaf celery can be grown for salad mixes/bunching and will overwinter in tunnels.
Sowing/ planting	Start early with heat (15°C) in January/February in modules or blocks, planting mid-March in tunnels under fleece for harvesting late May or June. Cold nights early on can cause bolting. For outside crop, sow in modules or blocks from early March–May for harvests through to autumn. **Distance in/between rows:** 30cm; plant self-blanching types in a block.
Soils/fertility	Celery is a marshland plant, so it likes fertile, deep, rich soil with plenty of organic matter. Doesn't tolerate compaction/poor soil structure.
Irrigation	Needs plentiful water throughout the season.
Weed control	Needs good early inter-row weed control or mulching, thereafter competitive against weeds. Good plant for intercropping with leeks or spring-planted garlic.
Pests	Celery leaf miner; encourage predators with flower strips. Slugs.
Diseases	Celery leaf spot (*Septoria*) can be severe. Healthy seed (hot-water treated) essential.
Harvesting/ storage	Use a good, sharp knife. Harvest whole heads from late May inside to October in the field. Put into plastic sleeves or pack tightly into crates to avoid moisture loss; remove field heat by cold storing.

Fennel

Florence fennel, the bulb vegetable rather than the herb, is increasingly popular and relatively straightforward to grow, if you choose the right varieties. It needs regular watering. If you can avoid it bolting, a well-grown fennel is a beautiful thing! Fresh leaves can be used in salad mixes.

Fennel for wholesale at Strawberry Fields.

Fennel	
Varieties	For early crops you need bolt-resistant types, often hybrids.
Sowing/ planting	Start early crops from mid-February in modules/blocks, sowing every 2 weeks until mid-June for the last field crop and twice in July for late tunnel crops. Avoid checks in growth – root-bound modules establish poorly and may bolt. Direct-drilling possible in June–July. **Sowing rate**: 18–20 seeds/m. **Distance in/between rows:** Early crops: 30cm. Field and late crops in tunnels: 30–40cm.
Soils/fertility	Prefers light soils with good moisture-holding capacity and reasonable fertility, manured for previous crop.
Irrigation	Needs plentiful water throughout the season. Mulching is beneficial.
Weed control	Needs early inter-row weed control or mulching, thereafter competitive against weeds.
Pests	Slugs can be problematic at planting. Rabbits love fennel, so will need to be excluded. Late sowings or plantings should avoid main carrot fly generation.
Diseases	Root rots can be an issue in waterlogged soils.
Harvesting/ storage	Will take minor frosts, but will need protection or harvest before hard frosts. When harvesting, use a sharp knife to cut off 1cm above ground and take off the scrappy outer leaves. A second harvest for salad bags can be made from regrowth, if plants are left in situ, which can be useful during the hungry gap (in tunnels). For marketing, fennel can be sold with its leaves on, accompanied by a recipe for fennel pesto.

Parsnips

This traditional root vegetable is a useful winter staple, which can be stored in the field and harvested as required from September to March. The trend is towards later sowing and smaller roots.

Sandy Lane Farm parsnips.

Parsnips	
Varieties	Not masses of choice in varieties, but shorter types available for shallower soils.
Sowing/ planting	Direct-drilled into beds or ridges from April (in Scotland) to early June in the south of England. Germination faster in warm soils. **Sowing rate**: 15–25 seeds/m. **Distance between rows:** 45cm/70cm on ridges.
Soils/fertility	Will grow on a range of soils, but prefers light, deep well-drained loams. Avoid manures, as roots will fork, though green-waste compost is okay.
Irrigation	Possibly needed to flush weeds in stale seedbeds and for germination, if dry, but be careful to avoid capping. Possibly required to increase yield.
Weed control	Stale seedbeds/thermal weeding advisable, followed by inter-row weeding.
Pests	Carrot fly is the major pest. Sowing times and crop covers are the main tools, used together with forecasting services. Early harvest can avoid late damage.
Diseases	Canker is caused by various pathogens and can get worse with long storage in the ground. Some varietal resistance. Avoid damage to the crowns when weeding and ridge up to cover crowns with soil.
Harvesting/ storage	Harvesting is easiest on lighter soils. Can be machine-harvested, undercut and/or hand-lifted depending on scale. Best harvested after the first frosts (for flavour) until late April, when they begin to shoot and become woody. Will store for 2–3 weeks in a clamp, or up to 6 months in a cold store (unwashed).

Poaceae

Sweetcorn

Gone are the days when you could only reliably grow sweetcorn south of a line between the Severn and the Wash. Thanks to breeding, the use of transplants and fleece, sweetcorn can be a successful crop almost anywhere. Due to it not belonging to any of the main-crop family groups, sweetcorn can be placed any-where in the rotation. It can be intercropped with squashes, or undersown with clovers. The advent of super-sweet varieties means that you no longer need to have the pot of water on the boil when you go to pick it, but freshness can still give the market

Sweetcorn 'Lisanco' bred under the Open Source Seeds licence.

grower an advantage. Most supermarket sweetcorn is stripped of its leaves and wrapped in plastic, but sweetcorn comes naturally ready wrapped!

Sweetcorn	
Varieties	Most breeding efforts have gone into hybrid super sweets; until recently, with the dehybridisation pro-gramme of Sativa and the Open Source 'Lisanco', there have been few reliable open-pollinated varieties.
Sowing/ planting	Sow into large modules/blocks 4 weeks before planting (when frost-free). Use early varieties for first sowing dates and early and later varieties together afterwards to spread the harvest. Avoid checks to growth by covering with fleece after planting, if cold. Plant deeply for access to moisture and to prevent rooks pulling out the plants. Direct drilling can start when soil temperatures reach 12°C. **Sowing rate**: 5–7 seeds/m. **Distance in/between rows:** 25cm × 60cm planted in a block.
Soils/fertility	Needs a deep, well-drained soil with moderate levels of P and K. Demanding of N. Best early in rotation, or after an overwintering vetch.
Irrigation	Drought-tolerant, though yield may be improved by irrigation in dry years.
Weed control	Stale seedbeds/thermal weeding advisable for direct drilling. Inter-row weeding with ridging or soil thrown into rows for intra-row weed control. Can be undersown with legumes (clover/trefoil etc.) after a couple of weedings.
Pests	Rooks can pull out transplants/seedlings. Aphids are sometimes a problem, but only in the outer layers of cobs. Electric fencing advisable against deer/badgers, which love the cobs.
Diseases	Few problems. Occasionally smut, but usually isolated plants.
Harvesting/ storage	Harvest when the silky tassels turn brown/black, cobs are full and colour is 'right'; until you get your eye in, strip back leaves a little and check for 'milkiness' by piercing corn with fingernail. Each planting needs to be picked over at least twice. If the plants are left in place after harvesting, the stalks provide good habitats for overwintering ladybirds.

Miscellaneous

Jerusalem artichokes

Some consider Jerusalem artichokes to be a perennial vegetable, but for growing purposes it is better to grow them as an annual crop. They can be planted with a potato planter in the spring and left to it until autumn, when the tops can be cut down. Harvest as required over the winter. Pigs can do a good job of cleaning up after harvest.

Agretti

Also known as saltwort or *Salsola soda*, agretti is a samphire-like vegetable that is increasing in popularity. It makes a good intercrop in a polytunnel and can also be grown outside. Sow in February/March in modules and plant out 30cm apart.

The 'wacky' stuff

There is an almost infinite list of things you *can* grow – lemongrass, ginger, Aztec spinach (huauzontle), achocha (try the giant Bolivian achocha!), magentaspeen (giant goosefoot), leaf amaranth, to name but a few.

Perennial vegetables

There are many reasons why perennial vegetables make sense. They are resilient, often with deep roots, being able to withstand droughts better than annual crops. Perennials usually require less work and soil-damaging cultivations. What's more, they often burst into life, when there is not much else around – the hungry gap. There are a lot more choices than you may think and we have moved beyond the question, which I found on a card of an old Trivial Pursuit game: 'What is the only perennial vegetable?' I think the answer was asparagus!

Asparagus

Asparagus is a great crop for those with sandy soils, or at least well-drained loams, cropping from late April/early May to midsummer; 1,500 plants will be enough to supply 500 boxes with 500g a week during the season. Plant them 30–45cm apart in rows 90cm apart; they can last 10–15 years.

Weed control is not easy as asparagus is shallow-rooted, so mechanical weeding needs to be gentle. At Kensons Farm in Wiltshire, they try to keep the beds as clean as possible until after harvest. They then mulch the beds with green-waste compost and sow short-term summer green manures in the paths, which are cultivated in before the next season harvest begins.

Cut down the fronds in late autumn. The main pest is asparagus beetle; ladybird larvae, predatory chalcid wasps and chickens are your allies. Harvesting can start 48 months after sowing, or 36 months if planting crowns.

Globe artichokes

Globe artichokes are a short-lived perennial, normally only cropped for around three years, so new plantings annually are recommended for continuity. Can be grown from seed sown in blocks or modules in late February, planting in late May 90cm apart. Good, fertile well-drained soil is essential, with plentiful additions of organic matter.

Globe artichokes will need protecting over winter from frosts with a thick layer of straw. Inter-row cultivations or hoeing keep weeds down and they should be mulched with compost in the spring. Harvest the immature buds from July to the autumn, cutting the king heads first, followed by smaller side shoots. Cut the flower stalks back before the autumn winds rock and damage the plants.

Other perennial vegetables

There are plenty of up and coming unusual perennial vegetables, many championed by Mandy Barber of Incredible Vegetables in Devon.

- Caucasian spinach (*Hablitzia tamnoides*) is a long-lived, very hardy perennial that produces heart-shaped spinach-like leaves on a vine. Early shoots can be harvested and eaten like asparagus. It thrives in shade and can be harvested from February to June. It can take three years to establish, but can go on for decades.
- Perennial kales and collard greens are huge perennial brassicas, which are grown from seed or cuttings. They can be very productive for up to five years and tend to be more resilient to pests and diseases than regular brassicas.
- Perennial nine-star broccoli produces a cauliflower-like head surrounded by smaller florets, that can be harvested each spring for up to five years.
- There are lots of perennial leafy greens, including Good King Henry, sea beet, sea kale, hostas and many more.
- Tuber options include tubers, such as yacon, oca, skirret, mashua, hog peanut, earthnut pea, Chinese artichoke, sweet potatoes, groundnut (*Apios americana*), as well as the aquatic wapato and chi-gu. These open up a wealth of possibilities for marketing to adventurous cooks and chefs.
- Perennial alliums such as Babington leek, three-cornered leek, wild garlic, Welsh onion and Poireau Perpétuel, a wild French perennial leek, offer a world of pungent potential.

Caucasian spinach (*Hablitzia tamnoides*) trained up vines.

Groundnut (*Apios americana*) tubers.

Chapter Fourteen

Economic and Environmental Sustainability

This may not be the most glamorous side of growing, but it is essential. To grow sustainably, you need to be financially sustainable. Good record-keeping is important to enable you to see how well your business is performing, to analyse and to make changes as and when required.

Record-keeping

Good record-keeping is also vital for organic certification purposes. Organic certification is an auditing process. Like many growers, I used to spend days and nights prior to the annual inspection feverishly gathering information from notebooks, invoices and transferring them to record sheets. The inspector will need to see:

- up to date farm map and field details
- any derogations applied for and correspondence with organic control body
- purchase invoices for inputs
- sales records/invoices out
- marketing materials
- certificates/trading schedules for organic suppliers
- separation plan (if both organic and conventional management on same land)
- cleaning procedures and records for storage facilities/equipment
- vermin control records
- complaints register

- crop-management plan (including rotations)
- field records/plant-raising (including inputs and yields)
- seeds/transplants/perennials (purchase records, labels, derogations)
- manure management (applications/storage)
- details of imported nutrients (bought-in manures, fertilizers, green-waste compost and so on, with non-GMO declarations where applicable)
- pest and disease control and application records
- details of growing media used.

While it may seem like a lot of bureaucracy, the data accumulated, if collected the right way, can not only save time and stress during the inspection process, but also be a useful tool to compare yields and inputs between years and differentiate spending patterns of customers.

Excel spreadsheets are the simplest way to organise your records. Ideally, they need to be regularly updated, with inputs, planting data, yields from the field and so on being entered, before the scraps of paper get lost. One option is to use a Cloud-based crop-recording system, such as Google Forms, which enables simple data entry direct from a phone or tablet in the field or in the packing shed into an online spreadsheet. It is a free tool and is easy to set up, with YouTube tutorials available online. Different team members can input to the same form through a weblink, or via the Google Forms app.

OPPOSITE: Where is the pot of gold to be found? Rainbow at Strode Valley Organics in north Somerset.

Box files of records, ready for the organic certification inspection at Glebelands Market Garden.

Economic analysis of farm performance

Gross and net margins can be calculated on an enterprise level, on a rotational level, or on a farm level. Deciding how you allocate your costs fairly to each enterprise can be difficult, however, and somewhat arbitrary. While looking at crop margins can be useful, some crops may have values to the farm beyond their financial returns – they might draw in customers to your shop or market stall, or help to provide variety to your boxes when not much else is available. It is wise to look at performance across a rotation, as you need to factor in the fertility-building crops.

As well as choice of crops and enterprises, there are many other factors impacting on farm performance:

Internal factors: These the grower has some control over. The biggest cost will be labour. The more that labour is directed towards planting and harvesting rather than weeding, the better. Factors that contribute to the quality of crops, such as optimum spacing and fertility, will impact on profitability.

External factors: While it may be possible to influence prices for local marketing, the prevailing market conditions will affect most growers. Recessions will impact on sales and you may have to work harder to convince your customers of the values of organic. The cost of fuels and fertilizers due to energy crises can impact conventional production more than organic, so it may be more the perception or prejudice, that organic is more expensive, which is the hurdle to overcome.

Relationships between enterprises: Enterprises can be competing, for instance requiring labour, machinery input or a place in the rotation at the same time. Similarly, enterprises may be complementary, such as crops benefiting the rotation in terms of fertility or weed control (for example, potatoes), or vegetables harvested during the hungry gap. Supplementary enterprises are those that have no impact on others. An example are perennial crops, which are outside the rotation and harvested during the hungry gap.

Full-cost accounting

In this complete-enterprise costing approach, all the fixed costs are allocated to individual enterprises. This enables the calculation of costs per unit of output produced on the farm and the calculation of break-even budgets. They can be useful, where contract prices are being fixed. It can, however, be difficult to implement and requires a great deal of detail to be recorded. Net profits per enterprise can also underplay the interrelated nature of organic systems.

Economic performance of small organic horticultural holdings

The economic performance of smaller organic vegetable producers can be hugely varied according to soils, locations, systems, skills and degree of mechanisation. While on a larger-scale organic yields

Planning ahead is vital. Good coffee is needed alongside planning tools and resources. Note a well-thumbed copy of Crowood's Organic Vegetable Production book to the right!

achieve 50–60 per cent of conventional yields, on a smaller scale yields can sometimes out-perform conventional, due to higher labour inputs, multiple pickings and a higher proportion of crop marketed.

A survey carried out by Organic Market Garden Data (OMG! Data) project (2019/20) reported in the *Organic Farm Management Handbook* showed an average turnover of £90,000/ha for smaller-scale growers, with staff levels of 1.8 Full-time Equivalent/ha and staff costs being 60 per cent of turnover. Small horticultural businesses can be profitable with good management skills and higher-value outlets.

Farm sustainability

There is an increasing number of tools available to help assess the sustainability of your business. It is important to be able to demonstrate that organic businesses are helping to tackle the big issues of climate change, increasing biodiversity, creating employment, enhancing food security and sovereignty, all while producing nutritious, affordable food. Not only can tools help us to make improvements to ensure that we are doing better, but they can help to provide evidence to policy-makers, customers and others that we are providing Public Goods (benefits to all). Whether public money is set aside to support Public Goods provision or not, it reminds us of why we do what we do.

Carbon footprinting

With rising awareness of global warming, carbon has become literally a hot topic. All businesses should aim towards 'net zero' and try to achieve a balance between the greenhouse gases put into the atmosphere and those taken out. In principle, organic growing businesses can even go beyond net zero and sequester more carbon than they emit. Grower Jonathan Smith, who founded the Farm Carbon Toolkit, emphasises a number of reasons why you should understand your business's carbon footprint and measure it regularly:

- You can't manage what you don't measure.
- It gives you great insight into your business.
- There's a moral obligation to do the right thing (organic growers tend to be quite good at this one).
- Saving carbon can save you money.
- Environmental credentials are good for business.
- Legislation enforcing change will probably be coming anyway at some point – get ahead of the game.

There are several free online carbon calculators, including the Farm Carbon Calculator, developed by Jonathan. They involve entering data into a form or spreadsheet, which then produces a report showing the carbon balance, comprising emissions and sequestration. There are, Jonathan says, a number of ways in which growers can reduce their carbon footprints, including cutting fuel use, using and/or generating renewable electricity, keeping buildings and machinery going as long as possible and ensuring that vegetable distribution is done as efficiently as possible. There are also opportunities to sequester carbon with perennial crops, woodland and hedges, as well as increasing organic matter through whatever means possible.

Circular economy

The Ellen MacArthur Foundation states that the circular economy is a systems-solution framework, which tackles global challenges like climate change, biodiversity loss, waste and pollution. In addition to carbon footprinting, it also includes Life Cycle Analysis (LCA) and understanding the environmental and social impacts of the business. The approach also includes co-creation, that is, engaging with customers to influence what crops or varieties are grown, products sold, prices and size of bags used and so on. It also focuses on materials bought in, recycling as much as possible and reducing single-use plastics. In that context, ask yourself whether crop wastes and out-grades are being used as effectively as possible.

Sources of information and advice change like the shifting of sands, especially in the digital age. There are many free resources online, but can you trust them? Here are a few pointers to reliable information, either research-based or based on growers' experiences. Not all the sources below are exclusively organic, so you will need to filter out what is relevant to you.

Agricology

Agricology is an independent knowledge platform, supporting UK farmers and growers to transition to more sustainable and resilient farming systems. The website contains a huge wealth of resources, case studies, videos and podcasts on agroecological practices and it can be searched or browsed by theme and filtered for compatibility with organic standards.

www.agricology.co.uk/

Agriculture and Horticulture Development Board (AHDB)

The AHDB is a statutory levy board, funded by farmers, growers and others in the supply chain. However, in 2022 Defra ended the levy in the horticulture sector, so activity has been wound down. The website contains now-archived but none the less very useful information, guides, resources, tools and data collated from the research and development work funded up to 2023.

www.ahdb.org.uk/

Biodynamic Association

Gateway to Biodynamic Certification, the Biodynamic Land Trust, the Biodynamic Agriculture College (BDAC), resources and more.

www.biodynamic.org.uk/

CSA Network UK

The CSA Network is a multi-stakeholder cooperative, dedicated to supporting and promoting Community Supported Agriculture (CSA) in the UK. It offers training as well as mentoring and support for establishing, running and expanding CSAs. It also hosts a great resource library, including an A–Z guide, case studies and masterclasses.

www.communitysupportedagriculture.org.uk/

Defra

Defra is the UK Government department responsible for safeguarding the natural environment, supporting the UK's food and farming industry and sustaining a thriving rural economy. Business advice, payments and support for farmers (England).

www.gov.uk/environment/food-and-farming

Garden Organic

A charity, formerly known as the Henry Doubleday Research Association, Garden Organic promotes organic growing and composting, citizen science and research, as well as seed conservation through the Heritage Seed Library. Useful knowledge hub containing archived research.

www.gardenorganic.org.uk/

Horticulture Wales

Horticulture Wales is a project funded by the European Agricultural Fund for Rural Development and the Welsh Government, managed and delivered by Glyndwr University. It aims to create improved access to local produce, stronger supply chains and increased collaboration.

www.horticulturewales.co.uk/

Innovative Farmers

Innovative Farmers is a not-for-profit membership network for all farmers and growers who are running on farm trials, on their own terms. Archive of trial results.

www.innovativefarmers.org/

Landworkers' Alliance (LWA)

The LWA is a union of farmers, growers, foresters and land-based workers with a mission to improve the livelihoods of their members and create a better food- and land-use system for everyone. While a lot of the LWA's resources are policy-focused, there are also many useful publications regarding business planning and marketing, specifically also for new entrants and so on.

www.landworkersalliance.org.uk/

LANTRA

The 'one-stop shop' for land-based training and careers.

www.lantra.co.uk

Nourish Scotland

Nourish Scotland is a charity focusing on food policy and practice. Useful resources and newsletter.

www.nourishscotland.org/

OASIS

OASIS offers support for farmers considering organic conversion and provides management advice and information for organic farmers.

www.organicinfo.org.uk/

OF&G (Organic Farmers & Growers)

Organic control body and certifier for Pasture for Life and other sustainable land-use schemes.

www.ofgorganic.org/

Open Food Network

Resources hub for everything you may need to manage a community food enterprise in the UK, from setting up to marketing advice.

www.openfoodnetwork.org.uk/

Organic Farm Knowledge

The Organic Farm Knowledge platform provides access to a wide range of tools and resources about organic farming and promotes the exchange of knowledge among farmers, farm advisers and scientists, with the aim of increasing the productivity, quality and sustainability of organic farming across Europe.

www.organic-farmknowledge.org/

Organic Growers Alliance (OGA)

The OGA is the only UK organisation that specifically represents the interests of organic growers. It is a peer-to-peer support network, run by growers for growers. The OGA is an ideal place to exchange information and experiences. Resources include:

- Quarterly magazine *The Organic Grower*, edited by the author, featuring articles from growers and others on a variety of relevant issues, as well as topical research and news from across Europe and beyond.
- The members area of the website features technical articles, reports and the indexed back catalogue of the magazine (back to 2007).
- Regular Organic Matters Conference with technical content, webinars and farm walks.
- Archive of webinars and conference sessions on YouTube.
- OGA forum for discussion and jobs/opportunities.

www.organicgrowersalliance.co.uk/

Organic Research Centre

The UK's only independent research organisation institution dedicated to organic farming. Produces bulletins, technical guides and the Organic Farm Management Handbook. Hosts Agricology, and administers the Dean Organic Fund.

www.organicresearchcentre.com/

Scotland's Farm Advisory Service (FAS)

The FAS is part of the Scottish Rural Development Programme (SRDP), which is funded by the Scottish Government, providing mentoring and land-management planning, information and resources aimed at increasing the profitability and sustainability of farms and crofts. Part of its remit is to provide organic advice and information.

www.fas.scot/

Scotland's Rural College (SRUC)

The SRUC runs an Organic Farming Masters programme with part-time distance learning. It also has an advisory arm called SAC Consulting, which hosts a number of technical resources related to organic farming and is a partner in Scotland's Farm Advisory Service.

www.sruc.ac.uk/

Scottish Organic Producers Association (SOPA)

Offers organic certification through OF&G; its Support Team provides free advice, business support and mentoring to SOPA Members.

www.sopa.org.uk/

The Scottish Organic Stakeholders Group (SOSG)

SOSG brings organic growers, farmers, processors and retailers together with organic certifying bodies and campaigning groups. It works with the Scottish Government on organic policy and growing the organic sector. It provides updates on progress and relevant information, both direct and through partner groups, including the Organic Growers Alliance.

www.organicstakeholders.scot/

The Seed Sovereignty Programme of UK and Ireland

The Seed Sovereignty Programme from The Gaia Foundation aims to support a biodiverse and resilient seed system and small-scale seed production across Britain and Ireland. Its website contains technical guides on seed production for growers, webinars and useful links.

www.seedsovereignty.info

Soil Association

In addition to its certification activities, the Soil Association charity has a Farming and Land Use team with farming and horticultural advisors. Licensees receive a technical services package, which includes the quarterly *Organic Farming* magazine, market reports, technical guides and information sheets. These services are also available to those not certified with the organisation through the Soil Association Producer Membership scheme.

www.soilassociation.org

Tyfu Cymru (Grow Wales)

Tyfu Cymru delivers industry-specific support and training to build the capacity and capability of the Welsh horticultural sector.

www.tyfucymru.co.uk/

UK Organic Market Gardeners Facebook page

This is a private group (you can request to join) with around 2,000 members and provides a lively forum for growers to pose questions and exchange information.

Vegan Organic Network

The Vegan Organic Network is the only organisation in the UK solely working for food to be grown the veganic way. It delivers resources, information on stockfree organic standards and certification and how to access advice.

www.veganorganic.net/

Chapter 1

Deane, T., 'The Heart of the Grower', *The Organic Grower* (No.1, Summer 2007, p.20)

FAO, *Agroecology Knowledge Hub* (accessed March 2023 through the FAO website http://www.fao.org/agroecology/en)

Frost, J., 'An Introduction to Korean Natural Farming', *Growing for Market* (October 2018, accessed March 2023 through the Growing For Market website https://www.growingformarket.com/articles/an-introduction-to-Korean-Natural-Farming)

Frost, J., *The Living Soil Handbook* (Chelsea Green, 2021)

Gonçalves Geiger, A. *et al.* 'Vegan Organic farming', *The Organic Grower* (No.55, Summer 2021, p.11)

IFOAM Organics International, 'The Four Principles of Organic Agriculture' (accessed March 2023 through the IFOAM website https://www.ifoam.bio/why-organic/shaping-agriculture/four-principles-organic)

Lampkin, N. *et al.*, *The Role of Agroecology in Sustainable Intensification* (Report for the Land Use Policy Group, Organic Research Centre and Game & Wildlife Conservation Trust, 2015)

La Via Campesina (accessed March 2023 through the La Via Campesina website https://viacampesina.org/en/)

Mollison, B., *Introduction to Permaculture* (Tagari Publications, 1991)

Organic Research Centre, 'Towards Farmer Principles of Health' (Organic Research Centre, 2016 accessed March 2023 through the ORC website https://www.organicresearchcentre.com/manage/authincludes/article_uploads/project_outputs/Health_booklet.pdf)

Sattler, F. and von Wistinghausen E., *Bio-Dynamic Farming Practice* (BDAA, 1989)

Sumption, P., 'Shumei – Naturally Different', *The Organic Grower* (No.28, Autumn 2014, p.34)

The Carbon Underground (accessed March 2023 through The Carbon Underground website https://thecarbonunderground.org/our-initiative/definition/)

Chapter 2

Borgstrom, G., *The Hungry Planet, the Modern World at the Edge of Famine* (Macmillan, 1965)

Davies, G. and Lennartsson, M. (eds), *Organic Vegetable Production: A Complete Guide* (Crowood, 2005)

Frost, J., *The Living Soil Handbook: The No-Till Grower's Guide to Ecological Market Gardening* (Chelsea Green, 2021)

Jeavons, J., *How to Grow More Vegetables* (Ten Speed Press, 1974)

Kuepper, G., *Farming with Walk-Behind Tractors* (Kerr Center for Sustainable Agriculture, 2018)

Leslie, S., *The New Horse-Powered Farm* (Chelsea Green, 2013)

Organic Growers Alliance, 'Small-scale machinery', *The Organic Grower* (No.56, Autumn 2021, p.27)

Raskin, B. and Osborn, S. (eds), *The Agroforestry Handbook* (Soil Association, 2019)

Woodward, W., 'Participatory certification is needed to protect the integrity of organic growers', *The Organic Grower* (No.53, Winter 2020, p.33)

Chapter 3

Aplin, J., 'Horticultural Hindsights: Jim Aplin', *The Organic Grower* (No.45, Winter 2018, p.5)

Beigel, S., 'Finding the Perfect Match between Farmers and New Entrants', *The Organic Grower* (No.58, Spring 2022, p.8)

Biodynamic Land Trust (accessed March 2023 through the Biodynamic Land Trust website https://biodynamiclandtrust.org.uk/)

Bowers, R., 'Horticultural Hindsights: Ric Bowers', *The Organic Grower* (No.56, Autumn 2021, p.30)

Chapter 7 (accessed March 2023 through The Land is Ours website https://tlio.org.uk/chapter7/)

Cooper, O., '8 steps for Farm Succession Planning', *Farmers Weekly Interactive* (*Farmers Weekly*, 2015, accessed March 2023 through the *Farmers Weekly Interactive* website https://www.fwi.co.uk/business/8-steps-farm-succession-planning)

CSA Network UK, 'S: Starting up', *Resource A–Z* (accessed March 2023 through the CSA website https://communitysupportedagriculture.org.uk/resource-a-z/)

Dean Organic Fund (accessed March 2023 through the Organic Research Centre website: https://www.organicresearchcentre.com/farming-organically/the-dean-organic-fund/)

Gladwell, M., *Outliers: The Story of Success* (Back Bay Books, 2011)

Lampkin, N. *et al.*, *2017 Organic Farm Management Handbook* (ORC, 2017)

Landworkers' Alliance, *How to Set up a Farmstart: A Handbook for Establishing and Running an Incubator Farm Site* (LWA, 2019)

Landworkers' Alliance, *Supporting the Next Generation of Farmers* (LWA, 2019)

Landworkers' Alliance, *New Entrants Survey April–June 2020* (LWA, 2020)

Landworkers' Alliance, *New Entrants to Agroecological Farming. Example Business Start-up Costs and the Case for Public Support.* (LWA, 2021)

Landworkers Alliance, *Business Planning Guide for Ecological Farm and Forestry Businesses* (LWA, 2022)

Landworkers' Alliance, *Agroecology Traineeship Programme. Horticulture Curriculum* (LWA, 2022)

Laughton *et al.*, *Planning Reform to Create Sustainable Farming Livelihoods in the Countryside* (LWA, 2020)

Rodker, J., 'Online and Farm-based Market Garden Courses: A Review (Part One)', *The Organic Grower* (No.46, Spring 2019, p.32). 'Part Two', *The Organic Grower* (No.47, Summer 2019, p.10)

Soil Association Land Trust (accessed March 2023 through the Soil Association website https://www.soilassociation.org/the-land-trust/)

Sumption, P., 'FarmStart: Growing Veg and Growers', *The Organic Grower* (No.57, Winter 2021, p.12)

Wetherell, S., 'The Forgotten Role of the Council Smallholding in Accessing Land for Agroecology' (Sustainable Farming Campaign Blog, 2021, accessed March 2023 through the Sustain website https://www.sustainweb.org/blogs/aug21-council-smallholding-urban-agroecology/)

Willis, G., 'Council Farms: What are They, and Why are They so Special?' (CPRE, 2018, accessed March 2023 through the CPRE website https://www.cpre.org.uk/explainer/county-farms-explainer/)

Yates, J., 'Share Farming: How it Works and Why it Could Reshape Farming', *Farmers Weekly Interactive* (*Farmers Weekly*, 2018, accessed March 2023 through the *Farmers Weekly Interactive* website https://www.fwi.co.uk/business/business-management/partnerships/share-farming-how-it-works-and-why-it-could-reshape-farming#tabs-1)

Chapter 4

Barn Owl Trust (accessed March 2023 through the Barn Owl Trust website https://www.barnowltrust.org.uk/barn-owl-facts/barn-owl-hunting-feeding/)

Billington, U., 'Pond Life Revives Hope for On-Farm Wildlife' (ARC 2020, 2021, accessed March 2023 through the ARC 2020 website https://www.arc2020.eu/uk-pond-life-revives-hope-for-on-farm-wildlife/)

Coed Cymru, *Shelterbelts. A guide to increasing farm productivity* (Coed Cymru, accessed March 2023 through the Coed Cymru website https://coed.cymru/images/user/IAR%20Shelterbelts%202016%20v3.pdf)

Coleman, E., *The New Organic Grower* (Chelsea Green, 3rd edition, 2018)

Collyns, K., *Gardening for Profit: From Home Plot to Market Garden* (Green Books, 2013)

Deane, T., 'Wireworm – in Theory and Practice', *The Organic Grower* (No.5, Summer 2008, p.32)

EIP-AGRI, 'Controlling Wireworm in Potatoes', *The Organic Grower* (No.61, Winter 2022, p.18)

Dollimore, P. Irrigation. *A Guide for New Growers.* (CSA Network UK, Gaia Foundation's Seed Sovereignty Programme and the Organic Growers Alliance, 2023)

Environment Agency and Defra, 'Check if you Need an Environmental Permit' (accessed March 2023 through the gov.uk website https://www.gov.uk/guidance/check-if-you-need-a-licence-to-abstract-water)

FarmHack UK (accessed March 2023 through the FarmHack UK facebook site https://www.facebook.com/groups/FarmHackUK/)

Geen, N. and Firth, C., 'The Vegetable Market and Marketing' in Davies, G. and Lennartsson, M., *Organic Vegetable Production: A Complete Guide* (Crowood, 2005)

GWCT, 'Beetle Banks´ (accessed March 2023 through the GWCT website https://www.gwct.org.uk/farming/advice/sustainable-farming/beetle-banks/)

Hayes, M., *et al.* (eds), *Organic Market Garden Start-up Manual* (GAK Nonprofit, 2013)

L'Atelier Paysan (accessed March 2023 through the L'Atelier Paysan website https://www.latelierpaysan.org/English)

Meyer- Graft, I., 'Bats on your Holding', *The Organic Grower* (No.22, Spring 2013, p.24)

Price, D., 'A New Pond on your Farm', *The Organic Grower* (No.60, Autumn 2022, p.26)

Sumption, P., 'Eliot Coleman at the AGM' *The Organic Grower* (No.59, Summer 2022, p.7)

Tolhurst, I., 'Shelter on the Farm Offers Better Crop Yields', *The Organic Grower* (No.24, Autumn 2014, p.34)

Tolhurst, I., 'Beetles You Can Bank On', *The Organic Grower* (No.32, Autumn 2014, p.14)

Tolhurst, I., 'Conversion of Pasture Land to Vegetable Production' in Tolhurst, I., *Back to Earth* (Tolhurst Organic Partnership CIC, 2016)

Weatherhead, K. *et al.*, *Thinking About an Irrigation Reservoir?* (Cranfield University/Environment Agency, 2013)

Chapter 5

ADAS, *Understanding Soil Fertility in Organically Farmed Soils* (Final Project Report to Defra, Project OF0164, ADAS, 2002 accessed March 2023 through the Organic Eprints website https://orgprints.org/id/eprint/8108/)

AHDB, *Factsheet Great Soils – Soil Structure and Infiltration* (AHDB, 2018)

AHDB, *Nutrient Management Guide (RB 209) Section 2 Organic materials* (AHDB, 2021)

Arriaga, F. *et al.*, 'Conventional Agricultural Production Systems and Soil Functions' in Al-Kaisi, M. and Lowery, B. (eds), *Soil Health and Intensification of Agroecosytems* (Academic Press, 2017, pp.109–125)

Baldivieso Freitas, P. *et al.*, 'Earthworm Abundance Response to Conservation Agriculture Practices in Organic Arable Farming Under Mediterranean Climate', *Pedobiologia* (Elsevier, Vol.66, January 2018, pp.58–64)

Bot, A. and Benites, J., 'The Importance of Soil Organic Matter', *FAO Soils Bulletin* (FAO, No.80, 2005)

Coleman, E., 'Eliot Coleman on Tillage, Compost, Green Manures and Balance', *The Organic Grower* (No.58, Spring 2022, p.24)

Crittenden, S. *et al.*, 'Effect of Tillage on Earthworms Over Short- and Medium-term in Conventional and Organic Farming', *Applied Soil Ecology* (Elsevier, November 2014, pp.149–58)

CSA Network UK, 'Composting for Small Farms – a Masterclass with Nicky Scott´ (CSA Network UK webinar, accessed March 2023 through YouTube https://youtu.be/IINqS__JoRA)

Davies, G. and Lennartsson, M. (eds), *Organic Vegetable Production: A Complete Guide* (Crowood, 2005)

Dowding, C., 'Compost or Green Manures?', *The Organic Grower* (OGA, No.13, Winter 2010)

FAO Plant Production and Protection Division, *An International Technical Workshop Investing in Sustainable Crop Intensification: The Case for Improving Soil Health – Integrated Crop Management Volume 6* (FAO, 2008)

Food Standards Agency, *Managing Farm Manures for Food Safety* (FSA, 2009)

Frost, J., *The Living Soil Handbook* (Chelsea Green, 2021)

Global Soil Biodiversity Initative, *Archaea* (accessed March 2023 through Global Soil Biodiversity Initiative website https://www.globalsoilbiodiversity.org/new-blog/2018/11/6/archaea)

Hitchings, R., 'Soil Analysis – Is It Worth It?', *The Organic Grower* (OGA, No.3, Winter 2007/08, pp.17–21)

ITPS, *Towards A Definition of Soil Health ITPS Soil Letter #1* (FAO, 2020)

Jonsson, P., 'Soil Health: The View from Sweden', *The Organic Grower* (OGA, No.54, Spring 2021, p.20)

Kassel University, 'AgroDiversity Toolbox – Subsidiary Crop Database' (accessed March 2023 through the Kassel University website http://vm193-134.its.uni-kassel.de/toolbox/SC_DB_home.php)

Measures, M., *Fertility Building Leys – IOTA Results of Organic Research: Technical Leaflet 9* (IOTA, 2014)

Measures, M., *Soil Management for Sustainable Food Production and Environmental Protection*, Winston Churchill Fellowship, 2018)

Measures, M. 'Soil Analysis in Organic Farming and Growing' *The Organic Grower* (OGA, No.52, Autumn 2020, p.14)

Merfield, C., 'Don't believe the Hype', *Organic Farming* (Soil Association, Winter 2007/2008, p.40)

NRM Laboratories, *Soil Health Handbook: A Guide and Interpretation for the NRM Soil Health Analytical Package* (Cawood Scientific Ltd)

Open Air Laboratories (OPAL), *Soil and Earthworm Survey* (OPAL, 2015a)

Open Air Laboratories (OPAL), *Earthworm Identification Guide* (OPAL, 2015b)

Pfiffner, L., *Earthworms – Architects of Fertile Soils* (FiBL, 2nd Edition, 2022)

PSMCC, 'Learn More About the Plant Soil Microbiome' (accessed March 2023 through the NC State University website https://cifr.ncsu.edu/plant-soil-microbial-community-consortium/about/background/)

Raskin, B., *The Woodchip Handbook* (Chelsea Green, 2021)

Rayns, F., 'Comfrey – Participatory Research and Fertility Building', *The Organic Grower* (OGA, No.49., Autumn 2019, p.26)

Rosenfeld, A. and Rayns, F., *Sort out Your Soil* (Cotswold Seeds, 2nd Edition, 2010)

Soil Association, *Organic Standards for Great Britain Farming and Growing* (Soil Association, 2023)

Sorensen, J. and Thorup-Kristensen, K., 'Plant-based Fertilizers for Organic Vegetable Production', *Journal of Plant Nutrition and Soil Science* (Wiley-VCH, Vol.174, Issue 2, p.321)

Stockdale, E.A. *et al.*, 'Soil Health and its Management for Organic Farming' in Atkinson, D. and Watson, C., *The Science beneath Organic Production* (John Wiley & Sons, 2020)

Sumption, P., 'Green Manures for No-till Market Gardeners', *The Organic Grower* (OGA, No.60, Autumn 2022, p.8)

Tolhurst, I., 'Composting Woodchips', *The Organic Grower* (OGA, No.13, Winter 2010, p.28)

Tolhurst, I., 'Soil Obesity – is your Soil Putting on Weight?', *The Organic Grower* (OGA, No.53, Winter 2020, p.13)

Vidacycle, *The New Science Behind Biodiversity, Cover Crops and Building the Soil Sociobiome: Learnings from Dr. Christine Jones* (accessed March 2023 through the Vidacycle website https://soils.vidacycle.com/soil-health/science-biodiversity-covercrops-building-the-soil-sociobiome/)

Vieweger, A. and Amos, D., 'Practical Soil Assessment Methods for Different Horticultural Systems', *ORC Bulletin* (ORC, No.124, Spring 2018)

Ward, C., 'Tackling the Nitrogen Problem – How Best to Manage This Brilliant but Volatile Element?', *The Organic Grower* (OGA, No.60, Autumn 2022, p.12)

Watson, C. *et al.*, *Soil Analysis and Management – Results of Organic Research: IOTA Technical Leaflet 4* (IOTA, 2009)

Westaway, S., *Ramial Woodchip Production and Use – WOOFS Technical Guide 1* (Organic Research Centre, 2020)

Westaway, S., *Ramial Woodchip in Agricultural Production – WOOFS Technical Guide 2* (Organic Research Centre, 2020)

Westaway, S., 'Can you Control Couch with Buckwheat?' *The Organic Grower* (OGA, No.52, Autumn 2020, p.30)

Younie, D., *Grass Clover Ley Species and Variety Selection and Management IOTA Research Topic Review* (IOTA, 2009)

Chapter 6

Davies, G. and Lennartsson, M. (eds), *Organic Vegetable Production: A Complete Guide* (Crowood, 2005)

Eghbal. R (ed.), *Ökologischer Gemüsebau* (Bioland, 2017)

Hayes, M. *et al.* (eds), *Organic Market Garden Start-up Manual* (GAK Nonprofit, 2013)

Hitchings, R., 'Crop Planning – Nightmare or Salvation?', *The Organic Grower* (OGA, No.8, Spring 2009, p.14)

Lott, D. and Hammond, V., *Water Wise Vegetable and Fruit Production* (University of Nebraska, 2013)

Mays, D., *The No-till Organic Vegetable Farm* (Storey Publishing, 2020)

Tolhurst, I., 'Relay Green Manures', *The Organic Grower* (OGA, No.5, Summer 2008, p.21)

Watson, C. *et al.*, *A Guide to Nutrient Budgeting on Organic Farms – IOTA Results of Organic Research Technical Leaflet 6* (IOTA, 2010)

Chapter 7

Adair, B., 'Soil Assisted Modules (SAMs)', *The Organic Grower* (OGA, No.21, Winter 2012, p.31)

Dollimore, P., 'Making a Dibber Peg Board for Module Trays', *The Organic Grower* (OGA, No.14, Spring 2011, p.22)

Eglington, S. 'Peat-free Soil Blocks', *The Organic Grower* (OGA, No.18, Spring 2012, p.29)

Hayes, M., 'Some Like it Hot! Hotbeds for Transplant-raising, Hungarian Style', *The Organic Grower* (No.22, Spring 2013, p.40)

Horticultural Development Department, *Modular Propagation – Technical Note April 2020* (Teagasc, 2020)

International Seed Testing Association, 'Detailed Methods for Germination Tests: Agricultural And Vegetable Seeds' (accessed March 2023 through the ISTA website https://www.seedtest.org/api/rm/ZTFM68H45TDMKJQ/appendix-1-ista-germination-table-5a-part-1-3.pdf)

Oxford Real Farming Conference, *Peat-Free Growing Media in Commercial Horticulture* (ORFC, 2023, accessed March 2023 through YouTube https://youtu.be/wZOiEPiWqs8)

Raskin, B., *The Woodchip Handbook* (Chelsea Green, 2021)

Real Seeds (accessed March 2023 through the Real Seeds website www.realseeds.co.uk)

Schofield, A., 'Plant-Raising … A Practical Approach for Growers', *The Organic Grower* (OGA, No.2, Autumn 2007, p.22)

Vaughan, J., 'Plant-raising and Substrates – the Choices', *The Organic Grower* (OGA, No.3, August 2007, p.10)

Chapter 8

AHDB, *The Encyclopaedia of Arable Weeds* (AHDB, 2018)

Balfour, N.J. *et al.*, 'The Disproportionate Value of "Weeds" to Pollinators and Biodiversity', *Journal of Applied Ecology* (British Ecological Society, Vol.59, Issue 5, May 2022, pp.1,209–18)

Dastgheib, F., 'Post-emergence Thermal Weeding in Onions (*Allium cepa*)', *Agronomy New Zealand*

(The Agronomy Society of New Zealand, No.40, 2010, p.177)

Davies, G., *et al., Weed Management for Organic Farmers, Growers and Smallholders: A Complete Guide* (Crowood, 2008)

Dibben, A., 'Using Pigs to Combat Couch Grass', *The Organic Grower* (OGA, No.20, Autumn 2012 p.38)

Dierauer, H. *et al., Creeping Thistle: Successful Control in Organic Farming – Technical Guide* (Organic Research Centre/FiBL, 2016)

Fortier, J.-M., *The Market Gardener: A Successful Grower's Handbook for Small-scale Organic Farming* (New Society Publishers, 2014)

Frost, J., *The Living Soil Handbook* (Chelsea Green, 2021)

Hauenstein, S. *et al.*, 'Transfer Mulch in Organic Greenhouses', *The Organic Grower* (OGA, No.55, Summer 2021, p32).

Hughson, G., 'Fighting Weeds & Pests with Plants' (as part of 'ORFC Goes Global'), *The Organic Grower* (OGA, No.54, Spring 2021, p.14)

Liebman, M. and Gallandt, E.R., 'Many Little Hammers: Ecological Management of Crop–Weed Interactions' in Jackson, L. (ed.), *Ecology in Agriculture* (Academic Press, 1997, pp.291–343)

Lindholm, N., *Ridge Tillage at Hackmatack Farm* (2014, accessed March 2023 through the Main Organic Farmers and Gardener website https://www.mofga.org/resources/fact-sheets/ridge-tillage-at-hackmatack-farm/)

Maughan, C. and Amos, D., *Weeds as Bioindicators – A Farmer's Field Guide* (CAWR, 2021)

Merfield, C.N., 'False and Stale Seedbeds: The Most Effective Non-chemical Weed Management Tools for Cropping and Pasture Establishment', *The BHU Future Farming Centre* (The BHU Future Farming Centre, No.23, 2013)

Organic-PLUS (accessed March 2023 through the Organic-PLUS website https://organic-plus.net/)

Rayns, F., 'Comfrey – Participatory Research and Fertility Building', *The Organic Grower* (OGA, No.48, Autumn 2019, p.26)

Rylander, H., *et al.*, 'Reusable Black Tarps Suppress Weeds and Make Organic Reduced Tillage More Viable', *The Organic Grower* (OGA, No.46 Spring 2019, p.14)

Schonbeck, P., *Knock Weeds Out at Critical Times* (accessed March 2023 through the eorganic website https://eorganic.org/node/2596

Sumption, P., 'Mulch Systems and Rotational No-till in Vegetable Farming', *The Organic Grower* (OGA, No.48, Autumn 2019, p.20)

Tolhurst, I., 'Relay Green Manures', *The Organic Grower* (OGA, No.5, Summer 2008, p.21)

Westaway, S., 'Can you Control Couch with Buckwheat?' *The Organic Grower* (OGA, No.52, Autumn 2020, p.30)

Chapter 9

AHDB, *Encyclopaedia of Pests and Natural Enemies in Field Crops* (AHDB, 2014)

Amos, D., *Aerated Compost Tea (ACT) to Improve Soil Biology and to Act as a Biofertiliser/ Biofungicide – Practice Abstract No.016* (Organic Research Centre/IFOAM Europe, 2017)

Carr, R., *Compost Tea: A How-To Guide* (accessed March 2023 through the Rodale Institute website *https://rodaleinstitute.org/blog/compost-tea-a-how-to-guide/)*

Collier, R. *et al.*, 'The Potential for Decision Support Tools to Improve the Management of Root-Feeding Fly Pests of Vegetables in Western Europe', *Insects* (MDPI, 2020, 11(6), p.369)

Dara, S.K., 'Advances in Biostimulants as an Integrated Pest Management Tool in Horticulture' in Collier, R., *Improving Integrated Pest Management in Horticulture* (Burleigh Dodds, 2022)

Davies, G. *et al., Pest and Disease Management for Organic Farmers, Growers and Smallholders: A Complete Guide* (Crowood, 2010)

Döring, T., 'Hide and Seek – Protecting Crops from Aphid Attack', *The Organic Grower* (OGA, No.32, Autumn 2015, p.26)

Gladders, P. *et al.*, *Diseases of Organic Vegetables* (ADAS, 2001)

Green, K. and O'Neill, T., *Management of Celery Leaf Spot – AHDB Factsheet 13/15* (AHDB, 2015)

Health and Safety Executive, *Plant Protection Products with Authorisation for Use in Great Britain and Northern Ireland* (accessed March 2023 through the Health and Safety Executive website https://secure.pesticides.gov.uk/pestreg/prodsearch.asp)

Jonsson, P., 'The Pros and Cons of Biostimulants', *The Organic Grower* (OGA, No.60, Autumn 2022, p.16)

Luka, H. *et al.*, 'Flower Strips to Promote Beneficial Insects in Brassica Fields', *The Organic Grower* (OGA, No.56, Autumn 2021, p.20)

Nicot, P.C. *et al.*, 'Advances in Bioprotectants for Plant Disease in Horticulture' in Collier, R. (ed.), *Improving Integrated Pest Management in Horticulture* (Burleigh Dodds, 2022)

Petitt, T. and Gladders, P., *Carrot Cavity Spot – HDC Factsheet 03/03* (HDC, 2003)

Sumption, P., 'The Great Cover-up', *The Organic Grower* (OGA, No.1, Summer 2007, p.10)

Sumption, P., 'Dutch Seed Open Days – 2018', *The Organic Grower* (OGA, No.45, Winter 2018, p.22)

Sumption, P., 'All the Trappings of Success – How to Control Pests in Horticulture, Oxford Real Farming Conference 2022 Report', *The Organic Grower* (OGA, No.58, Spring 2022, p.12)

Sumption, P., 'Eliot Coleman at the AGM', *The Organic Grower* (OGA, No.59, Summer 2022, p.6)

Symbio, 'Symbio – Bringing Life to your Soil' (accessed March 2023 through the Symbio website https://www.bioorganicgarden.co.uk/)

Chapter 10

Dollimore, P., 'Growing Glasshouse Fertility', *The Organic Grower* (OGA, No.17, Winter 2011, p.34)

Growing for Market, *Caterpillar Tunnel: An Inexpensive Variation on the Hoophouse Theme* (accessed March 2023 through the Growing For Market website https://www.growingformarket.com/articles/Caterpillar-Tunnel-Hoophouse

Hitchings, R., 'Protected Crop Planning', *The Organic Grower* (OGA, No.10 Autumn/Winter 2009, p.22)

James, O. and McKeever, M., 'Intercropping Vegetables', *The Organic Grower* (OGA, No.47, Summer 2019, p.31)

Lambion, J. and van Rijn, P., *Flower strips: A tool for pest control in greenhouses – Greenresilient Factsheet* (GRAB, 2021)

Manchett, R., 'The Movable Tunnel', *The Organic Grower* (OGA, No.9, Summer 2009, p.22)

Mefferd, A., *The Greenhouse and Hoophouse Grower's Handbook* (Chelsea Green, 2017)

Palme, W. and Stopper, E., *Winter-Harvest: Organic Vegetable Production in Unheated Greenhouses in Central Europe* (Biogreenhouse, 2016)

Tittarelli, F. *et al.*, *Soil Fertility Management in Organic Greenhouses in Europe* (BioGreenhouse, 2015)

van Marsh, D., 'Summertime Polytunnel Relay Cropping at Canalside', *The Organic Grower* (OGA, No.53, Winter 2020, p.18)

Wallace, K., 'Water Saving from Polytunnels', *The Organic Grower* (OGA, No.60, Autumn 2022, p.30)

Chapter 11

Aker, R., 'Farmers' Markets in Schools', *The Organic Grower* (OGA, No.28 Autumn 2014, p.14)

Bevan, J.R. *et al.*, *Storage of Organically Produced Crops* (Henry Doubleday Research Association, 1997)

Byczynski, L., *Market Farming Success: The Business of Growing and Selling Local Food* (Chelsea Green, 2013)

CSA Network UK (accessed March 2023 through the CSA website https://communitysupportedagriculture.org.uk/)

Dowding, C., 'Salad Bags – A Grower's Salvation', *The Organic Grower* (OGA, No.1, Summer 2007, p.8)

Dowding, C., 'Selling to Pubs and Restaurants', *The Organic Grower* (OGA, No.9, Summer 2009, p.28)

Exner, R., 'So you Think you'd Like to Start a Farm shop?', *The Organic Grower* (OGA, No.25, Winter 2013, p.20)

Food Standards Agency, 'Food Hygiene for Your Business' (accessed March 2023 through the Food Standards Agency website https://www.food.gov.uk/business-guidance/food-hygiene-for-your-business)

Frost, D., 'Growing for Caterers', *The Organic Grower* (OGA, No.16, Summer 2011, p.32)

Hashem, S., 'Ticking the Anti-globalisation Box', *The Organic Grower* (OGA, No.40, Autumn 2017, p.10)

Holmbeck, P., *Best Practice in Organic Public Procurement: The Case of Denmark* (IFOAM Organics Europe, 2020)

Larkcom, J., *The Salad Garden* (Penguin Books, 1984)

Larkcom, J., *Oriental Vegetables – The Complete Guide for Garden and Kitchen* (John Murray, 1991)

Little, T., 'Would your Mum Buy It? Producing Quality Organic Fruit & Veg', *The Organic Grower* (OGA, No.15, Summer 2011, p.32)

Open Food Network (accessed March 2023 through the Open Food Network website https://openfoodnetwork.org.uk/

Owen, A., 'A Story of Collaborative Working: Mach Vegbox', *The Organic Grower* (OGA, No.57, Winter 2021, p.36)

Reed, M., 'Smart Pathways to Market', *The Organic Grower* (OGA, No.53, Winter 2020, p.14)

Russell, R., 'Decentralised Home Delivery of Organic Food – An Idea Whose Time has Come', *The Organic Grower* (No.52 Autumn, 2020, p.22)

Smith, J. *et al.*, 'Growing for the Tourist Trade', *The Organic Grower* (No.34, Spring 2016, p.20)

Smith, J., 'Alternatives to Plastic Bags', *The Organic Grower* (OGA, No.58, Spring 2022, p.34)

Soil Association, *What You Can Say When Marketing Organic* (Soil Association, 2020)

Sumption, P., 'Storage to Extend the Season – Organic Matters Workshop Report', *The Organic Grower* (OGA, No.61, Winter 2022, p.11)

Taylor, A. and Seel, W., 'Growing Salads for Public Procurement in North-East Scotland' *The Organic Grower* (No.20, Autumn 2012, p.10)

van Diepen, P., *Organic Vegetable Storage in Wales – Opportunities and Constraints* (Organic Centre Wales, 2007)

Wangler, Z. and Payne, A., *Direct Sales and Short Supply Chains: An Introduction to Models and Management for Farmers and Growers* (The Landworkers' Alliance, 2020)

Chapter 12

Collyns, K., 'A Growing Family', *The Organic Grower* (OGA, No.38, Spring 2017, p.8)

Harries, R., 'Just Farm Labour', *The Organic Grower* (OGA, No.37, Winter 2016, p.26)

Hartman, B., *The Lean Farm* (Chelsea Green, 2015)

Hartman, B., *The Lean Farm Guide to Growing Vegetables* (Chelsea Green, 2017)

Naik, A., 'In Search of Wellbeing', *The Organic Grower* (OGA, No.38, Spring 2017, p.22)

OGA, 'Mental Health and Organic Growing', *The Organic Grower* (OGA, No.37, Winter 2016, p.34)

OGA, 'Better Together?', *The Organic Grower* (OGA, No.40, Autumn 2017, p.30)

OGA, 'Sustaining the Grower. How Can we Prevent Grower Burnout, Minimise Stress & Maintain Mental Health?' (OGA, OGA Organic Matters Conference 2022, accessed March 2023 through the YouTube https://youtu.be/WeK_UMJXpgE)

ORFC, *Farmerhood: Raising Crops, Animals and Children* (Oxford Real Farming Conference, 2021, accessed March 2023 through YouTube https://youtu.be/Yk5iPYdQEVc)

Rignell, E., 'Growing Together: Work Dynamics in Market Gardens (Part One)', *The Organic Grower* (OGA, No.46, Spring 2019, p.22)

Rignell, E., 'Growing Together: Work Dynamics in Market Gardens (Part Two)', *The Organic Grower* (OGA, No.47, Summer 2019, p.8)

Chapter 13

Barber, M., 'Incredible Vegetables – Perennial Vegetables and Future Food Crops', *The Organic Grower* (OGA, No.50. Spring 2020, p20)

Davies, G. and Lennartsson, M. (eds), *Organic Vegetable Production: A Complete Guide* (Crowood, 2005)

Deane, T., 'Drilling Sweetcorn ... Ontario or Bust', *The Organic Grower* (OGA, No.12 Summer 2010, p.22)

Dowding, C., 'Chicory, Under-grown in the UK', *The Organic Grower* (OGA, No.14, Spring 2011, p.32)

Eglington, S., 'Growing Runner Beans', *The Organic Grower* (OGA, No.27, Summer 2014, p.28)

Finckh, M. *et al.*, 'Organic Potatoes, Reduced Tillage and Mulch', *The Organic Grower* (OGA, No.33, Winter 2015, p.20)

Flintoff, L., 'Right on Cue' *The Organic Grower* (OGA, No.4, Spring 2008, p.24)

Flintoff, L., 'Growing Aubergines', *The Organic Grower* (OGA, No.11, Winter/Spring 2010, p.26)

Flintoff, L., 'Growing Sweet Peppers', *The Organic Grower* (OGA, No.26. Spring 2014, p.22)

Johnson, W., 'Roscoff Caulis for the Hungry Gap', *The Organic Grower* (OGA, No.31, Summer 2015, p.18)

Larkcom, J., *The Salad Garden* (Penguin Books, 1984)

Larkcom, J., *Oriental Vegetables – The Complete Guide for Garden and Kitchen* (John Murray, 1991)

McEvoy, K., 'Kate McEvoy's "Weird Shit"', *The Organic Grower* (OGA, No.47, Summer 2019, p.20)

Richards, N., 'In Defence of the Aubergine', and Stay, M., 'Aubergines in North Oxfordshire', *The Organic Grower* (OGA, No.57, Winter 2021, p.32)

Roberts, J. and Leslie, Y., 'Growing Fennel', *The Organic Grower* (OGA, No.21, Winter 2012, p.16)

Stickland, S., 'Growing Globe Artichokes in Mid-Wales', *The Organic Grower* (OGA, No.54, Spring 2021, p.35)

Sumption, P. *et al.*, 'Growing Climbing French Beans Inside', *The Organic Grower* (OGA, No.34, Spring 2016, p.18)

Sumption, P., 'Managing Potato Blight for Small Growers', *The Organic Grower* (OGA, No.42, Spring 2018, p.12)

Tolhurst, I., 'Asparagus Antics', *The Organic Grower* (OGA, No.3, Winter 2007/08, p.27)

Tolhurst, I., 'Squash in Storage', *The Organic Grower* (OGA, No.5, Summer 2008, p.30)

Tolhurst, I. 'Relay Green Manures', *The Organic Grower* (OGA, No.5, Summer 2008, p.21)

Tolhurst, I. ;Growing Broad Beans', *The Organic Grower* (OGA, No.19, Summer 2012, p.32)

Tolhurst, I., 'Tolly and the Kalettes', *The Organic Grower* (OGA, No.38, Spring 2017, p.18)

Tolhurst, I. *et al.*, 'The Humble Radish', *The Organic Grower* (OGA, No.39, Summer 2017, p.20)

Chapter 14

Davies, G. and Lennartsson, M. (eds), *Organic Vegetable Production: A Complete Guide* (Crowood, 2005)

Ellen MacArthur Foundation, *It's Time for a Circular Economy* (accessed March 2023 through the Ellen MacArthur Foundation website https://ellenmacarthurfoundation.org/)

Farm Carbon Toolkit (accessed March 2023 through the Farm Carbon Toolkit website https://farmcarbontoolkit.org.uk/)

Lampkin, N., Measures, M., Padel,S. (in press) *Organic Farm Management Handbook 2023* 12th Edition (Organic Research Centre, 2023)

Organic Market Garden (OMG) Data! survey 2019/20 (accessed May 2023 through https://organicgrowersalliance.co.uk/omg-data)

Smith, J., 'Carbon Footprinting for Organic Growers', *The Organic Grower* (OGA, No.53, Winter 2020, p.30)

Soil Association, *Soil Association Certification Inspection Guidance* (Soil Association, accessed March 2023 through the Soil Association website https://www.soilassociation.org/certification/farming/licensee-resources/inspection-guidance/)

First published in 2023 by
The Crowood Press Ltd
Ramsbury, Marlborough
Wiltshire SN8 2HR

enquiries@crowood.com

www.crowood.com

British Library Cataloguing-in-Publication Data
A catalogue record for this book is available from the British Library.

ISBN 978 0 7198 4311 2

Typeset by Simon and Sons
Cover design by Nick May/www.bluegecko22.com
Printed and bound in India by Thomson Press